THE EVERYTHING.
Grant Writing Book

Dear Reader,

Your individual reasons for wanting to learn more about grant writing probably vary. Whatever your motivation, we're delighted that you have purchased *The Everything® Grant Writing Book, 2nd Edition*. You'll find it full of valuable information about who and how to ask for grant funds for your nonprofit organization or social cause. We're excited to share with you what we've learned in more than four decades of writing grant proposals and other communications for businesses and nonprofit organizations in our community, and hope that you will apply these lessons to improve lives in yours.

This second edition brings you all the information contained in the first, plus an entire chapter on writing grant proposals for capital purchases and construction. We've also expanded the appendices to include not only a sample federal grant proposal and a sample foundation proposal, but also a complete sample challenge grant for a multimillion-dollar capital campaign. Though every proposal you write must be specific to the needs in your community, the samples we've provided will help you respond, in your own words, to some of the more difficult questions you may be asked in a grant proposal.

So read the book. Apply the lessons. And sit down to your keyboard to begin what you are sure to find a challenging, rewarding, and creative endeavor—that of a grant proposal writer. We wish you every success in your new venture.

Nancy Burke Smith   *Judy Tremore*

Welcome to the EVERYTHING® Series!

These handy, accessible books give you all you need to tackle a difficult project, gain a new hobby, comprehend a fascinating topic, prepare for an exam, or even brush up on something you learned back in school but have since forgotten.

You can choose to read an *Everything*® book from cover to cover or just pick out the information you want from our four useful boxes: e-questions, e-facts, e-alerts, e-ssentials. We give you everything you need to know on the subject, but throw in a lot of fun stuff along the way, too.

We now have more than 400 *Everything*® books in print, spanning such wide-ranging categories as weddings, pregnancy, cooking, music instruction, foreign language, crafts, pets, New Age, and so much more. When you're done reading them all, you can finally say you know *Everything*®!

QUESTIONS?
Answers to
common questions

FACTS
Important snippets
of information

ALERTS!
Urgent
warnings

ESSENTIALS
Quick
handy tips

DIRECTOR OF INNOVATION Paula Munier

EDITORIAL DIRECTOR Laura M. Daly

EXECUTIVE EDITOR, SERIES BOOKS Brielle K. Matson

ASSOCIATE COPY CHIEF Sheila Zwiebel

ACQUISITIONS EDITOR Lisa Laing

DEVELOPMENT EDITOR Katie McDonough

PRODUCTION EDITOR Casey Ebert

Visit the entire Everything® series at **www.everything.com**

THE
EVERYTHING®
GRANT WRITING BOOK

2nd Edition

Create the perfect proposal to raise the funds you need

Nancy Burke Smith and Judy Tremore

Avon, Massachusetts

To Tony Mazzarelli. You make me very proud.

An Everything® Series Book.
Everything® and everything.com® are registered trademarks of F+W Media, Inc.

Published by Adams Media, a division of F+W Media, Inc.
57 Littlefield Street, Avon, MA 02322 U.S.A.
www.adamsmedia.com

ISBN 10: 1-59869-633-5
ISBN 13: 978-1-59869-633-2

Printed in the United States of America.

10   9   8   7   6   5   4

Library of Congress Cataloging-in-Publication Data
is available from the publisher.

This publication is designed to provide accurate and authoritative information with regard to the subject matter covered. It is sold with the understanding that the publisher is not engaged in rendering legal, accounting, or other professional advice. If legal advice or other expert assistance is required, the services of a competent professional person should be sought.

　　　　—From a *Declaration of Principles* jointly adopted by a Committee of the American Bar Association and a Committee of Publishers and Associations

Many of the designations used by manufacturers and sellers to distinguish their products are claimed as trademarks. Where those designations appear in this book and Adams Media was aware of a trademark claim, the designations have been printed with initial capital letters.

This book is available at quantity discounts for bulk purchases.
For information, please call 1-800-289-0963.

Contents

13 Writing Action Plans and Timelines / 135

14 Designing an Evaluation Plan / 147

15 Developing a Budget and Budget Narrative / 157

16 Other Grant-Proposal Sections / 169

17 Capital-Grant Proposals / 183

18 Write It Well / 193

Acknowledgments

Thanks to all those wise enough to ask and all those generous enough to share what they know about fundraising and grant seeking, especially the members of the Philanthropy News Digest message board

Top Ten Reasons to Learn Grant Writing

1. Those who write grants are highly valued by employers and clients.

2. Grants bring money to your community and the causes you believe in.

3. Grant writing helps develop your skills as a writer, a small business person, and/or an administrator.

4. Whether the economy is good or bad, grant writers can easily find work. In fact, when the economy is bad, the need for services increases.

5. Securing grants for important organizations and projects helps you effect positive change in society.

6. Grant writing expands your network of professional and personal associations.

7. You can build your knowledge base of your community: Who's who, who's doing what, what's important, what needs to be done, and how things fit together.

8. Grant writing skills are transferable to private-sector work.

9. Grant writers can write full time for attractive earnings or part time for additional income.

10. Writing a grant exercises both your left and right brain—you can be creative and practical simultaneously.

Introduction

▶ THE TERM "GRANT WRITING" is a misnomer. No one actually writes grants. Those who seek funding write proposals; those who give funding write grant agreements and checks. But despite this fact, "grant writing" is the term everyone uses to describe the process of writing a proposal for funding a nonprofit organization's programs, operations, or construction projects. And "grant writer" is the term that everyone from the nonprofit sector will understand when you use it to describe your work.

"Grant writer" is not only inaccurate—it's insufficient. A grant writer does far more than write proposals for funding. A grant writer learns the philanthropic landscape of her community, enrolls to receive e-mail notices of grant funds, understands how to search for foundation and government grants, and knows how to cull through the search to select the most appropriate candidates. And all that is in addition to being a creative problem solver, a detail-oriented project supervisor, and a strong writer with a knack for brevity and clarity.

Today, there are hundreds of thousands of nonprofit organizations looking for funding and thousands of grantmakers looking for good projects to fund. But there are only a few hundred really good match-makers to bring them together—the grant writers.

It's no wonder that a grant writer is one of the most valued positions in any community. The grant writer helps nonprofit organizations seek and receive the funding they need to help others in the community live better, healthier, happier lives. Grant writers work for schools, hospitals, police and fire departments, religious institutions, universities, museums, symphonies, and others of the hundreds of nonprofit organizations in any mid-size U.S. city. They always have an abundance of work, regardless of economic conditions, and executives—from the mayor and police chief to the principal of a school—are always happy to meet the competent grant writer.

In short, by any name, this finding money and applying for it on behalf of nonprofit organizations in your community is a pretty fulfilling life. The rewards are not only monetary but also social and even spiritual.

By itself, reading a book will not make you a competent grant writer. Applying what you learn will. Practice will. Asking questions will. And you must start somewhere. *The Everything® Grant Writing Book, 2nd Edition,* provides a solid base of knowledge from which you can learn, practice, and develop intelligent questions to pose to seasoned professionals. This is a comprehensive "how-to" book that draws on the expertise of grant-writing professionals. You'll receive advice throughout the book from foundation program officers, grant reviewers, and a number of experienced grant writers. You'll read success stories, and you'll read stories about failures so you can learn to avoid the pitfalls. You'll get the know-how you need to effectively complete grant proposals to obtain the funding you need, to establish and build a thriving freelance grant-writing business, or to qualify for a full-time, paid staff position as a grant writer in a large nonprofit organization.

This is your first step into this rewarding, satisfying career. Enjoy the journey, and good luck!

Chapter 1

The World of Grant Writing

The first thing you try to learn when you intend to live in another country is the language. The same is true of venturing into the world of grantmaking: You'll need to learn the language. Key terms are listed in Appendix A, but you'll come to understand the "flavor" of the language as you read through this book. Chapter 1 provides the foundation you will need for learning more about grant writing.

What Is a Grant Proposal?

Grants are gifts made by a charitable-giving foundation or the government, most often to a nonprofit organization; that is, an organization designated a 501(c)(3) by the Internal Revenue Service (IRS). Grants are most often made to support the operations, special projects, or other activities of a nonprofit organization for a specific period of time. Grant proposals are submitted as requests for grant funding. Proposals include a narrative, forms, and attachments. It is the grant writer's responsibility to create, complete, and compile these documents.

Foundations are prohibited from making grants to individuals. Instead, individuals with needs such as housing, transportation, counseling, or health care must seek those services from a nonprofit organization. The nonprofit organization, in turn, seeks funding from grantmakers to provide those services.

Who Writes Grants?

While some individuals, such as inventors, and some businesses—particularly those in product development, research, defense, and construction—apply for grants, nonprofit organizations account for the majority of grant seekers.

That's because nearly all nonprofit organizations must seek grants to develop new programs or sustain operations. In smaller nonprofit agencies, the work of grant seeking and grant writing is often assigned to the executive director. Larger organizations often hire a fund development officer to do those jobs. On occasion, you'll find program directors assigned responsibility for seeking grants to support the organization's programs or ideas. Sometimes, a nonprofit's board of directors requests that staff pursue a specified number of grants or raise a specific amount of money through grant writing in any given year.

As executive directors of nonprofits have become busier and busier, the need for professional grant-writing services has grown consistently in the past several years, and shows no sign of slowing. That's where you come in.

Whether you're already a freelance writer and want to develop a new market for your work, grant writing is one of your job responsibilities, or you simply want to assist a favorite charity in a unique way, writing grant proposals can compensate you in two ways. You'll not only earn a living, but you'll also feel good about the contribution you make to improving your community and the lives of the people in it. And for many grant writers, that's almost as satisfying as the money itself.

The Grant-Writer's Market

Some individuals and businesses write grants, but your primary market is the nonprofit sector. Among those applying for grants are the following groups:

- Religious organizations
- Social service agencies of all kinds
- Schools
- Hospitals and clinics
- Governmental units (some also solicit and fund grant proposals)
- Colleges and universities
- Police/fire departments
- Public-access media
- Arts and cultural organizations

Four Absolutely Essential Skills

Above all as a grant writer, you must do four things and do them well and consistently.

First, have empathy for your readers. That means always writing directly to an audience. Learn who will be reading your grant proposals—often either a program officer at a foundation or a volunteer in a government office. Take care to understand what they need to know and how best to explain it to them.

Second, always meet your deadlines. If the grant arrives past the given deadline, even an hour late, it will not be reviewed! You may be able to resubmit the same grant to the same granting organization, but it's very likely that the next deadline will be a year or more away. Your nonprofit client will not be pleased; the organization may have been counting on that money for its next budget cycle.

Third, you must be able to read and follow instructions. This is more important than having a good writing style, good client relations, or even a successful grant-writing track record. While foundations are not as stringent, many government offices will throw your proposal into the trash unread, unreviewed, and, needless to say, unfunded, if you don't follow the instructions contained in the requests for proposals (RFP).

A fourth critical skill of grant writers is being a good "test taker." You must be able to read questions thoroughly, analyze the question for clues to the best answer, and provide the answer that best responds to the core of the question. A common downfall of many grant writers is that they answer questions with information they want to tell the granting agency, rather than with information the granting agency is requesting.

Interpreting the questions is the first step in writing a successful grant proposal and a skill that you'll perfect with experience. Focus on your audience and respond accordingly.

Grant Writing Versus Fundraising

A grant writer is most often a writer with a specialty, though she may also do fundraising. A fundraiser may write grants as part of his job. But most often, a fundraiser is a person on staff who is assigned to general fundraising duties.

Fundraising duties can include nurturing long-term donors, developing candidates and plans for bequests, planning and executing fundraising events or speaker series, managing a database of donors, developing year-end and mid-year letter campaigns, and other similar responsibilities.

Larger organizations usually have someone on staff assigned to fundraising, and often that person is called a development director.

While many development directors can and have written grants, they become so busy with the other requirements of their jobs that grant writing becomes a sideline for them or something they seek from an outside source, such as a professional grant writer.

Two Approaches

You will approach grant seeking in one of two ways: either as a response to a Request for Proposals (RFP); or proactively, through searching for matches between foundation guidelines and your nonprofit organization's mission. Government funding is most often accessed through an RFP process. Foundations sometimes issue RFPs for specific projects or initiatives, but most often present guidelines describing the location and types of organizations and projects they are interested in funding.

FACT

Some foundations are beginning to change their guidelines to look for ways to fund operations in nonprofits that are vital to the community or that have demonstrated "best practices" in their fields. However, most foundations still prefer to fund unique projects developed in response to a community need.

Whether you are writing to guidelines or an RFP, the grant proposal is formulaic; it includes instructions that, in the case of RFPs particularly, must be followed exactly. You also must use the accepted language and approach set forth by your reading audience.

Grant proposals are most often written to seek funding for a specific project within a larger organization. Projects may be capital (for construction, acquisition, or renovation of buildings) or programmatic (to support staffing, equipment, and other items that are necessary to launch a special project). Though it was once rare for grants to be made for operations (utilities, ongoing staffing costs, etc.), operating-fund grants are becoming more common today. Foundation grantmakers are just beginning a trend to ensure that the most outstanding and necessary nonprofit organizations are sustained with operating grants. This trend is an outgrowth of an increased emphasis by all grantmakers on sustaining programs once they are launched.

What Kinds of Projects Get Funded?

There are two key factors that often determine whether or not a grant proposal is successful: a creative response to a problem or need; and the potential for sustaining the project and its outcomes after the grant period ends.

Maggie is a freelance grant writer who works with various nonprofits to help them get grant money. In the early 1990s, Maggie received a call from a potential client in her state who wanted to meet with her to share his ideas and enlist her help writing grants to fund the project. He had already purchased a building and was in the process of renovating it into a hospital/orphanage for children born with AIDS.

As part of Maggie's interview with the client, she asked him why he had chosen this particular project. He responded that his primary reasons were that funders like projects that benefit children, that AIDS was a priority social/health issue of the time, and that the two together seemed a natural way for him to launch his new career in human services.

There's a reason that a statement of need or problem statement comes first in a grant proposal; all projects should identify and respond to a proven need in the community or identify a problem and its resolution. Make sure the need or situation can be supported with testimony or data before you write proposals for funding.

To Maggie, the project seemed opportunistic, manipulative, and motivated more by self-interest than interest in others. She did some research and learned that other long-standing service organizations had also discussed similar programs until they learned that a children's AIDS center was not necessary. One executive director told her, "We thought it might be an important contribution to society, but we learned that there are thousands of foster families that are more than willing to take in children with AIDS. We believe those children would be far better served in a family environment than an institution, so we simply scrapped the idea."

What are the attributes of "fundable" projects? A project and/or the organization proposing a project must have most of the following:

- Strong and recent data to support the need for the project or to describe the problem to be addressed
- An experienced project manager or other lead person such as the executive director of an organization
- A history of fiscal responsibility (or, if a new organization, comprehensive plans for fiscal oversight)
- A response (project description) that clearly addresses the identified need or a solution to the stated problem
- Collaboration with others in the community
- Community-member involvement in identifying the problem and the solution
- A plan for sustaining the project and/or the positive outcomes from the project after the grant period

There Must Be a Real Need

Maggie turned down the client. "Funders are not stupid. If I could learn with a few telephone calls that this was a 'phantom' need, they either already knew that or would learn it just as quickly."

Projects that don't address a real and pressing community, state, or national issue are not fundable. They might be creative. They might have strong possibilities for collaboration with potential partners. They might appear to address the priorities of a funder. But even with all these earmarks of a fundable proposal, they fall short unless the need is documented with supporting data.

Sustainability

A second major concern of funders is the ability of the nonprofit organization to support the program after their grant funding runs out. In the world of business, banks sometimes provide seed funding in the form of a loan. If the small start-up business is successful, it repays the loan and earns a profit for its owner. Though grants do not need to be repaid, the leader of a non-profit organization must think like the small business owner and be creative in developing ways that a project can earn revenues sufficient to continue without grant funds. Planning for sustainability can be very complex and difficult, but is a necessary discussion prior to seeking grant funds.

Trends in Funding

There are trends in funding priorities among both government funders and charitable foundations. During the 1980s and early 1990s, children's issues (child abuse and neglect, early childhood education, etc.) were priority projects for funding. While that focus has not disappeared, the trends have shifted to new priorities.

In the mid-to-late 1990s, closing the digital divide became a new funding priority, particularly at the federal-government level. Other recent trends include projects that support professional staff development, skills in chronically unemployed adults, economic development efforts, and projects that identify the potential for violence and work to prevent it, especially among teens. Since September 11, 2001, projects that address safety and security issues in communities throughout the United States have become especially important. And since the natural disasters of 2005, many grant opportunities have focused on rebuilding and restoring specific regions of the U.S.

Planning Is Critical

All Requests for Proposals (RFPs) have a deadline. Foundations, which most often provide guidelines rather than issue RFPs, frequently have deadlines as well. Sometimes the deadline for an RFP is months away, but more often you'll find that it's approximately thirty days after you hear of an RFP to its final deadline.

Short deadlines are deliberately designed as a sort of "natural selection" process. If the applying organization has not already planned for a project that responds to the focus of the RFP, they won't have time to plan, convene meetings of key partners, write the proposal, complete the forms, and send off a strong proposal in thirty days.

The First Steps

Develop your schedule by putting down a "ship by" deadline—not the actual due date. Then work backward. If you plan overnight shipping with next-day delivery, your ship deadline will be the day before the actual due date. If you plan to use the post office, shorten your deadline by three to five days. If you can hand-deliver grants to local foundations or drive to the final destination, you may be able to work closer to the actual due date. But be absolutely certain you'll be able to meet the deadline.

Remember, you have to allow enough time for first and second drafts, final tweaks to the narrative, completing forms, having forms signed, and developing and justifying budgets. It is also critically important to leave enough time for planning the project and identifying and securing commitments from community-partner agencies.

ALERT!

Before September 11, 2001, the federal government discouraged overnight shipping of grant proposals. Since mail delivery, particularly in Washington, D.C., has slowed for new inspection processes, the government now encourages overnight shipment and discourages the use of the postal service for time-sensitive materials.

Some RFPs indicate that they will accept a postmark date for the deadline. Be sure to read the instructions carefully and note whether it states "must arrive by" the date or "must be postmarked by" the date. If the project must be postmarked by a predetermined date, you must use the U.S. Postal Service for the postmark. Marks made by other delivery providers often will not fulfill this requirement.

A Typical Schedule

Following is the schedule for a typical grant-writing project. Let's say that it is due March 10, four weeks after you've received it.

Completion Date	Activity
2/2	Download RFP from Web site and review instructions.
2/3	Identify partnerships, plan program, and plan meetings, if necessary.
2/4–2/6	Draft brief (two-paragraph to one-page) proposal summary for partner meeting. Call State Single Point of Contact, if required.
2/8	Hold partners' meeting: present information; discuss roles of partners; secure commitments.
2/9	Write and distribute sample support letters from each partner. Request printout on agency letterhead and signatures by 2/24.
2/15	Submit first-draft narrative for review by colleagues.
2/18	Review grant and fill in blanks.
2/20	Submit second draft to partners for review and meet to discuss issues (also discuss financial needs for partner services).
2/24	Partner meeting to review draft two.
2/26	Finalize narrative based on partner input, check against rubric or evaluation criteria. Request assistance from a reader outside the organization to review draft against the evaluation criteria.
2/28	Meet with financial officer to develop final budget.
2/29	Write budget narrative, if required, for review by CFO.
2/30	Complete all application forms and tag for signatures.

Completion Date	Activity
3/3	Compile grant package and check against instructions. Proofread again. Make list of any outstanding letters of support or other items and schedule time to take care of these things.
3/5	Compile final grant package with original signatures on all forms. Make requisite number of copies. Include copies for State Single Point of Contact, if required.
3/6	Package original and required number of copies. Send overnight for arrival 3/10 in Washington, D.C., and at State Single Point of Contact, if requested.

Chapter 2

Finding the Money

Where do you find the money for the projects you're looking to fund? Maybe you already know of some sources, but you may also be overlooking some less obvious options. You'll soon learn the philanthropic landscape in your community and state. You want to know who gives out money, how much, and what for.

A Brief History of U.S. Philanthropy

The United States is unquestionably the most philanthropic nation in the world. Our long-standing tradition of caring for others and sharing our blessings dates back to Native Americans in the New World who were willing to share their harvests and knowledge with new settlers. The early religious leaders also brought a tradition of caring for others and sharing their blessings as they colonized the land, staked out farms, and populated early settlements.

The Federal Government's Role

With passage of the Federal Tax Act in 1913, the federal government established an income-tax program through which it collected money and then redistributed it throughout the United States to wherever it was most needed. Today, our government predetermines the types of projects and programs that need public support and then, through its various federal agencies, identifies exactly where the funding should go. The grant-seeking process starts when those agencies issue RFPs to nonprofit and governmental agencies in each of the states.

Private Philanthropy

The federal government encouraged private philanthropy when it passed the Federal Tax Act of 1969, which provides tax incentives to individuals and businesses for charitable giving.

Even before tax incentives were enacted, individual, family, and community philanthropy, which preceded government philanthropy, flourished. Ben Franklin was one of the earliest philanthropists, both with his time and his money. He gave to causes that would provide equal opportunities for community members and volunteered at his local hospital, library, and fire department. Andrew Carnegie was among the first of the turn-of-the-century industrialists to promote "giving back."

Subsequently, Carnegie was joined by such notables as John D. Rockefeller and Margaret Olivia Sage, wife of wealthy industrialist Russell Sage, who channeled his bequest to her into programs that strengthened education and encouraged social reform. These early millionaires established formal philanthropic foundations modeled after their successful business practices. The new foundations took the place of and provided more flexibility than the charitable trusts that had preceded them.

Government Funding Sources

The federal government issues RFPs to determine which of the various local and state programs that meet its predetermined requirements should be funded. That money is allocated from the government to its federal departments, such as the Department of Housing and Urban Development or the Department of Education, to be used in each department's various grant programs.

When seeking a federal grant, you may be tempted to put the grant writing off for a year if the deadline is rapidly approaching, knowing that the program will likely be offered again. It's often a good idea to submit anyway—you may request reviewer comments for failed proposals and use these suggestions to strengthen next year's proposal.

Often, the funded programs are available year after year, especially during a presidential or congressional term. When there's a change in leadership, priorities shift and money is often allocated to new priority categories and departments. For example, when President Bill Clinton was in office, funding technology-infrastructure improvements ("Closing the Digital Divide") was a priority. George W. Bush shifted the emphasis after September 11, 2001 to police- and fire-department projects in an attempt to strengthen "homeland security."

Many government grant programs go on for years, so you will have more than one opportunity to submit a proposal for funding or to resubmit a failed proposal.

Where Do You Find RFPs?

You may already be on a mailing list for appropriate RFPs. For instance, school districts receive most announcements issued by their state and the federal Departments of Education; large mental-health agencies are notified by the Department of Health and Human Services; and police departments will be given notice of grants available from the Department of Justice. As you develop these larger nonprofits as long-term clients, they'll begin to send you the RFPs and ask your opinion about whether they are qualified to pursue the grant program or if the proposed program is appropriate for their needs. Another way to review federal grant RFPs is to search the government's Web site: *www.grants.gov.* You can use program titles, departments, key words, or Catalog of Federal Domestic Assistance (CFDA) numbers assigned to each RFP to find available grants.

FACT

If you are working as a freelance grant writer, you can review RFPs on your own through Grants.gov, and call your clients and potential clients when you think one of the RFPs matches their requirements. While they are not obliged to ask you to write the proposal, they are just as likely to reward your notice with an assignment.

RFPs are published by each federal department and can be found on their individual Web sites or at *www.grants.gov.* You can also go to your local congressional representative's office and ask for time to review the office copy of the National Register, which contains all proposed grant opportunities for the upcoming year, regardless of which federal department is issuing them and regardless of whether it's secured funding or the actual levels of funding listed.

The Register is published or updated annually, but is not distributed widely. Instead, a one- or two-page announcement is mailed to pre-established mailing lists approximately 90–120 days before the grant deadline. The summary announcement contains a brief description of the program, its Federal Register number (CFDA number), the requesting department, a list of legal entities that may apply, the URL of the full RFP, and either an application or a telephone number so you can request an application package. It also contains information about any grant-seeker workshops or conferences that will take place and where they will be held. (See Chapter 6 for more information on these.)

You may also sign up with Grants.gov to receive regular notices of newly released RFPs. These notices come with a brief description of the grant program and a link to the request for proposals. Following is a sample announcement:

USDOJ
United States Department of Justice
Office of Justice Programs
National Institute of Justice
NIJ FY07 Solving Cold Cases With DNA
Grant
www.grants.gov/search/search.do?mode=VIEW&oppId=13313

Sometimes announcements of available grants are made and the RFPs are issued before the money is actually allocated by Congress to the department. And sometimes the grant program is funded at a smaller dollar amount than the department sought. Things can change during the review process, and there's nothing you can do about it except to be aware that these things happen. If you are enrolled with Grants.gov, you will sometimes receive e-mail update notices when deadlines, funding levels, or instructions change between the date of the RFP release and the due date for applications.

Philanthropic Organizations

Besides the government, philanthropic organizations, such as local foundations or the United Way, are a rich source of grants. Occasionally, in addition, people of wealth bestow grants without using a formal philanthropic organization or a grant-seeking process. A good grant writer is aware of these individuals in his or her community, but, because the needs and interests of these individual philanthropists vary widely—as do the best ways to approach them—they are not the subject of this book on grant writing.

Getting to Know the Funders

In Maggie's community, a midsized city in the Midwest, there are three major foundations: a large family foundation; a corporate foundation; and a community foundation. She has a local United Way agency and knows of several individuals who make large grants without using foundation governing boards. There are also numerous smaller foundations and corporate donors in her hometown. Maggie considers it a part of her service to clients to know what each of these local funders is interested in, what their program areas are, who is on their boards, and how often and when they meet to make decisions about grants.

Maggie got her information by meeting with funders, reviewing catalog listings of local funders, researching foundation 990s (tax statements indicating charitable gifts and their amounts available at *www.guidestar.org*), and talking with other clients about their experiences in local grant seeking. Her conclusions are not likely to be 100 percent applicable in your community, but they are worth sharing so you can look for similar patterns.

What Has Maggie Learned?

By doing her research beforehand, Maggie knows the following things:

- The major foundations have regular meetings in which they discuss projects and their planned portions of giving.
- Many of the smaller foundations wait to see what the corporate foundation does. They've come to understand and respect the staff person's approach to review and due diligence.
- When there's a really large capital project (such as an arena, convention center, or large university installation) that requires full community support, it becomes more difficult to get other special projects funded from the traditional sources.
- Staffs of foundations can't make promises or assurances on behalf of their boards.

- Changes in staffing (especially at the director levels) and trustee-board membership can affect grantmaking decisions and/or delay decisions.
- The foundations publish their values and mission statements and expect you to address the ways that potential projects fit with their vision and values.

Requests for Proposals

Sometimes foundations issue RFPs, which are often available either on the foundation Web site or through the Foundation Center. You can sign up at the Foundation Center (*www.foundationcenter.org*) to receive regular notices of foundation grant announcements. The announcements contain information about eligibility, a deadline, a brief description of the program, and a link to additional information, as shown in the following sample announcement:

California Community Foundation Invites Los Angeles Artists to Apply for Cover-Art Award

Deadline: May 4, 2007

The California Community Foundation's (*www.calfund.org*) Cover-Art Award is designed to support an emerging Los Angeles artist working in painting, drawing, or printmaking by purchasing an artwork that best reflects the foundation's annual theme: "Arts and Culture in Diverse Communities." This year's theme embodies CCF's goal to support initiatives that expand access to the arts for low-income populations, recognize nontraditional art forms among various cultures, and leverage the arts as a means of revitalizing neighborhoods. The foundation will feature the winning artwork in its 2007 annual-report cover, invitations, and other publications, and a limited-edition lithograph.

Cover-art award guidelines and application instructions are available at the CCF Web site.

RFP Link: *http://fconline.foundationcenter.org/pnd/10006747/calfund*

Usually, foundations issue RFPs only when they are planning special programs and need to identify appropriate grantees for their program. For instance, Pew Charitable Trusts in New York issued an RFP to midsized American cities requesting proposals to participate in a leadership-training program for nontraditional leaders. The RFP requested a description of the city leadership as it was, a process for identifying potential participants, and the means for ensuring long-lasting benefits to the participating communities.

Foundation RFPs vary in their information, but government RFPs usually contain the following information:

- Purpose
- Issuing agency/department
- Criteria for the program
- Total grant funds available and range of prospective grant awards
- Eligibility criteria for applicants
- Statements that must be signed by the applicant (regarding the enabling legislation, nonsupplanting, public comment requirement, etc.)
- Deadline
- Mailing instructions
- Outline of proposal content
- Points available for each section of the narrative
- Rubric (a chart of judging criteria and scoring) or other selection criteria for judges
- An application kit containing budget forms, cover sheets, and assurances
- Appendices/documents such as State Single Points of Contact, resources, call for reviewers, etc.

You may not deviate from the outline in the RFP—ever! If you don't follow the outline exactly, you can be assured that a grant proposal will be awarded funding, but it won't be yours. Remember, volunteers are often reading and scoring dozens of proposals at a time. They must be able to find the information where they expect to find it to assign it a proper score.

As a grant writer, you are most concerned with four sections:

- **The eligibility criteria.** You want to check it first to ensure that your employer or client meets all criteria for applicants, or that, with partners, they can meet the criteria.
- **The deadline.** You want to identify the deadline and develop your plan working backward from it.
- **The outline of content.** This third section is the most critical part of the RFP; think of it as the writer's instructions. Pay close attention to these instructions, and don't deviate from them.
- **The review criteria.** When you've completed your draft, you'll want to have it reviewed by peers and others both within and outside your organization. You do this to ensure that the narrative meets the highest level of the rubric scale.

Grant-Source Searches

Since RFPs, or at least announcements of their availability, are generally sent to qualified applicants, it's likely that your clients or employer will identify these grant sources for you or that you've found an appropriate grant opportunity through the Foundation Center or Grants.gov. But when it comes to compiling lists of other fund sources for your own files, you have a big job ahead of you.

To find foundation and other grant sources, you must check catalogs, software databases, and the Internet. As you begin to build your own knowledge base by asking for guidelines for various projects, you might consider putting foundation sources and their focus in a file cabinet (or electronic file) for easy reference or constructing a database that allows you frequent review.

FACT

If you intend to write grant proposals as a full-time pursuit either as a contract writer or as part of your job, it would be wise to organize information about fund sources in ways that make sense to you. Then, block out time on your calendar for annual or biannual updates to files on funders. Foundations often review their program guidelines and change them without notice to potential grantees.

Regional Associations of Grantmakers

The Foundation Center lists many U.S. foundations and information about them. In addition, catalogs and CD databases of foundations are available through organizations called the Regional Associations of Grantmakers (RAGs). Different RAGs cover different regions of the United States. You'll have to pay a fee to get these resources from your RAG, but they are worth it when you consider the time it would take you to hunt down every source on the Internet, and when you want to zero in on funders that cover a specific geographic area.

RAGs publish catalogs that list only those foundations that are members of the organization. The listings contain the following information:

- Name and address of foundation (usually in alphabetical order)
- Contact person
- Donor
- Purpose of the foundation
- Limitations (what the foundation will not fund)
- Fiscal year (the time in which the foundation must pay out its 5 percent)
- Assets
- Typical annual expenditures (includes grants and foundation operations)
- Grants made in previous year by focus area
- Range of grant funding
- Deadlines for submission and/or decisions about grants (grant cycles)
- Means of approach (letter of inquiry, request guidelines, submit full proposal, etc.)
- Typical grant size
- Officers and trustees

Following is an example of an entry in a RAG catalog.

XYZ FUND

P.O. Box 1

Somewhere, USA   123-456-7890

Contacts: John Doe, Foundation Manager

Donor(s): John Smith

Purpose and Activities: Support for health-care agencies, humanities, human-service agencies, public benefit, and religious organizations.

Fiscal Year End: 12/31

Assets: $1,234,567

Expenditures: $75,975

	Total	Somewhere, USA
Grants	$65,000	$25,000
Number of Grants	50	18
Humanities	5.00%	4.26%
Education	2.50%	4.26%
Health Care	11.33%	16.17%
Human Services	32.83%	30.64%
Public Benefit	13.33%	
Religion	35.00%	44.68%

Grant Range: $1,500–$15,000

Typical Grant Size: $3,500

Application Procedure: Initial approach with letter describing purpose of grant and tax-exempt status verification.

Funding Cycle: Grants made in January of each year.

Officers and Trustees: USA Bank

EIN: 123456789

The RAG catalogs (which may also be published and cross-referenced in an interactive CD) include such additional information as lists by geographical area of giving or lists by subject- or focus-area for giving.

You'll also find lists from the Council on Foundations, or on special CD/DVD research programs, such as those published for universities or medical-research facilities that may be of use.

ALERT!

In some catalog entries, the foundation states that it "gives to preselected organizations only." They are not open to reviewing unsolicited requests, so do not submit your grant proposals to them unless someone makes direct contact with the donor and has his or her permission to submit.

How to Begin Your Search for Grant Opportunities

To narrow your search using a RAG catalog, refer first to their index of subjects or areas of interest. For instance, if your client or employer is a women's health service, refer to the index of grantmakers in medical research, mental health, or general health, and also to the index of foundations that focus on women's issues.

Next, refer back to the individual foundations listed in those subject areas. Look at their limitations. If a foundation generally limits its giving to a specific city or region that your agency is not a part of, cross that foundation off your list of possible prospects. If they are listed as giving to "preselected organizations only," find out if your organization has any connection through friends, staff, or previous funding. If not, cross these foundations off your list, too.

Now, look at the range of grant funds and the allocation to health or women's issues to get an idea of what each foundation might do to assist financially. Look up the best prospects, in terms of shared focus and size of awards, on the Internet or by using the contact information. Then write to request guidelines from each of your final prospects, or, if possible, download guidelines from the Internet.

Once you have all the information about appropriate foundations and the size of the grants they tend to give, develop a plan for approaching them. Be sure to note such things as means of approach. (For instance, will you stress that your organization fills a health-care gap in your community or that it addresses critical women's health issues?) Also, note deadlines for submission and decision-making, and the amount you can or should request.

This sample guideline was developed by a Regional Association of Grantmakers (RAG) for use by any foundation within the geographical area of the RAG. Common grant applications generally have most of the same questions you will be asked to respond to in other foundation grant proposals; therefore, it's smart to do one of these first so you have text for subsequent proposals to other funders.

COMMON GRANT-APPLICATION FORMAT

Please provide the following information in this order. Briefly explain why your agency is requesting this grant, what outcomes you hope to achieve, and how you will spend the funds if the grant is made.

A. NARRATIVE

1. Executive Summary
- Begin with a half-page executive summary. Briefly explain why your agency is requesting this grant, what outcomes you hope to achieve, and how you will spend the funds if the grant is made.

2. Purpose of Grant
- Statement of needs/problems to be addressed; description of target population and how they will benefit.
- Description of project goals, measurable objectives, action plans, and statements as to whether this is a new or ongoing part of the sponsoring organization.
- Timetable for implementation.
- Who are the other partners in the project, and what are their roles?

- Acknowledge similar existing projects or agencies, if any, and explain how your agency or proposal differs, and what effort will be made to work cooperatively.
- Describe the active involvement of constituents in defining problems to be addressed, making policy, and planning the program.
- Describe the qualifications of key staff and volunteers that will ensure the success of the program. Are there specific training needs for this project?
- Long-term strategies for funding project at end of grant period.

3. Evaluation

- Plans for evaluation, including how success will be defined and measured.
- How evaluation results will be used and/or disseminated and, if appropriate, how the project will be replicated.
- Describe the active involvement of constituents in evaluating the program.

4. Budget Narrative/Justification

- Grant budget; use the Grant-Budget Format that follows, if appropriate.
- On a separate sheet, show how each budget item relates to the project and how the budgeted amount was calculated.
- List amounts requested of other foundations, corporations, and other funding sources to which this proposal has been submitted.
- In the event that we are unable to meet your full request, please indicate priority items in the proposed grant budget.

5. Organization Information

- Brief summary of organization's history.
- Brief statement of organization's mission and goals.
- Description of current programs, activities, and accomplishments.
- Organizational chart, including board, staff, and volunteer involvement.

B. ATTACHMENTS

1. A copy of the current IRS determination letter indicating 501(c)(3) tax-exempt status.

2. List of Board of Directors with affiliations.

3. **Finances**
   - Organization's current annual operating budget, including expenses and revenue.
   - Most recent annual financial statement (independently audited, if available; if not available, attach Form 990).
4. **Letters of support** should verify project need and collaboration with other organizations. (Optional)
5. **Annual report,** if available.

INFORMATION INCLUDED IN A COMMON GRANT APPLICATION

Date of Application:

Legal name of organization applying:
(Should be same as on IRS determination letter and as supplied on IRS Form 990.)

Year Founded: Current Operating Budget: $

Executive Director: Phone Number:
Contact person/title/phone number
(if different from executive director):
Address (principal/administrative office):
City/State/Zip:

Fax Number: E-mail Address:

List any previous support from this funder in the last 5 years:

Project Name:

Purpose of Grant (one sentence):

Dates of the Project: Amount Requested: $

Total Project Cost: $

Geographic Area Served:

Signature, Chairperson, Board of Directors Date

Typed Name and Title

Signature, Executive Director   Date

Typed Name and Title

GRANT-BUDGET FORMAT

Below is a listing of standard budget items. Please provide the project budget in this format and in this order.

A. Organizational fiscal year:

B. Time period this budget covers:

C. For a CAPITAL request, substitute your format for listing expenses. These will likely include: architectural fees, land/building purchase, construction costs, and campaign expenses.

D. Expenses: include a description and the total amount for each of the budget categories, in this order:

	Amount requested from this organization	Total project expenses
Salaries		
Payroll Taxes		
Fringe Benefits		
Consultants and Professional Fees		

Insurance

Travel

Equipment

Supplies

Printing and Copying

Telephone and Fax

Postage and Delivery

Rent

Utilities

Maintenance

Evaluation

Marketing

Other (specify)

E. Revenue: include a description and the total amount for each of the following budget categories, in this order; please indicate which sources of revenue are committed and which are pending.

	Committed	Pending
1. Grants/Contracts/		
Contributions		
Local Government		
State Government		
Federal Government		
Foundations (itemize)		
Corporations (itemize)		
Individuals		
Other (specify)		
2. Earned Income		
Events		

Publications and Products		
3. Membership Income		
4. In-Kind Support		
5. Other (specify)		
6. TOTAL REVENUE	$239,956	$607,952

You're finally ready to begin preparing your submissions. You should take the most complex proposal outline first. In it, you'll create responses to sections that you can use again and again on the other proposals, such things as the need statement, program description, evaluation plan, and other sections that only have to be tweaked slightly to fit the focus or emphasis of the other foundations.

ALERT!

As with RFPs, when applying for foundation funds, you must follow the instructions for submission (the outline contained in the guidelines) to the letter. Most foundations have established procedures for reviewing proposals and providing careful consideration by the right person at the foundation. If you deviate from their procedures or instructions, you may be harming your chances of getting the proposal to the right person.

Foundation Grant Guidelines

Grant guidelines are issued by most larger foundations, and are available by request or by search. They contain critical information for framing your grant proposal, including the following:

- Background/brief history of foundation
- Categories for funding/focus areas, with brief descriptions of types of programs
- Means of approach (such as letter of inquiry, meeting with funders, arrangement for site visit, full proposal requested)

- General requirements for funding
- Instructions for submission (outline of required sections)

"Cold Calling" Versus Responding to RFPs

Remember, there are two basic approaches to seeking grants: responding to requests for proposals or "cold calling" on foundations. In the former instance, you receive a request for proposals that clearly outlines the types of projects the funder is seeking and the requirements for each project. Then you work with your employer or client either to develop a new program that responds to the requirements or to modify an existing program to meet the requirements in the RFP.

Most often, the programs described in the RFP are those that have been found to work in other communities or that the funder wants to explore through several demonstration projects because they show great promise for systemic change. In these cases, you must design a program that is similar to or exactly like the one the RFP describes; the goals of your program and the goals of the funder must be the same.

A "cold call" is when you go to a foundation, either in person or in a letter of inquiry, describe the need you've identified in the community that is not being met by another agency, and tell what your organization would like to do about it.

A cold call is the only way that you will seek funding from a foundation that does not issue RFPs—in other words, from most foundations. It is also an opportunity for you to educate local foundations about a new need in your community, and to position your client as a responsive, engaged participant in coalition building and program activities.

When you cold call, you can create a program that responds to an identified need in your community. For instance, let's say data indicate that a large number of Polish immigrants have moved to your community recently. To help them resettle, you decide to call together an established refugee settlement organization, a Polish society hall, the Red Cross, a community-education program which teaches English as a Second Language (ESL), and several other local organizations to establish a comprehensive resettlement program. You want it to include English-language tutors, housing assistance, furniture and clothing banks, job-skill development, job-placement services, and other assistance needed by new residents.

The chance that an RFP comes out that exactly describes this sort of program is very slim. You might find a couple of them seeking to fund resettlement programs in general, but they probably wouldn't include Polish refugees as a target population; so, the best way to launch a program that responds to this specific need is to cold-call foundations.

You'll find that area foundations are keenly interested in learning about new needs in their geographic areas, and in responsive, creative programs that can help meet those needs. Cold-call grants can be extremely successful, and you'll feel great that you helped launch a program that's sure to be positively evaluated.

Chapter 3

Government Grants

Government grants are tax dollars redistributed to programs in your community. As such, they can be made by any entity that collects taxes: federal, state, and even local city or county governments. In general, the larger the government, the larger the fund available for grants and the larger the individual awards for projects.

3

Local-Government Funds

Local governments are your city, township, county, regional coordinating body such as a water district, or other such mechanisms. Local governments rarely have grant opportunities, and those that do provide only limited programs. But they do issue RFPs.

RFPs That Aren't for Grant Programs

Local governments are more likely to issue requests for proposals that are actually for work they wish to have completed. For instance, the city council or similar unit of local government might decide they need to build a new parking lot. They will send the job out for bids and call the process a "request for proposals," but of course, this is not a grant program.

ALERT!

Block-grant funding has become more scarce in recent years. And, even though a local government grants the money, grantees must comply with federal reporting requirements. Many now require extensive quarterly reporting on progress toward achieving outcomes.

Local Grants with Pass-Through Money

Don't cross local government off your list of grantors, however, because sometimes they receive larger grants from the federal government that they can redistribute locally, such as Community Development Block Grants (CDBG) or Local Law Enforcement Block Grants (LLEBG). The local government determines the priority issues to address with these funds and then issues requests for proposals to address those issues.

Block-grant funding comes from a source other than the local tax base. Usually it's state or federal money. Block-grant programs are often broad in scope and the issues they cover, such as housing, elder care, child welfare, and health. In addition, these programs are likely to be offered annually, and can be used as a source of operational funding for nonprofits that meet the criteria.

State-Government Funds

Grants from the state are among the easiest to apply for and receive. You'll find that your state is close enough to communities to have an understanding of what's going on and the problems they are having, yet large enough to provide grants in sufficient amounts to address problems that have been identified.

You can find state grant opportunities in nearly the same way as you find federal-government grants: by going from department to department. Most states have a Web site that lists departments. Pages within each department contain information about upcoming RFPs.

Some grants are awarded on what appears to be an "it's-your-turn" basis rather than merit. For example, a state department of education might give funding to different school districts on a rotating basis. When that's the case, it's better not to apply for the funding every time it becomes available; you'd be better off waiting four or five cycles, then trying again.

Intermediary Funds

State or federal governments occasionally provide funds to a nonprofit organization in your community, which the nonprofit then regrants to smaller nonprofit organizations. The intermediary is usually a larger, well-established nonprofit such as Family Independence Agency, United Way, your community foundation, or your workforce development board.

FACT

In recent years, the federal government has used intermediaries to help get grant money to small, faith-based community organizations. These organizations had difficulty competing for federal grants because they often did not have a financial officer or a means to comply with extensive federal reporting requirements.

When this happens, the local agency usually receives some of the grant as compensation for reviewing the mini-grant proposals, distributing the grant dollars, and ensuring that all reports and evaluations are submitted on time to the granting agent.

Funds Through an Intermediary Are Specific

Intermediary funding is always granted for a specific purpose, and made to a local agency, because that agency knows more about needs in the community. A local agency is also more familiar with the reputation of various service providers than any federal or state government could be.

Community Development Block Grants (CDBGs), for example, are meant to be spent locally, and are used to develop projects that respond to specific community needs. Block-grant money is passed from the federal to state government. The state awards some grants to rural or smaller communities, and passes the rest of the money to larger city governments and lets them administer their own programs.

Another example of intermediary funding was the large tobacco settlement. The money was earmarked for prevention and stop-smoking programs. Some states actually administered the tobacco-settlement funds. Other states, however, passed it to local agencies, such as community foundations. The foundations, in turn, passed it on to local nonprofits that had programs in place that addressed the targeted tobacco-use issues.

A Foundation Example

In Maggie's state, the tobacco settlement money first went to the local community foundation. The foundation then invited approximately twenty organizations to apply for grants, knowing they either already had programs in place or were capable of putting one together in short order. Technically, if an organization didn't receive an invitation to apply, it couldn't, but Maggie made a strong case for getting one of her clients added to the list.

"I had a client that had a strong program for educating teens about advertising and helping them use that knowledge to produce commercials that rebutted claims in the ads. Their program, however, was not well known." While her client had not specifically addressed smoking as an issue, she knew that eventually they would.

"I heard about the fund because another of my clients had been invited to apply. So I called the community foundation and told them about my other client's program. They were very nice about it. In fact, they welcomed the idea of teaching teens how to evaluate ads. They invited my agency to submit a proposal. It turned out that both of my clients got their grants, and the one that I had brought to the foundation's attention was awarded twice what they asked for."

Federal Grants

You will find that federal-government grants are where the money is and where the work is! Federal-government grants are meant to launch big programs; that's why awards can range from grants of less than $10,000 to grants of several million dollars.

Federal-government requests for proposals are published in the Federal Register (or Catalog of Federal Domestic Assistance), announced at various department sites on the Internet, and available at *www.grants.gov*. In addition, qualifying organizations often get advance notice of grants appropriate for their agency.

Ongoing Federal Programs

Some federal grant programs have been offered yearly for decades, and are provided to designated agencies based on their progress reports and annual reapplications.

QUESTION?

What's a DUNS number?
Required on all federal grant applications, a DUNS number is the non-profit organization's Dun and Bradstreet (D&B) number. You can apply by telephone or Internet for a DUNS number. D&B provides financial information about your organization to the federal government, eliminating the need for you to attach lengthy audit reports.

For instance, health-care clinics for the indigent may apply for a "330" designation by the federal government. Once they have that designation, they qualify to apply for ongoing funding through the aptly titled 330-program grants, which come up every year. While the 330 grants don't entirely support these clinics, they do provide a relatively stable source of ongoing funding. Head Start has also been funded for a number of years, with differing deadlines for resubmission based on geographic location.

New Grant Programs

Other grant programs are relatively new. Think about the new funding that became available once Congress passed the Homeland Security Act of 2002. This program increased funding already available to qualifying law-enforcement agencies through grants made by the Department of Justice. For the first time ever, firefighting units were also eligible to receive federal funding so that they could build up their capacity, purchase equipment, or receive additional training.

FACT

When the federal government opens up a new grant program, such as the Homeland Security Act, it often means that fewer dollars are available for other grant programs. Often, particularly after an administrative change, some grant programs are phased out and funding available for grants is redistributed to new programs.

Why You Should Watch Trends

Unless you are applying for designation and annual funding that is relatively stable, you should watch trends and allocations to the federal departments. When there is a large allocation made to one federal-government department, it's likely that large grant opportunities will be coming up within the year.

One-Time Opportunities

There are many one-time grant opportunities available from the federal government. These are usually multiyear awards—often of more than $1 million—given to demonstration projects throughout the nation.

A good example is the multimillion-dollar, three-year grant projects known as "Safe Schools—Healthy Students," created in response to the shootings at Columbine, as well as other school violence. The grant called for the school-district applicant to work in tandem with a mental-health agency and the local police or sheriff's department to address the entire life cycle (from birth to seniors) in its programs. They also had to develop a coherent program for using these tools to reduce school violence and improve the mental health of students and families.

Many of the districts funded under this three-year grant used the one-time money to purchase equipment or to develop materials they could use repeatedly, and to develop new programs and partnerships. At the end of three years, the school districts were ineligible to reapply for new grants under the program.

ALERT!

The success of a new program funded by a large-grant award can be short-lived if you don't plan for the continued funding you'll need to keep the project going after the grant funds are spent. Planning for sustainability—for funding and outcomes—should be a part of every grant writer's expertise.

Multidepartment grant applications are very difficult to write. Not only must the writer respond to all the requirements in the joint RFP, but she must also meet the individual requirements for each federal department.

Federal Register

The Federal Register contains all requests for proposals, from all federal departments, that are issued in a given year. It must be voluminous, but most writers have never seen the entire Register. Instead, you will receive or download individual RFPs for individual grant programs.

If you receive an RFP package in the mail, it is usually bound and saddle stitched as a small booklet; online, it comes as a simple PDF file. It contains all the information found in the Federal Register about that particular grant program, including the following:

- Program number (CFDA number)
- Enabling legislation
- Purpose of the grant program
- Outline for your narrative
- Evaluation criteria judges will use to select the programs that are funded
- Forms and assurances (that the organization practices equal opportunity or has an environmental policy, for instance)
- Listing of State Single Points of Contact, when contact with them is required
- Instructions for forms
- Instructions for appendices
- Mailing instructions and addresses

Sometimes the booklet also includes frequently asked questions and responses and/or government contact information so that you may ask questions by e-mail or telephone.

More often, you can download RFPs from the department's Web site. However, the package is not complete as a single downloadable file. You must download the RFP (usually listed by program title) and the forms (usually called "application package") separately. You also may choose whether or not you want to download additional pieces of information, such as frequently asked questions or other background information.

Over the past few years, the federal government has developed Grants. gov, which in some ways makes access easier and in some ways makes it more difficult. It is easier now to get notices of funding and to search all departments through the search engine at Grants.gov. However, now grant-seeking organizations must preapply for access to the complete RFP package, a process that sometimes takes several weeks. Also, different departments are limiting applications for some programs to online submission only.

ALERT!

Register your nonprofit organization with Grants.gov even if you don't think you'll be applying for a grant in the coming year. When you do find a grant opportunity, this will be one time-consuming hurdle out of the way.

The time will certainly come, likely in the next few years, when paper submissions for federal funding will be obsolete. The online submission process requires you to open, close, complete, and submit a dozen or more different documents and can be confusing and time consuming. Be sure to plan at least a day for uploading, and, to be safe, try to plan this activity for the day before the deadline in case the system goes down.

Other Sources of Information

Most reputable nonprofits are on mailing lists to receive notification of upcoming grant opportunities. They are also often contacted directly by the local, state, or even federal department with which they work. But you can also search for government programs and RFPs on your own.

How to Go about It

A good search engine is the grant writer's best friend. Key words that will help you find government grants include the following:

- The purpose of your program or project (for example, "lead hazards," "school violence," "prosthetics")
- The name of the department (be sure to specify "U.S." or name of state first to avoid getting a long list)

- The name of a similar program you know that has received funding. (When you search this way, you are likely to find out the name of the grant program they used and which department issued it.)

If your Web-surfing skills are weaker than you'd like, you might start out with some of the Web sites set up especially for grant writers. In addition to listing private, corporate, public, and community foundations, they often include federal agencies that have issued RFPs. Usually, you can search these sites by categories or topics.

There's no guarantee that a site will have links to all possible grant sources, but until you get a feel for what you can find on the Web, they may be a good place to start your search. At the very least, you won't be wasting time filtering through a lengthy list of grant topics pulled up by a search engine, only to discover that half the sites only contain news releases while the other half list grants with deadlines that have already expired.

Bookmark Your Results

It can take a while to locate different departments and agencies that issue RFPs, so be sure to bookmark sites that you know you'll want to return to. Also bookmark sites where you downloaded an RFP, so you can refer back to it throughout the writing process. Why do you want to do this? Sometimes deadlines are extended or modifications are made to the RFP, and the only way you will have of finding this out is to watch the Web site for updates.

Another Valuable Source

Your local representative's office can help keep you informed about upcoming RFPs. Members of Congress often have a local office as well as a Washington, D.C., office, and your hometown staff is there to assist constituents. They will be willing to put you on a mailing list or a computer listserv so that you can receive important announcements.

Chapter 4

Foundation Grants

A private charitable foundation engages in charitable giving from its "corpus," which is money
endowed to the foundation by a wealthy person,
family, or corporation. You'll learn more in this
chapter about how charitable foundations invest
those funds and, depending on the kind of foundation they are, how they use the proceeds to make
grants to nonprofit organizations like yours.

4

Funding from a Foundation

Charitable private foundations are required by tax law to pay out, through grant making, 5 percent of the total corpus (endowment plus earnings) each year. They usually invest their endowment funds. In years that the stock market does well, they earn more than the 5-percent payout requirement and are able to build the corpus of the foundation. In years that their investments, overall, earn less than 5 percent, they must dip into the corpus to meet the payout requirements. Poor earnings in a single year won't affect a foundation's corpus or its ability to award grants, but if the market continues to decline in subsequent years, those foundations that have no means of income other than earnings from investments will suffer, and so will the nonprofits that they fund.

While there are variations in type and size, in general, grant-making foundations are either private foundations or grant-making public charities.

Private foundations are nongovernmental, nonprofit, grant-making organizations managed by a board of trustees or directors that make grants for charitable purposes. They include corporate foundations, family foundations, private independent foundations, and operating foundations.

Grant-making public charities are 501(c)(3) nonprofit organizations that derive their funds from multiple donors, have a charitable purpose, and make grants. They include community foundations and public foundations.

Corporate Foundations

Although they are often linked with the founding corporation, corporate foundations are a separate legal organization subject to the same rules and regulations as other private foundations. Profit-making businesses, usually large corporations, establish corporate foundations to enable them to support projects in communities where they operate manufacturing plants, retail outlets, and other direct business. They are most interested in helping organizations in the communities where their employees live, though sometimes they expand grantmaking into communities where their customers live as well.

Corporate foundations have a board of trustees usually composed of current and retired corporate leaders. Staff often includes an executive director who reviews grants and makes recommendations to the board.

A corporate foundation is different from a corporate-giving program. The former has an endowment through which it earns income and makes grants. A corporate-giving program, on the other hand, makes grants of money or products based on its annual earnings. The gifts, therefore, fluctuate from year to year and may not be available at all during lean years.

FACT

Direct-giving programs do not accept grant applications, and they are not part of the endowment entrusted to the corporate foundation. Gifts of money and goods are allocated from the annual profits of the corporation.

Family Foundations

The largest group of private foundations is family foundations, which are usually established by one or two donors. Family foundations ensure that future generations continue to practice philanthropy, and are set up so that the endowment upholds values the donors believe are important. Most founders are successful entrepreneurs who want to use their fortunes to support the communities in which they and their families live. In return, they receive substantial tax benefits from the federal government.

Family foundations may be operated by a local bank, by the founder, by family members, or by a staff hired for that purpose. When a bank is in charge, grant proposals are mailed to a contact person at the bank. Staffed foundations will have an executive director and, as the corpus grows, will hire additional program staff. The board of trustees, which makes decisions about grantmaking, is usually composed of family members and sometimes includes third- and fourth-generation descendants of the donor. There also may be representatives from the community who were asked by trustees to serve on the board.

Some family foundations are established to make gifts to the same organizations the donor has supported for years. These types of foundations generally do not accept grant applications from nonprofit organizations that have not been preselected for funding. Some family foundations serve in this capacity for only a couple of generations; then they become so large that they must broaden their grant-making focus or endow the preselected charities directly.

Private Independent Foundations

Family foundations are a subset of private foundations, and many private independent foundations have derived from the growth of a family foundation. The differentiation between a private independent and family foundation is the composition of its board, and, informally, the size of its corpus. In a family foundation, the majority of the trustees are family members; in a private independent foundation, trustees are those selected from the community for their expertise in or shared values with the foundation program areas. Private foundations (including family and private independent foundations), collectively, make nearly 90 percent of all grants made by foundations in the U.S. annually.

QUESTION?

What are operating foundations, and how do they differ from the other types presented here?
Operating foundations do not make grants. Instead, they exist for one purpose, such as finding a cure for a disease, and commit their endowments to that effort and their own operations (including building the corpus through investment).

Community Foundations

Community foundations are a great example of strength in numbers. They are established by a number of donors in a community, and continue to grow through new gifts to the corpus such as direct donations, legacy gifts, or annual donations. All community foundations are focused on a specific geographic area and do not make grants to organizations that are outside of their geographic focus.

Major Players

Because many community foundations were founded decades ago and have grown with continued donations and investments, they have built up their corpuses to the point that they are now some of the largest foundations in their communities. The Cleveland Foundation is the oldest community foundation in the United States; the New York Community Trust is the largest in terms of assets.

ALERT!

Do not apply for a grant from a community foundation that is in a different geographic region or city than that of your nonprofit client. These foundations are set up by individuals who want to restrict their grants to organizations within their own communities.

There are more than 500 community foundations in the United States, all of which restrict their giving to the community in which they were founded or, at most, to the state in which they were founded. Their boards are composed of community leaders who often include representatives of the major banks and law firms in the city. A new trend is to include some representatives from area nonprofit organizations. Community foundations work hard to keep their boards a diverse mix of individuals who reflect the composition of the overall city or region.

Foundations Within Foundations

One of the operational hallmarks separating a community foundation from family, private independent, and most corporate foundations is that a community foundation both raises funds and makes grants. They also hold, administer, and grant money through separate "donor-directed" foundations.

You need to submit only one grant proposal to a community foundation to access funds held in a small foundation or trust. Part of the job of community-foundation staff is to match your needs with the interests of donors and make recommendations for funding. Sometimes you can get two grant awards with one proposal.

The grant-making process for these donor-directed funds is separate from the programs operated by the community foundation. Different boards and different values guide their giving. These smaller foundations within the community foundation benefit from having the community-foundation staff provide fiscal and grant-making oversight.

Public Foundations

Public foundations are generally small foundations established for a specific purpose, such as women's issues, or church funds. They raise funds and grant funds as a grant-making public charity.

Other Sources of Grants and Funding

There are also other places to find grants, such as:

- **Discretionary Funding:** Family foundations and large independent foundations often have set amounts of discretionary funds—grants that can be awarded on the decision of one person, rather than an entire board—for program officers, presidents, and some board members. Read their annual reports or call the foundation to learn who has control over discretionary funds and how you can request them. These small grants can be quite easy to get, as you only have to convince one person of the value of your proposed project.

- **United Way/Community Trust:** United Ways are not endowed and, thus, are not considered foundations. Through annual fund drives, they raise funds that are then granted to programs and organizations selected, most often, by a group of community members.

Billionaire Foundations

There are between fifty and sixty private family or independent foundations that have assets of more than $1 billion and make millions of dollars in grants annually. They are staffed with numerous program officers and often have communications departments, presidents, vice presidents, financial officers, and other departments and staff similar to that of a large corporation. Their sophisticated operations and programming can make the private independent foundation more difficult to reach, especially if the geographic or social reach of your program or activity is narrow.

Many of these larger billionaire foundations are now focused on world issues, such as developing philanthropy and a nonprofit sector in emerging democracies, finding a cure for HIV/AIDS, or saving the rain forests in South America. Often, even if your nonprofit organization is located in the same city as the offices of the foundation, you will have a difficult time getting their attention. Your nonprofit must have a really creative solution to a perplexing systemic problem and be as highly sophisticated in its operations as the billionaire foundation if you are to be successful in approaching these foundations.

Requesting Guidelines

A good way to identify foundations in your area is to request a catalog or CD from your Regional Association of Grantmakers (RAG). RAGs provide services to all the foundations within a region and develop catalogs that list them, often by city, alphabetically, and/or by type, and sometimes also by program area.

Once you've identified the foundations that operate in your area, you should request guidelines from each of them. If you just want to learn more about the foundation for future reference, request the guidelines by telephone or simply download them from the Internet. If, however, you have a particular project you intend to propose, you should write a letter. Briefly—preferably two paragraphs or less, but no more than one page—describe the project you hope to submit, then close by requesting a copy of their guidelines. In this way, the foundation can help you assess whether they'll be interested in receiving a proposal to learn more about the project. And—a big bonus—they sometimes even send a small donation without you ever having to submit a full proposal.

One format that identifies the project and also asks for guidelines follows.

Date
Name of Executive Director
Foundation
Address
City/State/ZIP

Dear Name:

ABC College, a liberal arts college founded in 1886, and DEF Theatre, a fifty-year-old performance and production theatre company, have joined together in your community to build a new performance complex on the ABC College campus. The complex will feature a 500-seat theatre and several classrooms/rehearsal halls, and will represent a new direction for education through the arts. The shared vision for the partnership is to enrich, educate, and entertain the community with dramatic arts that are innovative, creative, and accessible to all.

Both partners in this undertaking must grow to meet "customer" demands. In ABC's case, it must expand its curricula in dramatic arts, arts education, and arts management, and will be strongly positioned to do so with a performance-arts complex and its long-term collaboration with DEF Theatre. DEF Theatre operates a children's performing-arts program, a full-season theatrical production house, and hosts numerous visiting performances for a range of ages. Its current facility, Arts House, has seating for only 300 and cannot be expanded further, despite consistent sell-out performances. In addition, DEF is limited by the owners of the current facility to providing theatrical productions only from May through September. A school operates in the theatre off-season, and it too could improve programming in a facility dedicated to only one purpose. DEF Theatre and ABC College are also planning collaboratively with the Children's Museum, city public schools, member schools of area Intermediate School District, and other arts organizations in the community to develop curricula, joint programming, audience-engagement strategies, and future presentations.

The partnership between arts and educational organizations reflects a national trend toward cooperative efforts of nonprofit organizations to build audiences and help develop in individuals a deeper, richer involvement in the arts. When the facility is complete, ABC students—as well as the members of the larger community—will be afforded opportunities to participate in various aspects of dramatic-arts production or attend arts presentations that are relevant to and enrich their classroom learning. In addition, ABC and DEF Theatre plan teacher and student-teacher workshops with guest artists and staff to build parent/child relationships, incorporate the arts into the curricula, encourage creativity, and celebrate multiculturalism.

In January, the partners launched a joint $5.6-million capital campaign to construct and equip the performing-arts center and provide seed money for collaborative projects. At the close of year one of the campaign, the local community, including major donors, DEF Theatre patrons, and ABC alumni, has committed more than $2.2 million. Architectural renderings are complete, and site improvements preparatory to construction have begun.

ABC College and DEF Theatre are eager to tell you more or to answer specific questions about a project that promises to be one of the first of its kind in the United States—one that reaches new audience segments, engages them fully in lifelong learning and the performing arts, and provides a national model for organizational and community learning. We respectfully request that guidelines for a full-grant application be sent to our president, ABC College, 1600 Main Road, your town and state. Thank you in advance for your assistance.

Sincerely,   Sincerely,
College President   Theatre Director

Guidelines provide some or all of the following useful information:

- Name of a contact person and telephone numbers
- Description of program areas (the types of projects the foundation is interested in hearing about)
- Restrictions, or those projects, geographic areas, or types of organizations the foundation does not fund
- Range of grant awards and average grant award
- Assets of the foundation
- Previous projects the foundation has funded
- An application form
- An outline for a proposal narrative
- A list of required attachments for the grant proposal
- Deadlines for submission
- General indication of the time it takes from submission to approval or denial
- Foundation history, mission, values, board roster, or anything else that will help you learn what motivates their giving

Other Sources of Information

While you are exploring the range of foundations in your area, you may also be interested in learning more about foundations throughout the United States. Besides the Foundation Center Web site, a great source of information to help you explore is the Council on Foundations (COF), a national organization that supports philanthropy throughout the United States and provides services and publications to member foundations.

You may also wish to use the Internet to download the guidelines of your targeted foundations, but do so only for information gathering. If you have a project in mind, you really should request guidelines or write a letter of inquiry to make sure you aren't wasting energy. If the foundation is not interested in receiving a full proposal, they will say so. That keeps you from wasting your time on behalf of a project the foundation knows its board will not consider for funding.

Chapter 5

The Right Source

You want to be able to search out funding sources for special projects and, often, for operating funds. In this chapter you'll learn more about sorting through the vast amount of information available and narrowing your field of prospects.

5

When Is a Government Grant Appropriate?

Governments cannot be solicited for funds; instead, you must rely on matching your project with an appropriate RFP. Watch for RFPs not only from the most obvious department—such as Department of Education grants for school districts—but also from other departments. You might find an opportunity from the Department of Justice, for instance, that will allow a school district to apply for funding to provide drug- or violence-prevention programs.

Also work with others in the community. Federal grant providers nearly always want to know as much as they can about the nonprofit infrastructure in your community. Who's doing what? Where is the potential for duplication? And where is the potential for partnership and cost savings? While many of the larger foundations are also interested in multiagency approaches to community problems, the most likely source for funding to allow such an undertaking is the federal government.

When Is a Foundation Grant Appropriate?

Foundation grants are most appropriate for local projects, especially those from organizations the foundations have worked with in the past or for projects in which the foundations have a high interest.

In Maggie's community, nearly all the foundations support agencies that provide services for young children, including child-abuse/neglect prevention, early education, and children's health and nutrition. The community foundation also sponsored a task-force study on issues of children in the community. The study recommended that there should be a new interagency approach to treating child-abuse victims. Because of the community foundation's stature, several other funders joined in. Together they launched a new program that, in its ten years of existence, has enjoyed relatively stable funding from all of the original funders and others in the community.

Foundations, unlike government funders, can be solicited for funding and can have their interest piqued by your communications. Often, as you establish relationships with foundation program officers, you can simply pick up the telephone and query the program officers about ideas for new projects.

Never submit a grant proposal to a community foundation unless it is targeted to your own community. These foundations are endowed by local people, and their intent is that the money be spent on local projects.

Organizations outside the headquarters area of national funders like the W. K. Kellogg Foundation, the Pew Charitable Trusts, Gates Foundation, Robert Wood Johnson Foundation, or the Rockefeller Fund should only approach these foundations in response to an RFP or by a special invitation from the funder. An exception can be made for projects that promise to have a national reach or effect. Grants from these foundations are difficult to get without a truly strategic and trendsetting project.

A Checklist of Considerations

You need to consider several things while narrowing your field of prospects:

- Is your organization a qualified 501(c)(3) nonprofit?
- What is your organization's program focus, and where does it match funding programs?
- What type of funding is needed? (Use **TABLE 5-1** to identify type of funding.)
- How much funding is needed?
- Why would anyone—particularly a funder—be interested in this project?
- What kinds of other projects are going on that might benefit from a partnership or being merged as part of a "larger picture" of response?

Table 5-1: What Type of Funding Do You Need?			
Appropriate for	Government funds	Foundations	Other
Operations	Only as indirect allocation or from local government	Local only	United Way; annual fund drive
Large, costly projects	Yes	Only in partnership	Community members
Small projects	Occasionally	Yes	Internal funding
Capital projects	Rarely	Yes, local only	Community
Model projects	Yes	Yes (include national)	
Products/inventions	Yes, sometimes	No	Private investors
Research projects	Yes	Sometimes	By contract
Launch new nonprofit	Rarely	Sometimes	Board members, collaborations
Endowment	No	No	Community
Maintenance endowment	No	As part of capital drive	Community
Sustaining new programs	No	Sometimes	Community

Use systems thinking to resolve difficult social problems. The responses that work best are those in which the entire system mobilizes. It takes businesses, nonprofits, schools, hospitals, communications specialists, community members, and hundreds of others to see the problem—and the potential for change—from every viewpoint.

Narrowing the Field of Prospects

Sure, it only costs a stamp to write letters to every foundation or government agency listed in a grant-seeking catalog, but it's a waste of postage and your time if you're unlikely to succeed.

Mass mailings can really damage the credibility of your organization. It's very much like submitting a science-fiction novel to the publisher of Harlequin romances. If they remember your name, they are not likely to read any subsequent submissions that you send in—even if you've written the next *Gone with the Wind*.

A Better Approach

It's much better to target each letter or grant proposal to the individual interests and focus of each grantmaker. To do that, you have to read the guidelines or the RFP very carefully. When you've discovered several likely prospects, target your submissions to those funders and funding sources that are the most appropriate of all.

Maggie's Case

Maggie once had to advise her clients to seek a grant they didn't want to go after: "The leaders of the organization had read through the RFP, and they thought it was offered as a grant for providing programs for troubled teenage girls. But when I read through it, I saw that it was a grant to convene all the 'players' in the community and have them develop a systemic, cooperative approach to addressing teen girls' problems. My organization, however, had no experience in collaborating or operating focus groups or any of the things called for in the grant.

"When they understood what the grant was about, they decided against seeking the funding. I had to explain to them that if they received the grant, they could hire another organization with grant money to facilitate the meetings. Moreover, if they were successful in leading the effort, they could gain credibility with the other organizations in town and become a linchpin organization in addressing the needs of problem teens."

ALERT!

If you are a freelance grant writer, think like a consultant advisor. Your clients will be eager to go after every grant possible. You should advise them when a grant is inappropriate or when their planned approach is not in keeping with the goals of the program.

Maggie eventually persuaded the nonprofit to apply, and as a result, they were acknowledged statewide as the only applicant who addressed the true purpose of the grant. Three years later, they had state senators on the organization's board, and now they can raise money easily to support the programs they've developed.

Don't Make Random Attempts

Maybe you've been successful in garnering large federal grants, but don't start applying for anything and everything. If you see an RFP that you think you could do something with, but the deadline is in two weeks and you haven't even talked to others in the community about partnering, it's best to get some ideas going and start planning now for the next time that RFP is issued.

Reading Guidelines

After the Internet, the second place to search for appropriate foundations is with a national or regional catalog of foundations. These catalogs are available from publishing houses, your regional association of grantmakers, and the Council on Foundations. Catalogs are often available on CD for interactive keyword searches.

Read such listings carefully, beginning with the focus of the foundation. Often, the catalog has an index of lists by program focus (children, the arts, environment, and so on) that you can use to target the list of appropriate funders for your organization.

FACT

The Foundation Center (*www.foundationcenter.org*) provides an online search engine to identify foundations that might be interested in your project. The Center also hosts the Philanthropy News Digest Message Board (*http://members4.boardhost.com/PNDtalk*), where you can ask questions of experienced grant writers and fundraisers, share ideas, or reflect on issues associated with fund seeking.

Looking at the Profile

Next, look at each individual foundation's profile. First, read the purpose of the foundation; you want to make sure they share an interest in your project. You also want to check for hints about the best way to approach them. For instance, a foundation that has interests both in education and in environmental protection might be very interested in a summer-camp program that provides environmental education and experiences for young people.

What's in Their Purpose Statement?

Also, check the purpose statement to make sure that your project exactly fits their program interest. For instance, they might be listed as supporting education, but when you turn to the profile, you learn that their purpose is to strengthen community colleges in their region. Therefore, your program for a local high school is outside their area of interest and not a good fit.

Do They Target a Location?

Next, check for geographic priorities. If the foundation only makes local grants and your agency is on the other side of the state, cross its name off your list. If the foundation makes national grants, your project must have national importance if it is to be considered.

What about Limitations?

Next, look at the restrictions or limitations. Often, a listing contains one of three statements that should be used to eliminate the foundation from your list of prospects. The first two of these statements will say, "Grant funds are generally limited to charitable organizations already favorably known to the foundation," or "Grant funds are committed." Each of these statements means relatively the same thing—that the foundation is already working with established organizations and committing money to those organizations year after year.

The third statement you might see, "No unsolicited proposals considered," means that if you can't meet in person with the foundation principals to generate excitement about your proposal prior to submitting it, you should scratch this foundation from your cold-call list.

Other Restrictions

In addition, most catalog lists of foundations provide a paragraph on what each foundation will not fund. Restricted funding might include some or all of the following:

- Operating support
- Program-related investments/loans
- Endorsements
- Publications
- Conferences/seminars
- Underwriting for special events/sponsorships
- Grants to individuals
- Scholarships
- Fellowships
- Educational loans
- Endowments
- Travel or research grants
- Religious purposes

What Money Is Available?

Finally, look at the range of grants and the typical grant size. This information is published in the catalog, but rarely in guidelines received directly from a foundation.

If the grants range from $500 to $10,000 but the typical grant size is $1,000, you will probably approach this funder only when you are at the end of a large fundraising effort or if you have a very small project.

ALERT!

Most foundations prefer not to be the sole funder on a project; they want to see that you are asking others to support the effort, too. Be sure to keep a list of all the foundations from which you are seeking funding and the status of your requests (e.g., pending, not yet requested, committed) both to guide your work and to share with potential funders.

Develop a Strategy

Be strategic in your approach to foundations. Four or five well-targeted grants will serve you and your organization far better than one letter sent to 200 foundations. Expect to be able to narrow the broad field of prospects to about 10 percent. Then work that 10 percent with everything you have.

Reading RFPs

The first thing to read in the RFP is the purpose of the legislation and fund. What does the funder hope to accomplish with its money? If the stated purpose matches the purpose or mission of your program, continue reading. If it somewhat matches, continue reading to see if you can tweak your program to fit more closely.

Who Qualifies for Money?

Next, look at the list of qualified applicants. Often the organization qualified to apply is very specific. For instance, some grants call for the applicant to be a community mental-health organization (CMH); others for a local educational agency (LEA); and still others for "330" health clinics, as designated by the federal government.

If your agency doesn't fit the qualification, do not give up! For instance, let's say your organization addresses issues surrounding homelessness. You have a food pantry, free kitchen, a store or outlet for inexpensive clothing, shelter services, work-skill development programs, and substance-abuse programs. Your clientele, however, does not have access to health care, and your organization does not qualify to apply for grants that fund health care for the indigent.

Can You Find a Partner?

In this case, identify the agencies in town that are qualified to provide those services. Call them and suggest a partnership that would enable your organization's clientele to receive free or reduced-cost health care.

What Else to Note

Other important criteria to help you select the right RFP include the following:

- Deadline and amount of narrative required. Let's face it: You are not likely to do a good job on a 300-page grant if the deadline is just two or three weeks off.
- Funding allocation, average amount of awards, and probable number of projects. When the average grant award is several hundred thousand or a million dollars, you can be sure that thousands of qualified organizations will apply. You should calculate the odds of your project being chosen against the number of grants awarded and the time you will commit to writing the proposal.
- Match requirements. Often RFPs are issued for programs that require a certain local match and they will let you know what qualifies as a match.
- Sustainability requirements. Many federal grants require that an organization apply for a three- or four-year decreasing amount grant, in which case the applicant organization must commit to providing increasing amounts of its own money to continue the program over the four-year term of the grant.

Don't be afraid of the long shots. Even when only five grant awards are planned throughout your state, you can help create and "sell" a winning program.

Chapter 6

Grant-Seeker Workshops and Conferences

Almost every RFP issued includes announcements of grant-seeker workshops or conferences. Is it worth attending one of these workshops? Does it help you get the grant? In this chapter, you'll learn more about these grant-seeker workshops, how they can benefit you, and, in some cases, their drawbacks.

What Is a Grant-Seeker Workshop?

Most grant-seeker workshops are targeted to specific RFPs. Granting agencies sponsor workshops for grant seekers who plan to submit a proposal for funding in response to a particular RFP. These workshops are learning opportunities, and are usually held within sixty days of the deadline for proposals. They are not intended as a place where you can showcase or have peers review your work; you'd have to go to a grant-writing workshop for that.

Grant-writing workshops charge a fee and may well be worthwhile for developing and honing grant-writing skills. Fees usually average $150 for a half- or full-day session. Grant-seeker workshops are free and are focused on a specific RFP.

Grant-Seeker Workshops Are Free

You may be asked to preregister for a grant-seeker workshop, especially if the agency hosting the workshop expects a large turnout of grant seekers. If the grantor is a federal agency, the workshop is likely to be held in two or three different locations in the nation. If a state agency is sponsoring the workshop, it will probably be held in the state capital. If the local government or an intermediary issues the RFP, it will likely take place at one of the local agencies or a common meeting place. In some cases, you will be provided with a choice of dates and locations for the workshop.

Why Should You Go?

A grant-seeker workshop provides additional information about the proposal process that may or may not be available in the RFP. It is sometimes the place where an RFP is released for the first time. You can also count on the workshop leaders to give you pointers or tips on developing programs that respond to the RFP and to answer your questions about individual projects or to respond to frequently asked questions.

Who Holds Workshops?

In most cases, grant-seeker workshops are provided by the granting agency or consultants to that agency or government department. On occasion, however, a central support agency for a large group of similar nonprofit organizations, such as an intermediate school district, will provide grant-seeker conferences for its constituents when new funding opportunities become available.

Grant-seeker workshops are rarely mandatory; however, in a few instances, attendance at the workshop is an absolute prerequisite if you want your project to be considered. Read through notices carefully; if you miss an opportunity because of carelessness, you could disqualify your agency for consideration.

State Workshops

Grant-seeker workshops vary in size, site, and value depending on who offers them. State grant-seeker workshops are usually held in a convention center or another large site in a state capital. You'll find hundreds of people whose grant-writing skills vary from complete novice to professional writers attending on behalf of their clients. Grant-seeker workshops can last anywhere from a half day to a full day. Many of them include breakout sessions in which you and other members of the audience can ask more specific questions and get answers from workshop leaders.

Some national foundations will request a preliminary proposal and then invite the "short list" agencies to attend one of two or three workshops (for instance, one East Coast, one West Coast) prior to submitting their final proposal. Such grant-seeker workshops are mandatory.

If a federal department is issuing an RFP for a brand-new funded program, and if a lot of money has been allocated to the grant program, the department is likely to hold three or four grant-seeker workshops throughout the United States. Don't plan on any sightseeing, though—most of your day will be spent indoors at the convention center.

Local Grant-Seeker Workshops

Locally sponsored grant-seeker workshops are usually attended by no more than 100 people. They tend to be more valuable to grant writers for several reasons. The smaller audience allows more time for questions about specific projects, and even when it isn't your project being discussed, you can use the answers to frame your own narrative accordingly.

If you are invited to attend a personal meeting with a member of the foundation staff, always accept the opportunity. You'll get insight into what the foundation is looking for in proposals, tips on what to include, and the ability to form a professional relationship that you will value for years.

Eavesdrop on the Competition

A benefit to attending local grant-seeker workshops is that it's an opportunity to listen and learn what others are planning. You may hear about another project that meshes well with what your organization wants to do. If you can get together, it would give you an opportunity to collaborate with another agency in a unique and mutually beneficial way. At the very least, when you listen to others talking about their projects, you will be able to gauge the strength of your proposal in comparison to what others are submitting for the same funding.

Who Hosts Local Workshops?

Local grant-seeker workshops are usually provided by large supporting organizations such as city governments, arts councils, intermediate school districts, or intermediary grantees. Specialized funders such as local Rotary or Variety Clubs that offer once-a-year grants programs may also be hosts.

On occasion, some foundations will hold seminars for the grant-seeking public after they have changed their grant-making focus or process. Go to these seminars even if you don't have a grant-proposal idea in mind for the foundation.

When You Should Attend a Workshop

If any one of the following is true, you should plan to attend the grant-seekers workshop:

- The workshop is deemed mandatory by the grantor.
- You have questions about the RFP, funding limits, or the category you wish to apply for.
- You are new to grant writing.
- You have never written a proposal to that particular granting agency or governmental department.
- You're curious about who else is applying for competitive grants.
- The workshop is offered by a local foundation that has an announcement to make.

What Will You Learn?

Grant-seeker workshops usually begin with an overview of the RFP and announcements of any subsequent changes made to the program or funding allowances since the RFP was issued. These changes are valuable information that you'll find nowhere else, except perhaps in a press release buried somewhere on the Web.

A Good Source for Tips

You'll also receive tips on developing programs that respond to the RFP, as well as cautions about things that will be more difficult for you to justify as worthy of funding. The staff of the grant-seeker workshop will be able to tell you how you can make a new project fit the parameters of the grant, and they may also encourage you to try an approach that is more likely to receive funding.

When an RFP has several categories for funding, the workshop often includes breakout sessions you can attend that address each specific category. If you intend to apply in more than one category, and if the breakout sessions are being held concurrently, you have one of two choices. You can go to one session and hope to find out afterward what information was discussed at the other, or you can plan ahead and bring a colleague to the workshop so you can each cover one of the sessions.

Yes, Workshops Get Repetitive

As you become an experienced grant writer, you'll find the workshops become redundant, even when a new grant opportunity arises. Depending on who organizes and leads the workshops, the sessions can sometimes make you feel like you're attending a college lecture.

No matter how boring workshops can be, you are guaranteed to learn at least one vital piece of information. It will be something that has been added to or changed in the RFP since it was issued, or maybe an entirely new piece of information.

Sometimes, session leaders also attempt to present a mini course on grant writing. They usually provide the information in a half-hour Power-Point presentation led by a sociology professor from a local university. Usually, the information offers little of real value to a new grant writer. It certainly won't take the place of what you learn in this book or what you'll learn from experience in the field.

Advantages and Disadvantages

There are other advantages to attending a grant-seeker workshop, in addition to those that have been discussed previously in this chapter. They include the following:

- Marketing opportunities for a new grant-writing venture
- Potential for gaining a competitive advantage over grant seekers not in attendance. You'll get "inside" information or learn about others who intend to apply for the same grant.
- The opportunity to ask questions and learn from questions asked by others. That also gives you a valuable edge in writing your grant proposal.
- At least one new bit of information that you can use in writing this proposal or another down the line

Like everything else in life, there is a downside as well, and you have to take that into consideration. Disadvantages of attending a grant-seeker workshop include:

- They are time consuming, often taking at least a half-day or more (not including travel).
- You'll be in a crowd that has diverse and wide-ranging skills and experience; if you're a more experienced grant writer, you'll have to put up with elementary questions.
- They tend to be redundant after a while, particularly if you have already participated in workshops offered by the same granting agency or government department.
- Unless the workshop includes breakout sessions or coffee breaks, you may have little or no opportunity to talk to presenters and receive help or advice about specific questions.

You can't know, of course, before you go how good the grant-seeker workshop will be or what it will offer of value. Just keep in mind that these can be valuable, especially as you are starting to write your first grant proposal.

Chapter 7

Letters of Intent and Inquiry

Grant writers have to write a lot of letters, chief among them letters of inquiry and letters of intent. In this chapter, you'll learn the difference between the two and read some guidelines for writing each kind.

What's the Difference?

Many people get confused about letters of intent and letters of inquiry, but you don't have to worry. Just think of a letter of intent as a form stating that you intend to apply for a grant. In contrast, a letter of inquiry is more like a sales pitch, in which you describe your project in the hopes of being invited to submit a complete grant proposal.

Letters of Intent

In a letter of intent, you are telling the granting agency that you plan to respond to a request for proposals. These letters are often sent to governments, since they are the agencies that usually issue RFPs.

Sometimes the granting agency doesn't request a letter of intent at all. If they don't ask for it, don't send one. The agencies that do request letters of intent do so simply to learn how many project proposals they can expect to receive. Sometimes, they might also be interested in finding out from which geographical areas potential proposals will be submitted.

Letters of Inquiry

When you write a letter of inquiry, think of yourself as a sales representative. Your letter of inquiry describes your project and asks for permission to submit a grant proposal. These letters are usually sent to foundation-type funders. Increasingly, foundations are requiring letters of inquiry as the first step in their grant-proposal cycle.

Use a letter of inquiry when the foundation guidelines request this step and/or when you are unclear about whether the foundation funds the type of project you wish to present.

When to Send a Letter of Intent

There are three considerations regarding letters of intent. First, you may not be required to write one at all. Second, you may be requested to write the letter, but not required to send it. Third, you have no choice. In this case, the letter of intent is a necessity, and it will have an absolute deadline for reaching the foundation or government office.

If the instructions say nothing at all about letters of intent, you can assume that it is neither required nor requested. When one is requested but not required, the instructions about a letter of intent say something like, "You are not required to submit a letter of intent, and doing so does not commit you to applying for this grant."

Only submit a letter of intent when one is requested or required in the request for proposals. Pay attention to the deadline for submission of the letter; being late is the same as submitting no letter at all. Also differentiate between required and requested. If you do not submit a required letter of intent by the deadline, you will not be allowed to submit a full proposal for funding.

When a letter of intent is required, the instructions will say something like, "You are required to submit a letter (or notice) of intent to apply by 5:00 P.M. on January 20. Only those organizations submitting a letter of intent by the indicated deadline will be eligible to apply for funds under this grant program." Make no mistake—you must meet that deadline. If it gets there at 5:01 P.M., the letter will be too late.

Components of a Strong Letter of Intent

Letters of intent are short and to the point. They should be no longer than one page, and should contain the following pertinent information:

- Name of grant program
- Number of grant program (if available)
- Name of applicant
- Contact information for applicant
- Category of funding requested (when the RFP has separate categories)

Think of a letter of intent as a form (and in many cases, it actually will be a form), and include little beyond the required information. Don't request additional information or ask questions about your proposal.

Sample Letter of Intent

Increasingly, government agencies that require a letter of intent are supplying forms that you may complete and fax or submit electronically. They look something like this:

Notice of Intent to Apply for (2008–09) Program Grant

Submit this form no later than January 1, 2008, to assist Department of Education staff in determining the number of reviewers that will be necessary.

Submission of this notice is not a prerequisite for application of grant funds, nor does it obligate the organization to submit an application.

Organization:

Contact Person:

Phone:

Fax:

E-mail:

County(ies) to Be Served:

Mail or fax this form to:

Address:

Fax Number:

Following is a sample notice of intent from a grant seeker.

Dear Name:

The XYZ Nonprofit in City, State, intends to submit a grant proposal in response to program number 123456.9 in the Federal Register. Of the three categories for projects described in the designated RFP, XYZ plans to submit under category "C": Nonprofit community collaborations to address shortages of affordable housing.

I understand that this grant proposal will be due by 5:00 p.m. on March 31, year, in your offices. If supplementary information becomes available in the interim or if you have reservations about our qualifications to apply for this grant, please contact me by any of the following means:

Phone: 555-5555
Fax: 555-5566
E-mail: xyz@xyz.com
Thank you.
Sincerely,
Executive Director
XYZ Nonprofit

When to Use a Letter of Inquiry

It is becoming increasingly common for foundations to request a letter of inquiry (LOI) as the first step in the grant-seeking process. Sometimes, they just want a letter, other times they supply a format you should follow, which is similar to, but shorter than, a full proposal. The rationale behind LOIs is that the foundation really doesn't want you to go to the trouble of completing a long grant proposal if they know it is unlikely to be funded.

A letter of inquiry, unlike a letter of intent, should include a compelling summary of your program plans. Include potential links between your program and the goals of the funder, and, if you are writing the LOI in the form of a letter, request a discussion of the merits of the project.

Components of a Strong Letter of Inquiry

A letter of inquiry should be addressed to a specific person within the granting agency, most often the program officer. If the foundation is not staffed, find the contact person (perhaps a bank official or the founder) in the guidelines. Your letter of inquiry should include the following:

- The problem or need you are addressing
- A summary of the project
- Potential outcomes of the project
- A direct or indirect reference to the ways the project fits the goals or guidelines of the foundation
- An indication of the amount you hope to request and the structure of the grant (i.e., one year, three year, challenge, matching, etc.)
- A brief budget and breakdown of expenses and revenues, including other places the nonprofit has applied or plans to apply for funding
- Reference to partners in the project
- Outcomes of previous fundraising efforts, if any
- A request for a meeting or discussion of the merits of the project and a subsequent invitation to submit a full proposal

Sample Letter of Inquiry

Here is a letter of inquiry Maggie used when seeking a grant for one of her local nonprofit agencies. Note that Maggie links the project outcomes to the stated objectives of the granting agency found in their guidelines. Take care to do the same in your letters of inquiry.

Dear Program Officer:

Last fall, the XYZ nonprofit launched a mobile media laboratory, a van equipped with laptop computers, digital video cameras, digital-video editing software, educational software, and e-learning curricula.

The project was deployed in response to needs for technology education and educational enrichment in several areas of the community. In its scheduled visits to inner-city and other public and parochial schools, and community and youth centers, the project provides kindergarten to twelfth-grade enrichment in the subject areas, and Internet and video-production training for children and young adults who would otherwise lack access to equipment or connections.

While the educational outcomes for project participants are not yet available, they do appear promising. The project has been enthusiastically received by teachers, students, community members, and organizational representatives. Students have a natural interest in the cameras and computers and quickly learn to operate the equipment and to edit film. Project staff uses that interest to encourage further exploration and study in content-area subjects, as requested by the teaching and administrative staffs of the individual schools.

XYZ now proposes that it use the project not only to enrich academic studies but also to engage children and young adults in the creative process. Through a new program called [project name], staff plan to assist up to thirty at-risk middle and high school students in exploring their range of talent and in developing the artistic skills needed to support their natural abilities.

Students will participate in the new project five days a week for eight weeks. They will receive several one-act plays written by a local writer, a freelance playwright, and director, who will develop four to six "starter" plays on various topics of interest to young people. He will guide the students in writing the middles and ends to the plays they select. When they are finished, the group will read all the works and select a person to act as the playwright for the remainder of the project. All students will also study stage production, acting, directing, camera operation, and film editing with the playwright and a staff videographer, and through interactive teaching modules on the Internet accessed with project laptops.

Students may then select or try out for assignments related to producing the play and videotaping it as an artistic film. Some will become actors, others set designers, camera operators, costume designers, film editors, etc. Completed plays will be performed live and filmed and edited as short features for broadcast on public-access television or streaming to the Internet. Some components of the plays may be made into performing exhibits for display at the local partner agency. The completed curriculum and resulting work will be shared with other school districts that require new or enhanced arts programs.

Project outcomes include:

- Students will engage in the creative process, learn to work as a group, and come to appreciate their own and others' various talents and skills.
- Students will demonstrate a deeper and long-lasting appreciation for the arts.
- Schools struggling with budgets will have improved, rather than reduced, arts curricula and programming.

XYZ requires $_____ to launch the project, which will include the following:

- $_____Curriculum development (two months); development of interactive curriculum components and deployment to Web
- $_____ Vignettes and 8 weeks' program (five days per week), playwright
- $_____8 weeks' program, video production and broadcast
- $_____Miscellaneous (costumes, set design, vehicle expenses, etc.)

XYZ is just beginning to explore funding sources for this project. We hope to hear from you soon, not only to learn that you are inviting a full proposal for review by your board, but also to hear your ideas for additional partnerships or program refinements. Thank you for your assistance.

Sincerely,

Executive Director

Some foundations provide LOI forms and guidelines for writing a short narrative. As with grant proposals, follow the instructions and include all the information requested in forms like the sample that follows:

COMMUNITY FOUNDATION
Letter of Inquiry

_____

Legal Name of Organization

_____

Address of Organization

_____

Executive Director/President or CEO   Title

_____

Contact person (if different from CEO/Executive Director)

_____

Phone number

_____

Fax number

_____

E-mail address

_____

Attachments:
- Does the organization have 501(c)(3) non profit status?   Yes   No
  _____ (Please enclose a copy of the designation letter)
- Please attach a draft project budget.
- Please submit eight copies of your Letter of Inquiry.

Please use the following format to describe the issue you hope to address, limiting the description to two additional pages or less:
- Describe the issue that you hope to address with assistance from the Foundation. In what way is your identification of this issue and the proposed resolution based on credible data? (Please include a summary of the data)
- Please describe how this project addresses the Foundation's principles. If it does not address the principles, it is unlikely to be considered.
- How do you propose to address the issue?
- What will be accomplished through this project? How do you plan to evaluate your success?
- What is the proposed time frame for the project?

Which of the following roles do you foresee the Foundation playing in addressing the identified issue?

Convening

Advocating

Leveraging resources

Funding (if requesting funds, how much is requested? $_____

Leading an initiative

Please do not submit attachments other than those requested.

$_____ $_____

Proposed budget for the project Organization's current operating budget

_____

Signature of CEO/Executive Director or Board Chairperson   Date

Please forward this form, your narrative, and attachments to:

Community Foundation

City, State, Zip

Chapter 8

Components of a Grant Proposal

The grant proposal is your response to a request for proposals (RFP) or foundation guidelines. The RFP or guidelines contain your instructions and, most often, an outline of content. In this chapter, you'll learn what the outline usually looks like and get some tips for reading between the lines.

What to Expect

RFPs and guidelines can range from a single sheet to hundreds of pages of instructions and attachments. In nearly every case, the RFP or guidelines require that your proposal include a summary, a needs section, a project description (with goals and objectives), an evaluation section, and a budget.

The entire RFP package is instructional, so it's helpful if you read every word in it. Accomplished grant writers turn first to the outline to determine how much work will go into the proposal. Then they read the remainder of the packet to ensure that they are not missing important information.

> Freelance grant writers can use the outline to identify the extent of the work required. Based on the outline, they can determine (a) whether they can schedule adequate time to work on the proposal and (b) the cost estimate for their services.

RFPs from the Federal Register are several pages in length. Each page contains up to four columns of very small type. It will probably take approximately one hour to review the contents and make notes on important information that will help guide your writing process.

The outline for the proposal will be apparent, but additional directions may be scattered throughout the RFP. You'll find other important and relevant information such as the following:

- Paper size and composition (The Environmental Protection Agency, for instance, requires use of recycled paper.)
- Spacing (If not specified as double spaced, single space your documents and double space between paragraphs or indent the beginning of each paragraph.)
- Minimum size of typeface (and sometimes the font you must use)
- Deadline for submission (and whether by postmark or arrival date)
- Maximum number of pages

- Address and phone numbers for contact people and for submissions
- Formats
- Qualifications for grantees
- Purpose and goals of the grant program (These are critical, as you want your program to further the goals of the grantor.)
- Necessary forms and attachments
- Instructions for completing forms
- Additional sections required (such as compliance statements, tables of contents, abstracts, etc.)
- Instructions for the order in which you must compile the finished grant-proposal packet (sometimes also provided as a checklist)

You may find instructions in the back of an RFP for submitting to the State Single Point of Contact, as well as to the granting agency. The State Single Point of Contact is a person or office in your state with the responsibility of cataloging who applies for what grants and responding to questions during the application process.

Follow the Directions

A key rule to responding to an RFP is follow the directions. If you forget or ignore directions when you've gone through the instructions, your proposal may not be reviewed. If the instructions have an outline with Roman numerals, numbers, or alpha characters, your response should include the same designations for each section. If you find a section not applicable, you must enter the designation and a header for it before writing, "Not applicable." Grant reviewers use score sheets that are keyed to the instructions, so if your outline doesn't follow theirs or your information is in the wrong place, they may reduce your score.

Review Criteria

Some RFPs replace an outline for your narrative with review criteria or a rubric. Read the questions or qualifications contained in the criteria carefully. Try to determine the gist of each question the grantors are posing. Then respond to each question as completely as you can.

The directions may or may not include review criteria. If they do not, use the questions or headings from the outline to determine exactly how the granting agency wants prospective grantees to answer.

Sample of Need-Section Instructions

Following are instructions, in the form of review criteria, for the need section of an educational grant:

1. NEED (Ten points) "The proposal provides a brief explanation of why the project is needed. It summarizes the demographics of the district and the selected buildings that will be served by this funding; possible causes for an increase in the number of students requiring special-education services or a decrease in state-assessment reading scores; and the need for new resources and programs for students who are not achieving in reading or who are at risk of reading failure."

Include Relevant Data

In following the instructions, you will provide relevant data, first about the district and then about the building(s) in which you will implement the program. Relevant data in this example would include the number of children and the percentage by building of children failing state assessment and other tests of reading. Other relevant data would point out possible causes for the need.

In addressing the last part of the criteria, you'll want to talk about what programs the buildings have tried in the past and why they haven't worked or helped children achieve as much as the principals had hoped. When you complete this section, you'll be set up to begin writing in the project description, addressing why this project will succeed where others have failed.

Follow the Outline

Be sure to follow the outline as closely as you can. Don't write a narrative description of your program—grant proposals are not literature. No matter how good your instincts usually are, if an outline calls for the "need" section to be followed by the description of the program, don't decide that it makes more sense to tell them "what" before you tell them "why."

ALERT!

Use the same headings the outline does. If they have a heading marked with "B" or Roman numeral "II," make sure that your heading also says "B" or "II." If they give you subheadings marked "a," "b," and "c," create subheadings marked exactly the same way.

The outline is provided to ensure that you address every item on which the proposal will be judged. Following it exactly means that you have responded to all the questions.

There Is No Outline?

Don't panic; a few RFPs don't come with outlines. The Small Business Innovation and Research (SBIR) grant offered by the federal government through several departments is one of them.

In these cases, request or look up on the Internet previous grant-proposal submissions. Often, the contact person will fax or mail you a copy of a successful proposal and you can use its general outline as a guide for your proposal writing.

A Last Resort

If you cannot locate or acquire a previous submission, base your response on the common elements of a grant proposal or a business plan. Discuss the need or potential market for a product. Describe the project or product. Talk about what remains to be done and how you expect to accomplish it.

Develop a budget and explain how you derived the numbers you included. Discuss at length the qualifications of the organization and its staff to carry out the project plan.

Finally, discuss an evaluation of the project or product—what you hope to learn from it and what you'll do with the evaluation once it's complete. Be sure to use headings and subheadings. They will assist readers in navigating the document.

Review Criteria Can Help

Sometimes you'll receive only review criteria without an outline. In these cases, you are expected to follow the review criteria as outlined in the RFP. Summarize the content of each criteria as your headings and subheadings, rather than writing out the entire statement. For instance, the following are review criteria for the first section, "Statement of Need." You may use one or several subheadings within each criterion:

Review Criteria	Suggested Subheadings
The extent to which the applicant specifies the goals and objectives of the project and describes how implementation will fulfill the purposes of the Early Learning Opportunities Act (ELOA). The applicant must demonstrate a thorough understanding of the importance of early learning services and activities that help parents, caregivers, and childcare providers incorporate early learning into the daily lives of young children, as well as programs that directly provide early learning to young children.	Goals and Objectives/Implementation Plan
The extent to which the applicant demonstrates the need for assistance, including identification and discussion of its needs and resources assessment concerning early learning services. Relevant data from the assessment should be included. Participant and beneficiary information must also be included.	Need for Assistance/Target Population

Review Criteria	Suggested Subheadings
The extent to which the applicant describes its resources assessment and the relevance of the results as the basis for determining its objectives and need for assistance.	Needs Assessment

Review Criteria	Suggested Subheadings
The extent to which the applicant demonstrates how it will give preference to supporting activities/projects that maximize the use of resources through collaboration with other early learning programs, provide continuity of services for young children across the age spectrum, and help parents and other caregivers promote early learning with their young children. The applicant must provide information about how decisions will be made about who will provide each early learning service and/or activity funded through this grant.	Partners and Their Roles/Maximizing Resources

Review Criteria	Suggested Subheadings
The extent to which the applicant demonstrates that it has worked with local education agencies to identify cognitive, social, emotional, and motor-developmental abilities that are necessary to support children's readiness for school; that the programs, services, and activities assisted under this title will represent developmentally appropriate steps toward the acquisition of those abilities; and that the programs, services, and assisted activities provide benefits for children cared for in their own homes as well as children placed in the care of others.	Review of Literature/Lessons Learned

Essential Components

A good grant proposal, like a good news story, tells who, what, where, when, why, and how.

"Who" is both the organization you are describing and the target population whose needs you expect to address with your project. You'll answer that in the needs section of the proposal.

"Where" is a description of the city or region in which the project will take place. You have to address where in the needs section.

"What" describes your project in detail. You'll place this in the project-description section.

"When" is your timeline of activities and it is contained in the project description.

"How" and "why?" You'll be answering these in various places throughout the RFP, like so:

- How many (people, units of service, hours)?
- How much (change is expected in the population/environment/outcomes)?
- How will you know? (evaluation)
- How much does it cost? (budget)
- How does your program fit the goals of the grant program?
- Why did you choose this particular program?
- Why is your organization the best one to do the work?
- Why do you think the project will work?
- Why should the grantor care?

You will be asked to describe all the essential components listed here in every grant proposal. Some RFPs, however, will also ask such things as the history of the organization, the genesis for the project, the roles of partners in the project, and the input by constituents or the target population into the design or evaluation of the project.

You might be asked to include your plan for disseminating the results of your evaluation. Some agencies want to know what literature you used in developing your project. You'll also be asked how you will sustain the program after grant funds are expended.

A new trend in grant proposals, especially among foundations, is a question about constituent input into program design and/or the evaluation process. This is to help nonprofit-organization staff begin to realize that they are not the final arbiters of someone else's need.

Federal Register Instructions Example

The sample RFP shown here is one of the tougher ones, in part because the language of the RFP is that of experts. Maggie suggests that only those who are experts in the field of child care attempt this grant proposal as a first project.

20527 Federal Register / Vol. 67, No. 80 / Thursday, April 25, 2002 / Notices

Part III General Instructions for Preparing the Uniform Project Description

ACF is particularly interested in specific factual information and statements of measurable goals in quantitative terms. Project descriptions are evaluated on the basis of substance, not length. Extensive exhibits are not required. Cross-referencing should be used rather than repetition. Supporting information concerning activities that will not be directly funded by the grant or information that does not directly pertain to an integral part of the grant-funded activity should be placed in an appendix.

The Project Description Overview Purpose

The project description provides a major means by which an application is evaluated and ranked to compete with other applications for available assistance. The project description should be concise and complete and should address the activity for which federal funds are being requested. Supporting documents should be included where they can present information clearly and succinctly. In preparing your project description, all information requested through each specific evaluation criteria should be provided. Awarding offices use this and other information in making their funding recommendations. It is important, therefore, that this information be included in the application. Pages should be numbered, and a table of contents should be included for easy reference.

A. Project Summary/Abstract/Geographic Location

Provide a summary of the project description (a page or less) with reference to the funding request. Describe the precise location of the project and boundaries of the area to be served by the proposed project. Maps or other graphic aids may be attached.

B. Objectives and Need for Assistance

Clearly identify the physical, economic, social, financial, institutional, and/or other problem(s) requiring a solution. The need for assistance must be demonstrated, and the principal and subordinate objectives of the project must be clearly stated; supporting documentation, such as letters of support and testimonials from concerned interests other than the applicant, may be included.

Any relevant data based on planning studies should be included or referred to in the endnotes/footnotes. Incorporate demographic data and participant/beneficiary information, as needed. In developing the project description, the applicant may volunteer or be requested to provide information on the total range of projects currently being conducted and supported (or to be initiated), some of which may be outside the scope of the program announcement.

C. Results or Benefits Expected

Identify the results and benefits to be derived. For example, specify the number of children and families to be served and how the services to be provided will be funded consistent with the local needs assessment. Or, explain how the expected results will benefit the population to be served in meeting its needs for early learning services and activities.

D. Approach/Evaluation Approach

Outline a plan of action that describes the scope and detail of how the proposed work will be accomplished. Account for all functions or activities identified in the application. Cite factors that might accelerate or decelerate the work and state your reason for taking the proposed approach rather than others.

Describe any unusual features of the project such as design or technological innovations, reductions in cost or time, or extraordinary social and community involvement.

Provide quantitative monthly or quarterly projections of the accomplishments to be achieved for each function or activity in such terms as the number of people to be served and the number of activities accomplished. When accomplishments cannot be quantified by activity or function, list them in chronological order to show the schedule of accomplishments and their target dates.

If any data is to be collected, maintained, and/or disseminated, clearance may be required from the U.S. Office of Management and Budget (OMB). This clearance pertains to any "collection of information that is conducted or sponsored by ACF."

List organizations, cooperating entities, consultants, or other key individuals who will work on the project, along with a short description of the nature of their effort or contribution.

E. Evaluation

Provide a narrative addressing how the results of the project and the conduct of the project will be evaluated. In addressing the evaluation of results, state how you will determine the extent to which the project has achieved its stated objectives and the extent to which the accomplishment of objectives can be attributed to the project. Discuss the criteria to be used to evaluate results, and explain the methodology that will be used to determine if the needs identified and discussed are being met, and if the project results and benefits are being achieved. With respect to the conduct of the project, define the procedures to be employed to determine whether the project is being conducted in a manner consistent with the work plan presented, and discuss the impact of the project's various activities on the project's effectiveness.

F. Additional Information

The following are requests for additional information that need to be included in the application:

- Staff and Position Data: Provide a biographical sketch for each key person appointed and a job description for each vacant key position. A biographical sketch will also be required for new key staff as appointed.

- Plan for Continuance Beyond Grant Support: Provide a plan for securing resources and continuing project activities after federal assistance has ceased.

- Organizational Profiles: Provide information on the applicant organization(s) and cooperating partners, such as organizational charts, financial statements, audit reports or statements from CPA/licensed public accountants, employer identification numbers, names of bond carriers, contact persons and telephone numbers, child-care licenses, and other documentation of professional accreditation, information on compliance with federal/state/local government standards, documentation of experience in the program area, and other pertinent information. Any nonprofit organization submitting an application must submit proof of its nonprofit status in its application at the time of submission. The nonprofit agency can accomplish this by providing a copy of the applicant's listing in the Internal Revenue Service's (IRS) most recent list of tax-exempt organizations described in section 501(c)(3) of the IRS code, or by providing a copy of the currently valid IRS tax-exemption certificate, or by providing a copy of the articles of incorporation bearing the seal of the state in which the corporation or association is domiciled.

- Third-Party Agreements: Include written agreements between grantees and subgrantees or subcontractors or other cooperating entities. These agreements must detail scope of work to be performed, work schedules, remuneration, and other terms and conditions that structure or define the relationship.

- Letters of Support: Provide statements from community, public, and commercial leaders that support the project proposed for funding. All submissions should be included in the application OR by application deadline.

G. Budget and Budget Justification

Provide line-item detail and detailed calculations for each budget-object class identified on the Budget Information form. Detailed calculations must include estimation methods, quantities, unit costs, and other similar quantitative detail sufficient for the calculation to be duplicated. The detailed budget must also include a breakout by the funding sources identified in Block 15 of the SF–424.

Provide a narrative budget justification that describes how the categorical costs are derived. Discuss the necessity, reasonableness, and allocation of the proposed costs.

Chapter 9

Preparing to Write

Always review the guidelines or RFP closely before you begin writing the first draft. Learn as much as you can about your audience—are they foundation trustees and staff or volunteers who may be your peers? Read between the lines of the RFP or guidelines to help you determine what they need and want to know about your organization and its programs. Focus on their interests rather than on what *you* need or want to tell them, and you're on your way to writing a successful grant proposal.

Know Your Readers

The first rule of all good writing is to know—and understand—your audience. How much do they already know about the subject? How much do they want to learn from your document? What are their biases? What are their interests?

For your purposes, there are two different kinds of grant readers: one reads foundation proposals, the other, government responses to RFPs.

Foundation Readers

Foundation staff, and occasionally, trustees, read foundation grant proposals. It helps, therefore, to read the guidelines, annual reports, or Web information thoroughly to learn as much as you can about their personal and collective interests before you submit a proposal.

Often, you can go to the local foundation to meet staff and discuss your proposal. Then you can revise it before they present it to their trustees. Alternately, program officers may come to your office (called a "site visit"), or ask you to meet in theirs so they can get more information to share with their trustees and to support their recommendations regarding funding.

These program officers are the critical people to impress in the foundation grant-seeking process. Listen to all of their requests for additional information and respond in a timely manner. If they want you to rewrite an entire proposal, do so. They are not the enemy; they know their boards and what the members want covered in proposals. Their job is to go before the trustees with solid reasons for recommending funding or declining the proposals—give them the tools to help you.

Government Grants

In the case of government grants, the proposal readers are the decision-makers or judges for each proposal. They are the most important figures in the entire process. They award points for each section, total the points, and average them with the scores of the other readers to come up with a final score. That final score must total an established number for the project to be funded. Recommendations of the judges don't have to be supported by the reviewers or questioned by the funding agency.

In most cases, these proposal readers are experts in their fields who have responded to a call for readers or been recruited by the issuing department. Proposal readers often represent a cross-section of geography, expertise, and interests, and are usually peers of those who are submitting proposals.

FACT

Very often, RFPs will include a supplementary call for readers. That means that any person who receives the RFP may also apply to become a judge. If the reader also represents an agency that has applied for the grant, he or she will not be assigned to review his or her own organization's proposal.

A research grant submitted to the National Institutes of Health, for instance, will be reviewed by a panel of scientists, Ph.D.s, and/or physicians. A proposal submitted to the U.S. Department of Education will be reviewed by educators and curriculum experts. If your proposal asks for funding for computers in schools, you can expect that along with educators, computer-software experts, technicians, and others familiar with computers will be reading the proposals.

A Tight Timeline for Readers

Proposal reviews usually take place in less than a week. Readers are sent ten or more proposals to read and score and return to the funding agency for final tallying. Usually, each proposal has three to five judges. Reviewers are provided score sheets to guide their judging, often in the form of rubrics or review criteria identical to that provided in the RFP, and a cover sheet or space to write comments. While they are not required to justify their scoring, they often do provide comments that you can use later to strengthen a failed proposal.

Scoring an RFP

While grant proposals are competitive, the individual proposals are not judged one against another. The final score is the average of all scores awarded by all readers of that proposal. That is the only criterion upon which funding is based, except in cases where the funding agency further ensures geographic equity.

A high score, however, does not always guarantee funding. If, for instance, 1,000 proposals are submitted and 500 of them score 90 out of 100 points, the benchmark for funding will be raised—to 95 or higher. If the grant has limited funds, it means that the grantmaker will fund only the best of the best projects, not all of the good projects.

FACT

As used in RFPs, a rubric is a chart that contains various classifications and explanations and the range of points that may be awarded to each category in the grant proposal. The readers of proposals use the rubric to guide their awarding of points to each section of your proposal. It is provided to grant writers to help them ensure that their responses to each section are as comprehensive as possible.

In the case of government grants, it is important to remember that you are writing to your peers or, in the case of freelance grant writers, to the peers of your clients. If your clients understand and support the narrative, chances are that the judges will be equally impressed.

Outlining

Outlining a grant proposal is the easiest thing you have to do. Simply follow the outline provided in the RFP or guidelines exactly.

Every Roman numeral in the RFP should have a corresponding Roman numeral in your outline. The same is true for all alpha characters and numbers. You also may want to include the point value for each question or some of your notes to the outline. You can delete them later.

Brainstorming

Once you have an outline and questions, sit down with other members of your organization and potential collaborators to brainstorm ideas for the program. This is not your typical brainstorming session in which "anything goes."

For this session, you should lay out the program mandates from the grant on one page of a flip chart and the components of programs your organization currently has in place on another page. Begin by comparing the two to see how you can modify existing programs to fit more closely with the program sought in the RFP.

If there is information that you aren't sure of, or areas you know less about, ask other staff members for their assistance so you can make sure you have the most complete data possible.

If you're working as a freelancer, you'll want to schedule a meeting with your clients to gather information. Provide feedback to the group with comments such as, "I hear you saying that the program should focus on 'a' rather than 'b,' is that right?" Don't end the meeting until you feel you have enough information to write a solid first draft.

Your brainstorming group can and should become your grant-seeking team. You'll need help with a lot of tasks throughout the writing process; often, one or two members of the team can give you a hand. If you're freelancing, make it clear to team members that the more they help, the fewer hours you will have to spend on nonwriting tasks and the lower your final invoice for services.

Tasks you can assign the team members include the following:

- Calling other organizations for data
- Locating internal data
- Developing budgets and moving draft budgets through internal approval channels
- Reviewing drafts
- Locating library resources if needed
- Providing anecdotal evidence of need

Planning Responsive Programs

You are the person most familiar with the requirements outlined in the RFP, and as you gain experience writing grants, you will become very familiar with what local foundations will and will not fund. You'll be able to use this knowledge to guide you as you help develop programs and new ideas for collaborations with other groups.

An Example RFP

One of the family foundations in Maggie's town published guidelines for an environmental program. Its goal is to protect the environment and encourage better land-use planning. According to their guidelines, their grant-making interests include:

- **Regional land-protection efforts that:**
  1. Preserve quality farmland and forests
  2. Protect ecological corridors and valuable environmental features
  3. Enhance water quality
  4. Enhance access to the natural environment by the public
- **Regional or statewide public policy or advocacy that:**
  1. Protects or improves the ecological health of natural areas
  2. Results in the more sensible use of land through farmland preservation and more efficient and sustainable urban development
- **Land-use education projects of potential regional significance**

To be responsive to these program guidelines, a project that proposes to protect land must work in a geographical area targeted by the foundation and must address the listed criteria.

What Would You Do?

If you have an idea for a project to preserve and restore inner-city homes, could you make a case for the ways in which such a program would preserve farmland and forests, protect ecological corridors and environmental features, enhance water quality, and enhance access by the public to the natural environment?

Maggie did: "I learned that most often farmland is lost because it's sold to developers for residential centers. Usually, these bedroom communities also create long commutes that use additional gasoline and contribute to air pollution and oil runoff into lakes and streams. So I proposed that an effort to improve an inner-city neighborhood would reduce the demand for semi-rural construction and, thus, if successful, save farmlands. It was a tough sell, but we eventually won the foundation over by doing our homework."

Another Example

Now let's look at a federal grant RFP. In this case, you could not "fit a square peg into a round hole." You must follow all the criteria exactly in planning your program and ensuring that it provides each and every service described.

According to the guidelines, the purposes of the grant program are:

- To increase the availability of voluntary programs, services, and activities that support early childhood development, increase parent effectiveness, and promote the learning readiness of young children so that young children enter school ready to learn
- To support parents, child care providers, and caregivers who want to incorporate early learning activities into the daily lives of young children
- To remove barriers to the provision of an accessible system of early childhood learning programs in communities throughout the United States
- To increase the availability and affordability of professional development activities and compensation for caregivers and child-care providers
- To facilitate the development of community-based systems of collaborative service-delivery models characterized by resource sharing, linkages between appropriate supports, and local planning for services

What to Do

List each of the criteria on a large flip-chart sheet and post them in the room during your team's brainstorming session. Have members respond to ways in which the proposed project already answers these requirements. Then have the team suggest ways that they could strengthen the program to ensure that it meets all the criteria to the highest degree possible.

What's the Deadline?

Plan backward from the deadline. The closer the deadline, the more you should call on your team to assist you. Work backward from the shipping date, not the deadline for arrival at the grantor's office, unless it's a local office where you can drop off the proposal.

Your schedule must include: meetings; time to write at least two drafts; draft-review times for team members; time to complete forms and get signatures; time to get and, sometimes, write support letters; and time for gathering attachments and copying and collating. A typical schedule that Maggie would provide a client looks like this:

Date	Process/Activity	Responsibility
2/2	Complete draft 1 with questions and blanks for first review	writer
2/6–2/9	Return draft with suggestions for revisions	team
	Meet to discuss issues/questions	team and writer
Week of 2/9	Revise draft	writer
	Begin preliminary budget	team
Week of 2/16	Review draft 2	team
	Meet to discuss attachments, narrative, potential list of support letters, etc.	team and writer
Week of 2/23	Revise draft	writer
	Request support letters, locate additional attachments	team
	Finalize budget	team and writer
3/2	Finalize draft and attachments and submit for approval	writer
3/6	Compile completed narrative for final review, page allowance, attachments, and forms	writer
3/6–3/9	Outstanding forms, signatures, letters, etc.	writer and team
3/10	Ship date for arrival by 3/11	writer

A Checklist of Procedures and Tasks

The following tasks will become second nature as you write more and more grant proposals. Here are some of the things you must be sure to accomplish prior to writing:

- Outline the grant following the outline of the RFP/guidelines.
- Brainstorm and list potential collaborations.
- Contact potential collaborators to participate in project-design meetings.
- Develop a calendar of draft submissions and reviews with anyone who has agreed to review the proposal.
- Develop a list of outstanding documents. Establish who or where these documents will come from.
- Write letters of support, send them to signers, and set a deadline for return of signed originals.
- Set up a file folder with separate sections for narrative drafts, forms, original letters and attachments, RFP/guidelines, and background materials.
- Make a list of data required and potential sources for data. Include phone numbers and contact names in case you can assign this job to a grant-seeking team member.

Chapter 10

Planning for Letters of Support

Experienced grant writers will tell you that if you fail to plan ahead for your letters of support, you'll pay with added stress and travel on proposal-mailing day. You must identify and contact people, and sometimes even write their letters of support! You should plan on addressing this early in the process to ensure that all the letters arrive in time to be sent with your grant package.

What Is a Letter of Support?

There are generally two types of letters of support. One is from an organization that is a partner to the project. Recently, this type of letter has been supplemented or replaced with a formal partnership agreement, which is required by some grantmakers.

> If another nonprofit organization is partnering with yours to deliver services, that organization must put its commitment to the project in writing either through a letter of support or an interagency agreement. Never submit a grant proposal from a partnership without written agreements between the partners for how the project will be implemented and how grant funds will be expended.

The second type comes from community leaders, program collaborators, or organizational-service recipients. These letters of support validate the need for the program. In addition to providing support for the proposing agency and/or its program, they may also indicate ways in which others in the community are willing to support the project.

Who Should Write It and Sign It?

The letter of support can be written by anyone. Since the grant writer is most familiar with the program and what has already been stated in the narrative, he or she often writes this letter. The letter must, however, be signed by the head of the supporting organization. It also must be printed on that organization's letterhead and supplied as an original document; you may not rely on faxed copies. Therefore, you must make certain that the originals arrive at your office in time for you to attach them to the proposal.

Perhaps because the letter is not a particularly difficult part of the project, it tends to be put off by both grant writers and executive directors until the very end of the process. If either one of you procrastinates, it gives you less time to make certain executives at the supporting organizations write their letters of support, sign letterhead copies, and get you the originals. Your best bet is to take charge early in the process.

QUESTION?

Is it difficult to get people to write letters of support?
It's not difficult to get people to commit to writing letters of support. Everyone wants to see fellow organizations secure grants, since government grants return tax revenue to their community. It is more difficult to get people to follow up on their commitments.

If you do write all the letters of support as a service to your client or employer, make sure they are all different. The best way to do that is to interview the agencies involved. That way you can learn unique things about each one and incorporate that information into the letter.

When to Start Soliciting Letters

As soon as you know how many collaborators you'll have on the project, you must begin soliciting their letters of support. If you are writing them, you should e-mail your copy to them so they can print it on the organization's letterhead.

As you develop your schedule for completing the grant, add in a check-back point for those agencies that have agreed to write a letter of support but have not yet sent it in. Request that the original letters be sent by mail or courier directly to you or to your client's office. Stress that they should be unfolded and sent in a large envelope. Your other option is to pick them up from each agency.

Writing a Support Letter

Some support letters are overly generic. You don't want the judges to read, "This is a great project, so please fund it." Letters must be specific so that it's clear to the reader exactly what the organization is supporting.

For instance, is the letter-writing organization providing some sort of collaborative service to the project? Is it supporting the need statement and stating that its own constituents would take advantage of the proposed project? Is the letter a letter of agreement to jointly provide services? Or is it a letter from a leader in the community who is vouching for the organization's track record?

Letters of support should not be generic. Encourage your writers to state their commitments specifically. Provide them information or a draft proposal so they can link their commitments to those made in the proposal. Or, if that fails, write the support letter and ask that the author of record review it, print it on his or her organizational letterhead, and sign it.

Support letters must state the fundamental components of the program that they are supporting so that the reader knows the agency is familiar with the project and knows exactly what they are committing to doing.

Sample Support Letters

The following examples show four different types of support letters. Each has a different function. In the first letter, the proposing agency and its primary partners signed the same letter and asked those affected by the program to sign in support of the project:

Date

We, the undersigned, understand that the XYZ project requires a strong network of caring individuals and service providers if it is to help create systemic change, improve the XXX community, and serve as a model of effective practices for reducing prostitution and its resulting social problems. We, therefore, commit ourselves and the organizations and agencies we represent to building and strengthening that network, to participating in the XYZ Advisory Committee, and to providing services judged important to helping prostitutes rebuild their lives.

Sincerely,

Chief of Police Department   University School of Social Work

Neighborhood Association   Social Work Agency

The second sample letter supports a need for services proposed by one agency and states that a local school district would take advantage of such services if they were available. You can tell that the writer has clearly read the proposal and knows what the grant writer has said about the school district and the planned project. She affirms the need for the project in the school district and links program outcomes to the district's student outcomes.

Date

Dear name:

On behalf of XXX Public Schools and our students, I strongly support the Mobile Media Laboratories planned for launch by the XYZ Nonprofit Organization in Fall, 2007. As you already know, our students come from families that range from wealthy to indigent. At one of our ten elementary schools, more than 90 percent of students participate in the Federal Free/Reduced Lunch program; at another, only 22 percent participate. The Mobile Media Lab will help us "level the playing field" for students who don't have access to home computers, high-speed Internet connections, or digital video cameras.

Every graduate of XXX Schools must meet our exit standards, which mandate that students are effective communicators (expressing and listening), personal managers, quality producers, global citizens, critical/creative thinkers, and self-directed learners. Our job is to provide the tools that help students meet these standards and to change those tools as students, culture, and future worker requirements change. The Mobile Media Lab will assist us greatly in providing tools that will help our students gather and analyze information, make informed decisions, engage in creative communications, and explore new vehicles for teaching and learning.

The opportunity to link, through the lab's wireless connections, with XYZ's television and radio stations or directly to the Web, is sure to generate excitement among our students. Media can be a strong motivator for more reluctant scholars, and broadcasting is sure to help some of our students overcome shyness and improve their self-esteem.

We look forward to working with you and participating in an ongoing evaluation of the Mobile Media Lab and its programs.

Sincerely,

Assistant Superintendent for Curriculum and Instruction

The third letter comes from a community leader in support of a local agency. In this case, the author is president of a local foundation and is familiar with the work of the proposing nonprofit. A letter from a community leader or fellow funder has greater importance when sent to a foundation in the state or region; in other words, peer to peer. Such a letter would not be as necessary to a federal grant project.

Date

Dear name:

I strongly encourage the City Foundation to consider XYZ's grant application for improvements to the structure and programming at their Youth Center.

This program is critical to preventing juvenile delinquency and building the self-esteem of inner-city youth in our community. When it was conceived nearly sixty years ago, it was the first in the nation to use police officers in the roles of mentors to at-risk youngsters; it remains a model for other communities in the nation for its success, longevity, and unique niche in meeting the needs of young people.

The XXX Foundation, one of the state's largest family foundations, has supported programming at the center despite the fact that the foundation does not generally support programs for teens, but rather, focuses its charitable giving on programs that provide early childhood development. This support is testament to XYZ's importance to prevention services in our community.

If I can answer any questions or provide additional information, please do not hesitate to contact me.

Sincerely,

Foundation President

The fourth sample is really two samples in one. The letters were required by the federal government and are, in essence, an agreement to partner on the project proposed.

Date

Dear name:

The process of grant-proposal development is often beneficial, and the FAST opportunity has proved to be perhaps the most beneficial development process ever. As a result of discussions about our various programs, efforts, and goals, the state Small Business Development Center (SBDC) and the state Economic Development Corporation (EDC) have joined in partnership to focus on commercializing technologies developed by state-based entrepreneurs.

The state SBDC will continue to work one on one with potential and current small-business owners, and, with four new staff members, will intensify its efforts and expand its support network for technology innovators. The support network for technology innovators is automatically strengthened by the partnership with the state EDC, which has initiated the state Life Science Corridor, the Emerging Technology Fund, Smart Zones, and Venture Quest, among its other efforts to strengthen our state's place in the "new economy."

The SBDC operates from twelve regional offices and thirty-one satellite offices throughout the state, each of which is affiliated with a regional college or university. Four technology-resources counselors (two hired by the state SBDC and two hired from grant funds, if we are successful) will cover the entire state, working closely with regional directors, small-business counselors, and innovators to deliver the right combination of services needed to develop and commercialize innovative technologies.

We look forward to our working partnership with the state EDC, as we believe this is the best way to identify, reach, and support technology innovators and, ultimately, to bring life-enhancing and, sometimes, life-saving innovations to people who will benefit from them.

Sincerely,

State Director

Date

Dear name:

The state Economic Development Corporation (EDC) is proud to announce its newly created working partnership with the state Small Business Development Center (SBDC)—a strong addition to the statewide network of initiatives already launched in support of technology innovation and economic development in our state.

The state's economic-development entity, the EDC, has developed several entrepreneurial initiatives, including the state Life Science Corridor, Emerging Technology Challenge Fund, Smart Zones, Venture Quest, and a number of venture- and angel-capital-formation activities, as well as support for SBIR/STTR and other R&D grant seeking.

While we have undertaken creation of this large, statewide support system, we have not had a great deal of one-on-one experience with technology innovators. The partnership with the state SBDC allows us to deploy responses and resources individualized to the needs of each technology innovator.

The two organizations share a goal for commercializing technology innovations and securing the state's place in the "new economy." We are excited about this emerging partnership and its many possibilities.

Thank you for your review of our enclosed grant application. We look forward to your response.

Sincerely,

State EDC President

Knowing How Many Letters You Need

You must have letters of support from every formal partner and every organization highlighted as a collaborator in the grant-proposal narrative; it sends up red flags if they are not included. Listen to what a program officer at a local foundation says about a grant proposal that did not contain such letters:

"I did a site visit after receipt of a program proposal I thought fit our mission well and held promise for providing early education services through a local college. The proposing college had stated that it was collaborating with three local agencies focused on child care, child abuse/neglect, and systemic services for indigent families.

Some letters of support are really partnership agreements and are required by the grantor. Make sure that, if you write them, you outline the scope of work for both partners and that both partners read, understand, and agree to the division of responsibilities, their roles in the partnership, and the dispersal of grant funds.

"Something didn't feel right during the site visit. The proposers were evasive in their answers to some of my questions, particularly regarding the roles of their partners. I decided to investigate further. I called all three collaborating organizations and learned that they had never even heard of this project, let alone been asked to collaborate.

"Needless to say, the trustees of the foundation turned down the proposal."

It's also a good idea to provide as many letters as you can that support the case for need for the service you are proposing. Letters of support from leadership agencies and individuals are simply "icing" and can be attached or not, as you see fit.

Be sure to check the instructions for page limits on attachments. Select from the very best and most critical support letters if you have a limit. Also encourage all support-letter writers to keep their missives to one page only.

Chapter 11

Writing a Statement of Need

Usually, the first section of a grant proposal, the statement of need—also called a "case statement" or a "problem statement"—is your chance to introduce your organization and community to the proposal judges. Most often, federal grants are awarded to communities where the need is greatest. In the case of foundations, grants are most often successful when they clearly outline a social or community problem and propose a creative, workable solution. Either audience needs strong data to support the problem or need statement.

Introduce the Organization

In many foundation guidelines, information about your organization comes last in the outline, and the directions in a federal grant RFP usually don't have a section in which you can introduce your organization. So the best place to tell them who you are and what you do is in the needs statement. Not only is the needs statement most often the first section of the proposal, it's also where you will describe your community and your target population. Use this section to "set the stage" so that readers of the proposal begin to visualize how and why your proposed program will work.

Use data to introduce your organization. Tell the reader how many people you serve, what percentage of the population you reach, how many more people there are that you need to target for services, and any other numbers that help you introduce the organization and state the need for funding its services.

Selecting Appropriate Data

Data is the evidence you present to make your case. Find supporting data from your organization and other nonprofit agencies in your community. Just as in a court case, you must present irrefutable evidence of the need for action, and thus, funding.

The RFP will describe some necessary data, but you must be the judge of what other data you can gather to support your case. Some of the more unusual data Maggie has been asked to supply include the following:

- Rate of suicide or suicide attempts among high school students
- Blood lead levels among children living in a specific area of the city
- Rate of volunteerism among alternative-education students
- Purchase date of every piece of computer equipment in a building
- Number of individuals in the United States who use a prosthetic arm or leg
- Number of people in a city who speak a language other than English

- Infant mortality rate by ethnicity, age of mother, family income, and native language of mother
- Number of active prostitutes in a city

You will be asked to supply numbers to support your case and to form your evaluation of the program. Along with being a good writer, you will have to develop your research and mathematics skills. First you have to find the data and then you have to "crunch the numbers." For instance, you will often be given raw numbers when the RFP requests percentages or vice versa.

Locating Data

Locating appropriate data can be difficult. Census data are helpful, but often they are not current or specific enough to support an emerging need. When a community has a low unemployment rate during the year of the census, for example, but then unemployment rates steadily rise over the next several years, census data can actually harm your case for a job-training program. While your local United Way may collect the data, they often must rely on information provided by member organizations, and generally the United Way does not verify those numbers.

Best Sources for Data

Individual and specific organizations are generally the best source for reliable data. For instance, if you need to know how many students receive the federal lunch program in a school district, you simply have to call the central district office to find out. Call the police department for crime statistics; the juvenile court for teen delinquency rates; or the YWCA for domestic-abuse cases.

Sometimes you'll just have to estimate. In those cases, tell the reader how you arrived at your estimate. For instance, to determine the number of prostitutes in a city, first find out the number of men and women arrested for prostitution. Go over the list with the police officers who cover the area where prostitutes are known to hang out. They will tell you which of the arrests are repeat offenders and will also provide you a more accurate estimate than the arrest numbers indicate. You'd write something like, "In 2002, the police made more than 300 arrests of approximately 280 women and 20 men. Officers working with the population estimate that the number of active prostitutes on city streets and in known houses of prostitution is between 500 and 700 people."

Another good source of data can be a local or nearby university. Telephone the social sciences department and ask to speak to a researcher. Some really helpful university departments will assign graduate students to help you update old data or extrapolate pieces of data from aggregates.

Clip Published Reports

You can also clip newspaper articles that you encounter throughout the year that may be related to the people your organization reaches. The reporter has already gathered the data to support his or her article, so you can just clip the information and file it in a notebook, saving it for later so you have a source to go to the next time you need data for a grant proposal.

Use Data to Support Your Case

It's not enough just to put the data requested in the RFP. Your next step is to use it well so that you can demonstrate that your community needs the particular service or program your organization is proposing.

Analyze why the RFP has asked for certain information and how relevant the data that you've gathered are to your program. For instance, you may have the data on teens who have attempted suicide, but do you use it to justify a case for additional computers in the schools? Typically, you would use that data in grants about something like health or mental-health services in the schools, but there are exceptions.

Sometimes your data are counterindicative. In other words, the data suggest that your organization or community does not have an overwhelming need for the services or programs for which you are applying. You can work around this. For instance, in the sample needs statement that you'll find at the end of this chapter, the writer states that the school district scored high on a state assessment of availability of computers in classrooms. But then the writer goes on to say that even though there are computers, test scores haven't improved and the computers are clearly not enhancing or improving learning. Now the writer has used the data to make a case for improved teacher-training programs, perhaps for additional or improved software, and for targeted computer-assisted learning programs in the content areas.

State Your Case

You must pull all the data together to form a picture of the situation and to set the stage for your proposed program. Make sure that the data support the program you are proposing. If you tell the reviewers, for instance, that 90 percent of prostitutes are drug abusers, then you should have a drug-abuse treatment or intervention program in your overall program.

Be coherent. This is where you lay a foundation for understanding why you selected the program you are now proposing. As with the foundation of a building, if you don't make a strong case here, everything you add later is in danger of collapse.

Use a Gap Analysis

When you don't have a lot of data to support your need statement, you can pull together a team of people who are collaborating on the grant and have them help you perform a gap analysis.

A gap analysis is a means to identify hindrances or other roadblocks that might otherwise prevent you from achieving a desired goal. It forces a realistic look at the current situation and helps identify the things that need to be done to arrive at the desired future/goals. Use your data (the present state of affairs), your outcomes (the desired future), and the gaps between them (the need). Following is a step-by-step method for a gap analysis.

Identify the Future State

Where do you want to be? What's the desired outcome? Add detail to your goal statement. List the information and thoughts and details in a box labeled "Desired Future."

Identify the Present State

How are things now? Describe the same components featured in the future state, but do so in present terms. For instance, state that you know that 90 percent of prostitutes are drug users. You know that approximately 2 percent of prostitutes are male transvestites. And you know that there are gay male prostitutes but that they are not on the street and you have no way of counting them or analyzing the extent of the problem. Again, be very detailed. Post the ideas generated in a box labeled "Present State."

Focus on the Gaps

Ask teammates and collaborators to talk through the following points:

- What are the gaps?
- What are the barriers to achieving the goals?
- What's missing in already-existing services?

Write a Needs Statement

Use the results of the gaps you focused on to assist in writing your needs statement. In the above example, the teammates found that there were no services that addressed the need for child care while prostitutes were in drug rehabilitation. Although they had other data, they were more interested in addressing the greatest barrier they found, that relating to prostitutes seeking drug-rehabilitation services.

Citing Resources

While you don't have to cite every source of data or create a research paper with bibliography and footnotes, it is important to cite any experts you quote and to credit published reports from which you take data. Add just a few resources and citations if they are available. For example, if you are writing about prostitution in your city, add some statistics about prostitution in general.

Nationally, police departments are estimated to spend approximately 40 percent of their budgets on enforcing prostitution laws. It is time-consuming police work, requiring in many cases that officers pair up, obtain a solicitation form, and make an arrest of a suspected prostitute. Then they have to transport the woman to the police station or jail, complete fingerprinting and identification, write and file a report, and testify in court. Teams of police officers in other cities are estimated to spend twenty-one officer hours on each prostitution arrest. ("Prostitution Control Costs," Hastings Law Journal, April, 1987.)

Be sure when you cite national statistics to link them to the case in your own community. In the above example, you might say: "Here in City, State, the police department receives no special budget allocation for battling prostitution. Instead, it works with courts, social-service agencies, and others to share and reduce costs. It has also streamlined the arrest process to reduce the amount of time officers spend completing paperwork. Last year's 300 arrests cost the city only $10,000 (after fines were paid); police officers spent approximately fourteen hours per arrest."

Sample Needs Statement

Use the first paragraph of the sample needs statement to introduce the organization and the community it serves.

City Public Schools (CPS) is a public school system serving nearly 6,000 children and young adults in kindergarten through twelfth grades, alternative education, preschool, and adult-education programs. The district is composed of portions of the cities of City A and City B and of Township A. CPS includes eight elementary, two middle, one alternative, one alternative charter, and two high school buildings.

The predominant service area is the city of City A, which was built as a suburb of City just after World War II and was composed primarily of "tract" housing modeled after Levittown, New York, developments. Although City A now has more diverse housing options, some industry, and much retail, according to experts on land-use trends, it is becoming increasingly poorer as upwardly mobile families move to more distant suburbs. Whereas in 1970, city residents earned exactly the average regional median income, by 1990, they earned only 87 percent of the regional median income. This decline is indicated in the City Public Schools as the number of children participating in the federal free/reduced lunch program has increased from approximately 10 percent in 1970 to 26 percent in the 1996–97 school year and to more than 29 percent in 1998–99.

Nevertheless, the City community has a history of supporting educational institutions and initiatives. Although many communities of comparable size have only one high school, City voters have continually approved school-support millages and bond issues that enable support of two high schools of 700–900 students, which Carnegie Institute researchers have found to be the most appropriate size for learning. One elementary school has garnered national attention for its experimentation with a longer school year and nearly 100-percent parental involvement. Parent participation at CPS elementary school conferences regularly exceeds 95 percent.

The community has also supported increased technology resources and learning opportunities for its children. In 1992 and 1997, the CPS community passed two bond issues for a combined total of $57 million ($14 and $43 million respectively). These bonds were used to provide computer connectivity (LAN/WAN network) in and across all CPS educational and support buildings, to purchase computer hardware, and to remodel, repair, and add to existing school buildings. Today, each school building has a twenty-five-station networked computer lab in its media center. One elementary school has an additional three to five computers in each classroom. The two middle schools have a second lab in addition to the one in the media center, and the two high schools have two labs in addition to the computers in their media centers.

Community support has enabled CPS to score "high-tech" on the STaR chart in the areas of connectivity and hardware. Computer-to-student ratios in buildings ranges from twelve-to-one in Elementary 1 to four-to-one in Elementary 2. The eight CPS elementary schools serve nearly 2,600 students (K–5) with approximately 370 computers. The combined ratio of computers to students in the elementary schools is seven-to-one.

To date, the hardware and connectivity have improved only the technological "look" of CPS schools, but they have failed to improve learning as measured on standardized tests. In fact, in all but a very few instances, test scores among CPS elementary students, despite additional tutorial resources and testing strategies, fell dramatically between the 1996–97 and 1997–98 school years.

The following chart indicates the percentage of CPS elementary students scoring satisfactorily on various sections of the 1997–98 State Educational Assessment Program (SEAP) and the percentile change between those scores and 1996–97 school-year scores. As is evident, all building scores declined in math. All but one declined in reading (and in the case of the one building that increased, scores are still less than 60-percent satisfactory). Only three buildings improved writing scores, though all buildings continue to exceed 60-percent satisfactory. Only two buildings improved in science and, in both cases, fewer than half of students scored satisfactorily despite increased annual scores.

Building	Math 1997-1998	Percentage Change	Reading 1997-1998	Percentage Change
Elementary 1	84.6	−7.7	57.7	+25.8
Elementary 2	92.9	−8.6	60.5	−33.6
Elementary 3	82.9	−4.8	70.7	−21.9
Elementary 4	63.9	−20	38.5	−21.6
Elementary 5	75.4	−16	51.7	−23

Building				
Elementary 6	70.2	−10	53.2	−3.2
Elementary 7	50	−17	38.2	−9.9
Elementary 8	88.5	−11	68.5	−4.8

Building	Writing 1997-1998	Percentage Change	Science 1997-1998	Percentage Change
Elementary 1	78.9	+30.8	47.4	+9.4
Elementary 2	80	+20.8	32.3	−1.7
Elementary 3	63.9	−40	41.7	−2.9
Elementary 4	73.3	−14	49	+2.7
Elementary 5	66.7	−36	46.2	−16
Elementary 6	66.7	−43	36.7	−1
Elementary 7	62.5	−11	17.5	−20
Elementary 8	93.3	+7	57.4	−21

To mitigate the effects of rising poverty levels and improve SEAP scores, CPS must put the hardware and LAN/WAN network to use as the learning tools they are meant to be. All CPS school buildings score "low-tech" in the areas of content/software, professional development, and instructional integration and use. CPS's first technology plan (1997) held outcome objectives for students to become computer proficient, but it did not emphasize the use of technology in content areas as tools to enhance learning. Since that plan was written and filed, CPS has had several changes in administration, including a new technology director and a new assistant superintendent.

The assistant superintendent comes from direct experience in the schools, specifically as principal of a model elementary school, and understands the importance of integrating technology resources to improve academic outcomes. Both new administrators are in the process of revising the long-range technology plan and are committed to acquiring software, providing "just-in-time" training for teaching staff, and integrating the use of technology resources into all areas of instruction.

Note how the grant writer weaves in information about land use and makes it relevant to a grant proposing to address a need for technology resources among school children. Additionally, a STaR chart was used by the state to help schools measure the number of computers they had, the age of the computers, the uses of the technology, and the comfort level of teachers with the equipment. The numbers were then compiled into a final measure of low-tech, medium-tech, and high-tech to demonstrate need in the various categories.

Chapter 12

Writing Goals, Objectives, and Outcomes

No part of the proposal is more important than the goals, objectives, and outcomes, which are usually a part of—and integral to—the project description. The granting agency wants to know what their money will achieve, and they want to know what evidence you'll be supplying to ensure them they've made a difference.

What's the Distinction?

Goals are broad statements about what the program will accomplish or your mission(s) for the project. Outcomes are planned changes in the environment or people, and should be measurable. Objectives are the things that you'll plan to do in order to achieve outcomes, and must also be measurable. Other words you may encounter in describing goals, objectives, and outcomes include these:

- **Benchmarks:** The places along the way that will mark your progress. Think of them as mini goals.
- **Activities:** The specific steps you will take to achieve objectives in the grant.
- **Indicators:** The measures you will use to determine whether you have met the objectives or outcomes of the grant.
- **Inputs (resources):** The items you'll need to carry out the objectives or activities (such as surveys, money, staff time, volunteer time, etc.).
- **Outputs:** Direct products from program activities (number of service units, number of participants, products developed, curricula developed, etc.).
- **Timeline:** A schedule for completion of objectives/activities with assigned responsibilities.

In the last decade, "measurable outcomes" have taken the place of "goals and objectives" in many RFPs; however, others still ask for all three.

Writing Goals: What Will You Accomplish?

Goals are the broad, overarching statements of purpose for your program. Ask yourself what the program will accomplish. For instance, a lead-hazard program may state its goal as "reducing the risk of lead hazards to children in inner-city homes." A health clinic may state a goal as "ensuring translation services to all non–English-speaking clients."

Goals don't need to be measurable, and can be fairly broad since you must include support for each in the form of objectives, activities, outcomes, benchmarks, and/or indicators. Keep your goals realistic for the time frame of the grant and the money you are requesting. Remember that you must report on progress toward goals and outcomes at the end of, and sometimes during, the grant period, so you'll want to make sure that the goal statements describe objectives that your organization is relatively sure it can meet.

Writing Outcomes: What Will Change?

Outcomes are the basis for your evaluation plan. Ask yourself what will change as a result of your project and use the answers as outcomes. Then ask yourself how you will measure the change.

If you are implementing a project to make your local high school safer from school violence, you might plan on the following changes and measures that can be combined into an outcome statement:

- **What will change?** Students will not bring weapons to school.
- **How will we know?** Reduced number of students expelled for weapons; findings of random locker checks.
- **Outcome statement:** As an outcome of the safer-schools program, results from four random locker checks will yield fewer weapons and at the end of year one; fewer students will have been expelled for weapons violations on school grounds.
- **What will change?** Teachers will be able to identify behaviors indicative of propensity for school violence and take appropriate intervention measures.
- **How will we know?** Number of teachers attending workshops provided by FBI school-violence specialist; number of teachers scoring high on workshop learning reviews; number of students referred to counseling for suspicious behaviors.
- **Outcome statement:** As a result of workshops conducted by FBI school-violence specialists, teachers will be better equipped to identify behaviors that signal school violence and make appropriate system referrals for troubled students as indicated by an increased

number of teacher referrals to counseling specialists and the reasons for referrals.

- **What will change?** Fighting on school grounds will decrease.
- **How will we know?** Fewer suspensions/expulsions for fighting; referrals for counseling; number of students participating in peer-dispute resolution sessions.
- **Outcome statement:** Fighting on school grounds will decrease as indicated by comparative data on school disciplinary actions and by the number and results of student peer-dispute resolution sessions.

Some outcomes cannot be achieved during the grant period, even in a three-year funded project. When you report on your outcomes, you should be sure that you report progress toward the outcomes even when you cannot report having achieved the change(s) permanently.

Writing Objectives: What Will You Do?

Objectives are a running list of activities, projects, seminars, and other events or items you will produce, participate in, and/or use to achieve the goals and outcomes of a project. Objectives must be measurable.

Using the example of a safer-schools program, some objectives might include the following:

- At least 80 percent of staff members will attend at least one of three FBI-led seminars focusing on identifying indicators for school violence and possible actions teachers can take.
- At least thirty more students than last year will be referred for counseling services because of indicators for violence.
- At least fifty students will be trained to perform peer mediation. At least 400 students will participate in peer-mediation services in year one.
- Random locker checks will be performed four times during the school year.
- The school will rewrite its policies and procedures for dealing with violence on school grounds. New guidelines will be distributed to all

students, signed, and returned to homeroom teachers. New guidelines will be mailed to 40,000 households in the school district that receive the district newsletter.

Note how the objectives include numbers so that the organization can quickly assess their progress any time during the project. Clear measures are also important to the grant writer if he or she is to write progress reports to the funder. Unlike outcomes, you must achieve as many of the objectives as possible and to the degree that you state. So while you're writing, be realistic.

> Writing objectives is a balancing act. You have to promise to do enough to interest funders, yet not promise too much, setting your organization up for failure. The objectives must also link back to the statement of need or problem and forward to the budget, so that the plan of work makes sense to the proposing organization and its potential funder.

It's nice to promise, for instance, that 100 percent of the teachers will attend a seminar, but it is more likely that at least 10 percent won't. If the teachers are not being reimbursed for their time, you may not be able to expect more than a 50-percent turnout. Discuss these eventualities candidly in your review of the writing to make sure that your client or employer can truly commit to the objectives.

Putting It All Together

Following is a program outline for Museums Are Fun for Everyone that includes goals, objectives, outcomes, and indicators. Note the differences in language used to respond to an RFP that called for a purpose statement, services, outcomes, and indicators.

PROGRAM TITLE

Museums Are Fun for Everyone

PROGRAM PURPOSE (GOAL)

The Museum provides a series of workshops about its programs for mothers and two- to five-year olds from the Hills High School parenting program and Cabot Park neighborhood to increase visits by local families and to increase the museum comfort level of mothers who rarely or never visit the museum.

PROGRAM SERVICES (OBJECTIVES)

1. Make outreach visits to Hills High School and Head Start parent meetings.
2. Provide three Saturday workshops for target mothers and children.
3. Provide three after-school workshops for target mothers and children.

INTENDED OUTCOMES

Mothers from Cabot Park and Hills High will feel more comfortable bringing kids to the museum, and these families will use the museum more.

INDICATORS

(a) The number of participating mothers who report their comfort in bringing kids to the museum increased to at least four on a five-point scale, and (b) the number of Cabot Park and Hills High visitors in Kids' Week 2002.

DATA SOURCE(S)

(a) Questionnaire and phone survey for all mothers who participate in a workshop and (b) random exit interviews of adults who visit the Museum with children during Kids' Week 2001, repeated in Kids' Week 2002.

TARGET FOR CHANGE

(a) Participants' reported comfort level goes up 75 percent or more from workshop one to six weeks after workshop three, and (b) visits by target families increase from less than 1 percent in Kids' Week 2001 to 10 percent in Kids' Week 2002. In the project described above, the goal is to increase the comfort level of mothers visiting the museum, with the longer-term goal of increasing museum visits by families. The project will ask mothers who participate in the workshops to rate their comfort level in the museum on a simple scale ("five equals very comfortable, one equals not at all comfortable") to show that mothers feel more comfortable in the museum after the workshops. During Kids' Weeks 2001 and 2002, it will compare information about where visitors live to see whether the workshop series increased visitors from the target neighborhoods.

Questionnaires and interviews provide the opportunity to ask other important planning questions and can be very short. There might be other explanations for a rise in local Kids' Week attendance, but if the museum did not make major changes in the program or publicity, it would be reasonable to think the workshops made a difference. Outcome-based evaluation has different goals from research or many visitor studies—it seeks to document the extent to which a program achieved its purposes.

Completing a Project Description

While the goals and objectives and outcomes are the most critical part of the project description, they are not the only components. You must also provide a narrative introduction and explanations, often a timeline of activities, and a rationale for why you've chosen one method or project over another.

Explain what the need is and link the response and the need statement through measurable objectives. Report local data using footnotes to support the use of research material, and describe how your community's needs are the same or worse than others in the nation.

You may be asked to address several other issues or requirements within the section, including but not limited to the following:

- Stakeholder involvement in project design
- Partners to the project and their roles
- Research findings regarding the project
- Projected benefits to constituency
- Professional development activities related to the project
- Strategies
- Programmatic divisions and separate goals for each

The following sample is in response to a state Department of Education RFP that required a purpose statement and goals and objectives but that did not request outcomes. The available funds were targeted more toward capital expenses for technology equipment or infrastructure.

In this sample response, the granting agent did not assume that an investment in technology would yield social or behavioral change, so it did not request outcome-based measurement.

PROJECT DESCRIPTION

The purpose of the school district's technology project is to equip the district with a fiber-optic WAN/LAN and to deliver the professional development/training its staff requires to meet the following goals:

(a) incorporate technology to teach to the state and district outcome standards;

(b) report student achievement of standards to parents, district, and state officials;

(c) improve teaching strategies and methodologies for all students; and

(d) improve communication channels and outreach with parents and community members

All teachers will be required to attend at least fifteen hours of training in one or more of the following, depending on their proficiencies: CIMS, Word, Excel, PowerPoint, Internet, distance learning, using e-mail and listservs, Web site development, and multimedia. Teachers will also participate in multimedia training that will enable them to incorporate voice/video/data opportunities into their classrooms.

Four of the elementary buildings, for instance, have environmental projects dealing with plant life, water resources, air quality, and wetlands. Fiber-optic lines would provide video capabilities to enable the teachers to share their school-ground environmental laboratories across the district. Teachers could also use the voice-video-data transfers to address shared concerns, become members of interdistrict learning groups, or communicate with the administrative office or parents of their students.

Classes for teachers on distance learning and maximizing their use of the fiber-optic WAN/LAN will be offered during the school year on release time or on an alternate schedule as proposed by staff.

Within one year, teachers will submit information about curriculum, homework, and standards for addition to the district Web site. Teachers will be encouraged and supported to develop their own Web sites to enhance communication with students, parents, and community members. In addition, teachers will develop e-mail connections between themselves and parents/students so that parents might contact teachers regarding specific questions about their children and students can submit homework or questions electronically.

Students without home computers will be encouraged to access Web sites from the multimedia computer labs in the upper-grade buildings and from the media-room computer in elementary schools. All students, beginning in third grade, will participate in at least one e-mail correspondence with their teacher(s).

GOALS AND ACTIVITIES

Goals and activities/objectives are summarized here:

1. Incorporate technology to teach to the state and district outcome standards; to report student achievement of standards to parents, district, and state officials; and to improve teaching strategies and methodologies for all district students.

- Objective 1.1: By December, 2002, install fiber-optic WAN-LAN to intra- and interconnect all school buildings.
- Objective 1.2: By August, 2003, connect Student-Report System software for tracking student achievement of standards, attendance, course outlines, and syllabi. Select software that can look for trends among standards and desegregate student achievement by standard.
- Objective 1.3: By July, 2003, connect all computers to the district's intranet and to the Internet.
- Objective 1.4: By June, 2004, provide professional development courses in distance learning and use of VVD lines to share classroom activities.

2. Improve communication channels and outreach with parents and community members.

- Objective 2.1: By December, 2003, establish a district-wide e-mail system.
- Objective 2.2: By December, 2003, require teachers to submit information for inclusion on district Web site.
- Objective 2.3: By June, 2004, establish listservs to facilitate communication between teachers and parents.

Tips that you can learn from this sample include the following:

- Whenever possible, provide concrete examples of program activities or strategies. It makes the project come alive for the reader and assures them that you really plan to move from theory to action.
- When neither the grant money nor the organization can ensure equal access to programs or equipment by all the target population, you must provide a solution. In this case, kids without home computers can use the media center at the school in the evening.
- It's not enough to apply for grants to purchase computers because your school needs them. Explain what you'll use them for and how they will improve educational outcomes for all students.

Chapter 13

Writing Action Plans and Timelines

Most RFPs request a fully detailed plan of action—
a step-by-step explanation of what the grantee
organization will do and when. An action plan is
the detailed map to achieving your goal. In this
chapter, you'll learn various ways of developing a
detailed plan of action that answers the requirements of the RFP.

What Are Action Steps?

In the same way that objectives are the steps toward achieving a goal, action steps are the next level of detail, the steps your organization will take to achieve the objective. For each objective you've listed, ask yourself how you will achieve that objective. For instance, following is the list of hypothetical objectives from Chapter 12.

- At least thirty more students will be referred for counseling services because of indicators for violence than were last year.
- At least fifty students will be trained to perform peer mediation. At least 400 students will participate in peer-mediation services in year one.
- Random locker checks will be performed four times during the school year.
- The school will rewrite its policies and procedures for dealing with violence on school grounds. New guidelines will be distributed to all students, signed, and returned to homeroom teachers. New guidelines will be mailed to 40,000 households in the school district that receive the district newsletter.

The next step is to develop a plan to describe how you will achieve the objectives. Think about what it will take to do that. What will it take for a school to perform four random locker checks during the school year? At minimum, they will have to do the following: (a) identify a means for random selection of lockers; (b) plan a schedule to ensure that they perform the inspections four times within the nine-month school year; (c) identify what inspectors should look for during the inspections; (d) communicate the plan and goal to inspectors; and (e) develop a plan for reporting findings.

To fulfill the spirit of the objective, they also must have a plan ready for what they will do if they find drugs, guns, knives, or other contraband in the lockers. This step, however, would be better if made a part of the fourth objective to rewrite the school's policies and procedures for dealing with violence on school grounds.

Who's Responsible?

An integral part of an action plan is assignment of responsibility, and by definition, accountability. In the example of random locker checks, assignment would likely go to the high school principal. It would be up to the principal to then assign inspectors, help identify the means of random selection, and ensure that the objective is met with no fewer than four locker inspections during the year.

Remember that you are adding additional responsibilities to someone's job by assigning action steps. Try to have high-level administrators at your organization check with people before redefining or expanding their responsibilities. Grant money won't be used to increase pay for increased work.

Responsibility for training teachers to fulfill the first objective would fall to the district administrators. After training, it would fall to the teachers, and then, ultimately, when you address accountability for achieving the objective, to the principal directly in charge of the teachers.

The organization implementing a funded project must assign responsibility for each objective or each step in the action plan, whether requested by the RFP or not. You can do that during the writing process by developing a grid or narrative that assigns responsibility. You can always change those reporting channels later if you need to. For instance, if between application and funding, the principal retires, the district might want to reassign responsibility to the vice principal, because she has been in the school and is familiar with personnel and existing procedures.

The granting agent rarely, if ever, cares exactly who is responsible for achieving an objective, so long as the person is judged competent by position, education, or reputation. But they will care very much if the objective goes unfilled. Ultimately, if the funded organization fails to achieve its objectives, someone will be held accountable!

How Long It Takes to Achieve Goals

No one has to tell you that nearly everything takes longer than you think it will. It's true about writing the grant narrative, and it's especially true about implementing a project. Grant awards are most often for one year or three years. If you have a one-year grant, you have to be very realistic in writing your plans about what can be accomplished in one year. With three-year grants you have more latitude in planning your timeline and meeting your goals.

One-Year Projects

With a one-year project, you must make sure that your agency can accomplish what it sets out to do and that it can achieve or make progress toward the outcomes in one year or less. One-year action plans must be very detailed. Think of the year as being the first step in a long process of change—it will take longer than the grant period to reach your desired outcomes. Therefore, action plans should list just those steps your organization can make in one year, not all the effort that will take place later to achieve the outcome.

Assign every step, from developing a job description for a new position to hiring that person; from sending out product bid requests to purchasing them. This is a good way to give your organization time to plan and put things into place before you launch the project.

One way to handle this task is by structuring the timeline for a year-long funded project by each month of the year, beginning in the month that the organization is likely to receive the grant funding.

Multiyear Projects

If you are applying for a multiyear grant (usually three years), you must submit a three-year action plan. In three years you can come closer to achieving an outcome for change, so you can use many of your objectives and outcomes as the framework for a three-year action plan.

You don't have to be exact in your timeline. Provide a month-by-month break-down for year one, and a much more generic timeline for years two and three, incorporating only recurring activities and next steps in the process that began in year one. At the end of the first year, write out a detailed action plan for year two. This will help you accomplish your stated goals in the time allotted.

Detailed Action Plans

If you are asked to write a detailed action plan, it's implied (if not stated) that the grantor wants a timeline of activities. It's sometimes easier to develop a plan of action by asking yourself what needs to be done first, second, third, and so on, so your thought process becomes the structure of the plan. The third sample at the end of this chapter provides a simple illus-tration of a timeline-centered plan of action.

Illustrating Goals

As stated earlier in this chapter, sometimes the questions about action plans, persons responsible, and the time frame of activities are asked as separate questions. More often, the RFP requests "a detailed plan of action that includes objectives, measures, persons responsible, action steps, and a time frame for accomplishments."

Using Grids

In these cases, a grid is the most efficient way of communicating all the required information in a short amount of space. Cells or tables available in most word-processing computer programs make such illustrations simple. Remember, however, that you will sometimes have six or more columns if you separate each topic.

FACT

Print grids horizontally. Extensively detailed action plans are best con-structed on landscape-oriented pages. You may even want to write the entire grant narrative on landscape-oriented pages so readers don't have to turn pages.

Using Diagrams

Process-oriented projects often require a diagram to illustrate the steps in planning. Continuous improvement, for instance, is a cyclical rather than a linear process. Grids don't work to illustrate concepts like the process of planning, implementing, checking, and revising, which can be ongoing and may start anywhere in the process. Instead, illustrate these concepts with simple diagrams like the one below.

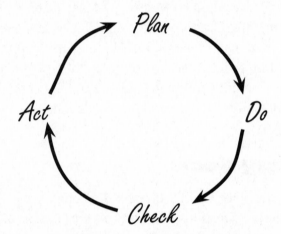

Using Typeface and Gray-Scale Techniques

Most RFPs will specify that they do not want color graphs or charts. But when illustrating levels of information, you can use various fonts, typefaces, simple black-and-white graphs, gray-scale shading, and tables. Just be sure that your illustrations photocopy well. Copy that's lost in an improperly shaded box, for instance, counters your attempts to be clear and concise in your action plan.

Sample Action Plans

The first sample action plan was developed for a health-care clinic. Organized by life-cycle stages (perinatal, pediatric, adolescent, adult, and geriatric), it begins with a problem statement. Each problem then has a set of goals, objectives, action steps, and evaluation measures.

ALERT!

Remember if you are instructed to double-space your proposal, you must also double-space all grids, tables, and graphs. Though foundation funders will not be overly particular about this, government funders often are and may reject your proposal immediately.

Note that timelines and the person responsible for each step are incorporated into the chart. For instance, each objective begins with "By this month" (in correlation with the timeline), and each evaluation statement tells who is responsible for evaluating progress toward the objective. Timelines and responsibility assignments also may be called out separately in action plans.

These three different ways of presenting a timeline demonstrate the flexibility you'll have for presenting the requested information clearly and concisely, in a form that does not eat up excessive amounts of your page limits.

Following is an action plan organized under a problem statement, showing a set of goals and objectives for the named problem.

Life-Cycle-Stage Organization

Problem/Need Statement: "The population of this state ranks highest in the U.S. in incidence of chronic disease illness. 'Healthy County 2010' targets reducing preventable chronic disease incidence and mortality, focusing on cancer (173.8 per 100,000), cardiovascular disease and stroke (231.6 per 100,000), and diabetes (approximately 26,570 individuals). The poverty and cultures of the clinic's geriatric patients contribute to their high risk of developing one or more chronic illnesses. The clinic sees many patients for episodic care only and has developed objectives to increase prevention services to these patients."

Goal (funding): "To increase education about prevention and treatment for clinic's geriatric patients, thereby working to reduce incidence and mortality due to chronic diseases. (CHC funding)"

Objectives	Action Steps	Evaluation and Data	Comments
J1: By December, 2008, 70 percent of all patients who visit will have had an annual risk assessment completed during an episodic visit in a calendar year. Risk assessments will include, as applicable: offers for health-maintenance exam; pap test; immunizations and boosters; cancer screening; anemia testing; cardiovascular screening; prostate screening; mammograms; diabetes screening; and screening for depression, ADL, smoking/alcohol/substance abuse, oral nutrition, and morbid obesity.	J1.a. Revise risk-assessment forms for geriatric life cycles (change colors each year to indicate calendar year in which each risk assessment was completed). J1.b. Providers document risk assessments performed. J1.c. Providers document risk-management plans in place, if indicated.	J1. Quarterly audits of ten randomly selected geriatric patient charts performed by coordinator. Results reported to medical director.	See appendix for sample risk assessment sheets that are currently being revised.
J2: By December, 2008, provide medication review for 8 percent of geriatric patients at risk of drug interactions.	J2.a. Add appropriate questions to patient-progress note forms; e.g., "Has patient seen other providers since last visit?" "What medicines has patient been prescribed by other providers?" "What over-the-counter medications is patient taking?" Document responses. J2.b. Audit progress notes to ensure that providers ask questions.	J2. Revised patient progress notes: clinical coordinator to audit quarterly ten randomly selected geriatric patient charts. Results reported to medical director.	See appendix for same risk assessment sheets, which will be revised.

Horizontal Landscape

The second example is from a community problem-solving organization. This horizontal (landscape) timeline is a good way to graph activities that are scheduled to take place over a period of months, a year, or more. You'll see activities for five months in this sample.

	Month 1	Month 2	Month 3	Month 4	Month 5
Activity A	Observe funder staff systems thinking workshop	Participate in leadership planning for final visioning retreat	Synthesize learning from previous activities	Identify and attend at least one community meeting	Continue community engagement; triweekly design-team meetings
	Hold ABC focus groups		Identify and attend at least one community meeting		Identify and attend at least one community meeting
Activity B	Triweekly meetings of design team for community engagement process		Hold first systems thinking workshop for 24 diverse leaders as nominated/selected from advisory committee and leadership	Synthesize learning from first systems thinking workshop	Synthesize learning from community meetings
	Identify and attend at least one community meeting				
Associated costs		$3,000 (facilitators, food for activity B)	$12,000 (facilitator materials, food, lodging, logistics, for activity B)	$5,000 (facility, facilitators, publicity, and materials for activity A, which continues for several months)	

Timeline Example

The last sample is a simple timeline of a year's activities for each of the first twelve months. Begin a timeline with the month in which funding is likely to be approved. Whether as dots on a chart or in narrative form, be sure to identify recurring activities throughout the project. Also, continuous improvement is, by definition, recurring and continuous. Be sure to illustrate evaluation steps that lend themselves to constant review and program revision.

JUNE: Announce to local media memberships of partner organizations and citizens, the grant award, and launch of the commission. Finalize job description and seek applicants for project coordinator.

JULY: Interview and select project coordinator.

MONTHLY: Convene meetings of commission; select and schedule speakers and/or expert consultants for gathering information and sharing lessons learned.

AUGUST–JANUARY: Gather data from Information Infrastructure providers, businesses, and others needed to identify current infrastructure.

JANUARY: Map current public-access sites and disseminate to sites frequented by those who are believed to lack access to computer equipment. (Note: This activity is funded by the Community Foundation.) Hold "town meeting" to encourage input by commission nonmembers on issues regarding technology infrastructure and digital divide.

JANUARY–APRIL: With professional facilitator and available data, develop vision, key findings, and recommendations for the Information Infrastructure.

APRIL: Perform SWOT on data, findings, and draft recommendations; identify gaps between preferred infrastructure and existing infrastructure.

MAY: Begin mapping process for inclusion in commission report. Report evaluation of the planning process and grant expenditures.

Balancing Ambition with Realism

Often, once an organization has been granted funding, its members suddenly feel overwhelmed looking at the action plan and think, "How are we going to get all this done in a year?" This is a common struggle. Most nonprofits just don't have the capacity to be ready to launch a new program the minute they are awarded the funding. Often, the project implementation schedule is two or three months, sometimes more, behind the schedule (timeline) that was included in the proposal.

The grant writer must strike a balance between setting forth an action plan and schedule that are sufficiently ambitious to get the grant and setting a schedule that is realistic. And it's not only because the organization will struggle to get started—many grants are turned down because the action plan is unrealistic.

Set aside the first month or two of your action plan for tasks your organization can accomplish quickly or somewhat easily while you prepare to implement the newly funded project. For instance, include time to post a new job opening and interview candidates, or announce the grant award to the media.

Be thorough and detailed. Promise enough work on behalf of your client or employer to accomplish the stated goals, but not so much that even the grant readers shake their heads in disbelief.

Also be sure to write a paragraph about the capacity of the organization. Will it need additional staff to lead or carry out the project? Schedule at least thirty days early in the action plan for finding those people.

Chapter 14

Designing an Evaluation Plan

How will you know if your program is working? Almost no layperson knows how to develop and write an evaluation. In this chapter, you'll get guidance on the language and approach to evaluation plans and the assurance that you can, indeed, write one with confidence.

14

The Language of Evaluators

Evaluators have their own language. It's important that you learn to use this language when writing grant-program evaluations, not only because the evaluation is a critical part of the grant proposal, but because using the language of evaluators adds authority to your grant writing.

This list includes some of the most common terminology:

- **Qualitative:** Means of measuring objectives with "soft" data, including opinion surveys, anecdotal stories from participants and staff, etc. Remember the root word "quality" to determine the difference between qualitative and quantitative.
- **Quantitative:** Means of measuring objectives with "hard" data (that is, numbers). Remember the root word "quantity" to determine the difference between quantitative and qualitative.
- **Operationalize:** Act of forming measurable outcomes from aims and goals of the grant program.
- **Longitudinal study:** Study of change over a specified time period.
- **Anecdotal evidence:** Stories from participants or staff. A part of a qualitative (soft data) measure.
- **Indicators:** Selection of measures that will determine success.
- **Learning history:** Particular type of evaluation, useful for projects that are highly process oriented and do not lend themselves to quantitative evaluation. Formed from written documents such as meeting minutes and interviews of participants. This type of evaluation is mostly qualitative.
- **Assessment:** Measurement tool.
- **Continuous improvement:** Use of indicators and evaluation to determine ways the project can improve its services.
- **Benchmarks:** Data on the current status of the problem that the evaluator can use to measure subsequent changes.

You don't have to be a professional evaluator to write an evaluation, but you do need to speak the language.

Types of Evaluations

There are internal, external, and national evaluations. Internal evaluations are those performed by project personnel as a part of the project. External evaluations are performed by a consultant hired by the organization to perform the service.

National evaluations are cross-organizational, cross-project evaluations performed by the granting agency to determine the effectiveness of a particular type of project in its various geographic locations. These types of evaluations are called "cluster evaluations."

FACT

National evaluations are strong learning tools for all participants. They share results of all their evaluations as well as plans, remedial efforts to fix what doesn't work, and success stories. The comparisons between similar projects implemented with different populations and in different locations are interesting and often provide information that you can use in the your next community problem-solving effort.

Mandatory Evaluations

Sometimes an RFP will mandate an external evaluation or both an external and a national evaluation project. If an external evaluator has to be called in, the granting agency will mandate a budget line item and most often will cover the cost. It's often a percentage of the overall grant request. If your agency participates in a national evaluation project, there are no extra charges.

External Evaluations

When an external evaluation is commissioned, it is likely to be performed by a nearby or state university/college department, by the local United Way, or by a national organization under which your organization operates (such as a media-technology support organization, a health-studies group, etc.). When the type of evaluation is not predetermined, you and your organization can choose the most appropriate means of evaluating the project, as well as the person who will perform it.

Evaluating Small Projects

Generally, the smaller the grant request the less stringent the grantor is about the form of the evaluation. Small grants may be evaluated by something as simple as a survey developed by project staff that asks participants about their impressions of a new building façade or what they learned at a seminar or whatever else was funded.

Sometimes, you can write a grant proposal requesting money just for evaluation. If your project is up and running, you might ask the local United Way or community foundation to fund a learning history or a cost-effectiveness study. If you think your project might have potential for replication of results in other communities, you might ask an independent foundation to fund an evaluation to determine all the factors that contributed to your success.

Asking the Right Questions

The best way to begin an evaluation plan is to ask yourself what you and the grantor hope to achieve or learn, then develop a process to identify and measure your success.

The following list of questions was developed for a long-term community-improvement project involving public transportation. The agency recognized that it would take a number of years to see any meaningful changes taking place in the use of public transportation and the habits of people in the community. Nevertheless, the agency wanted to measure any small steps taken in that direction. To do it, the agency decided to conduct an annual evaluation.

- Have we developed a shared vision statement for improving transportation that is accepted by the entire community? Is the statement applicable to all social, environmental, and economic issues?
- What has been our work with existing community initiatives? Has there been progress in merging like initiatives, particularly those that are cross-cluster or cross-sector? Is participation in these initiatives increasing, and does participation reflect the community's diversity?
- Are participants in events and meetings surrounding the project and its action teams diverse in age, opinion, ethnicity, income, gender, and residence?
- Are problem-solving models and strategies readily available? Are they being requested? Used?
- Have we collected and shared data? To what degree? What is missing?
- What are the agreed-on measures of success? Are benchmarks available for all areas of agreement?
- With what communities have we communicated to share information and lessons? What new connections among individuals, organizations, and/or sectors have grown from the project and its transportation action team?

Weigh both the grantor and grantee goals. Be sure to ask both questions: what your organization hopes to learn, and what the granting agent hopes to learn. Hopefully, they are the same. If not, blend the questions together to form the basis for your evaluation plan.

Determining Results

Once the questions are listed, ask yourself how you can find the answers. For instance, in the questions posed above, how will the organization find out if its action teams are diverse? Clearly, the organization must survey participants about their opinions, ages, ethnicity, income, neighborhood, and gender.

If the organization asks about gender, it will become apparent after just a few meetings if it lacks women. Then it can target that group to ensure (the operative word signaling success of the evaluation criteria) that the action teams become a good cross-section of participants.

In the first evaluation sample at the end of this chapter, one of the things the organization wants to learn is the long-term effect of a ninth-grade adventure-camp experience. The evaluator, therefore, might be asked to develop a series of surveys and other evaluative tools to test the effects. One could take place at the end of the camping experience, a second at the end of ninth grade, and the others could be scheduled annually thereafter. This might be the best way to determine whether the learning at the adventure camp has changed the lives of its participants, either for better or worse, and whether any short-term changes were sustained over time.

An evaluation of a hypothesis (for instance, that ninth graders will have a life-altering experience at an adventure camp) need not be proven true in order to have a successful evaluation. The evaluation is a success even if the hypothesis turns out to be false.

Linking Evaluation to Goals and Objectives

If you've written strong goals and objectives, half the work of writing the evaluation section is complete. Return to your project plan. Pull out every objective or outcome, and repeat it in this section. Use the indicators you developed for the objectives/outcomes, if any, or establish indicators in the evaluation section as the measures of effectiveness for each of your objectives.

The strongest grant proposals make the link between the project goals and objectives and the evaluation plan. If your goal is to increase use of the public transportation system and you have objectives regarding marketing, additional stops for buses, new times for bus routes, and similar efforts, you can develop an evaluation plan that addresses the overall success toward reaching your goal. In this case, you would measure ridership both before (baseline) and after implementation of the objectives. Then you can determine whether the steps the transit authority took had the desired effect on the goal (that is, increasing use of the public transportation system).

Sample Evaluation Plans

The following sample of a narrative evaluation plan was written to address an RFP mandate for a local (external) evaluator to be hired by the project. The RFP also stipulated that the evaluation would be coordinated with a national evaluation process for all similar projects in the United States that were designed and funded by the federal grantor.

This grant proposal lists the numerous components of a program that addresses the entire life cycle (infants to seniors) and, therefore, requires extensive evaluation to address each of the components.

The school district and its local partners to the project agree to participate in a national evaluation of the Safe Schools–Healthy Students Initiative, which will collect data on student-risk indicators and outcomes of the programs implemented across sites on an annual basis. Further, the local evaluator will:

- Help district strategically plan activities that will achieve the program goals and objectives
- Respond to the direction of the national evaluator to ensure the collection of high-quality core data
- Design and implement a process evaluation of the local program with assistance from the national evaluator to show results achieved as appropriate
- Provide district with data that can be used to make adjustments in service delivery and improve the overall program
- Design and conduct an outcome evaluation to determine whether an intervention is producing its intended effects

Specifically, the local evaluator, Dr. T. of State University's School of Public Administration and director of the Office of Community Research, will assist the partnership in all forms of interim, annual, and final evaluations. She will teach staff how to gather and log appropriate data to track the progress of the district's Safe Schools–Healthy Students Initiative and all students.

Academic and other appropriate data on all students will be gathered continuously by district staff as advised by the local evaluator and reviewed quarterly in reports to the project partners to ensure immediate responses to weaknesses in the plan.

The Search Institute survey of assets was given to district seventh, ninth, and eleventh graders in 2004 and in 2006 and is scheduled to be given again in 2008. In this way, the district is able to gather comparative data on cohorts of young people (i.e., the ninth graders tested in 2006 were mostly the same seventh graders tested in 2004). The year 2008 asset-survey responses will provide a baseline measure of assets early in the proposed process of involving the entire community in building assets. A fourth survey (second during the grant period) in 2008 will measure the effect of the community process on the youth.

Healthy Communities–Healthy Youth has compiled the following list of fifteen characteristics of asset-building communities. The local evaluator will operationalize these characteristics to establish benchmark measures for the city community in the first year of the grant. By the end of the three-year process, the district and its partners will have demonstrated progressive development in each of the characteristics listed:

1. All residents take personal responsibility for building assets in children and adolescents.
2. The community thinks and acts intergenerationally.
3. The community builds a consensus on values and boundaries that it seeks to articulate and model.
4. All children and teenagers frequently engage in service to others.
5. Families are supported, educated, and equipped to elevate asset building to top priority.
6. All children and teenagers receive frequent expressions of support in both informal settings and in places where youth gather.
7. Neighborhoods are places of caring, support, and safety.
8. Schools—both elementary and secondary—mobilize to promote caring, clear boundaries and sustained relationships with adults.
9. Businesses establish family-friendly policies and embrace asset-building principles for young employees.
10. Virtually all youth ten to eighteen years old are involved in one or more club, team, or other youth-serving organizations that see building assets as central to their mission.
11. The media (print, radio, television) repeatedly communicate the community's vision, support local mobilization efforts, and provide forums for sharing innovative actions taken by individuals and organizations.

12. All professionals and volunteers who work with youth receive training in asset building.
13. Youth have opportunities to serve, lead, and make decisions.
14. Religious institutions mobilize their resources to build assets both within their own programs and in the community.
15. The community-wide commitment to asset building is long term and sustained.

Within the first six months of the grant period, the local evaluator will design a plan for evaluating all components of the initiative including, but not necessarily limited to:

- A longitudinal study of the effect of ninth-grade retreat camp on the students' high school careers and number of assets
- A sample population study of at least thirty toddlers from high-risk families and the effect of parent training/counseling and educational intervention on development and/or kindergarten readiness
- A comparison of all sociological and academic data gathered in each of the three years of the grant project indicating reductions in such things as truancy/expulsion, dropping out, disputes in schools, teen depression, teen pregnancy, experimentation with alcohol/drugs, juvenile crime, reports of abuse/neglect, and increases in state-assessment test scores and academic performance against district outcome standards
- A sample study of at least ten high-risk teens identified as potentially violent and the effect of intervention services on behavior and attitude
- A comparative study on reported feelings of "safety" among students in each of the building levels: elementary, middle, freshman, and high school

Here's another sample evaluation plan. This one employs what is known as a "log frame" model. A log frame, or logic model, uses the goals and objectives of the organization's work plan as the basis for continuous evaluation and improvement. You can learn more about logic-model evaluation from your local United Way.

Defining and Measuring Success: This project will employ a Log Frame Model (also known as Logic Model) and Participatory Evaluation Process to evaluate effectiveness against a set of indicators. The methodology employs an independent evaluator working with program participants, ensures that evaluation is continuous, and involves program participants (e.g., family members, staff, and collaboration partners).

The independent evaluator will work with an evaluation team composed of neighborhood captains, family members from affected households, program staff, and members of the collaboration throughout the process. He or she will create the Log Frame Model and meet twice monthly with the evaluation team to track progress on the Logic Model and to measure effectiveness against indicators the team will establish to determine progress toward and effectiveness of the planned outcomes, goals and objectives, and activities of the project plan.

Evaluation Dissemination and Project Replication: Quarterly, the evaluator will provide a written report to the collaboration steering committee. The evaluator will provide an annual compilation report that will be made available to the collaboration steering committee and project funders. It will be the responsibility of the collaboration steering committee, working with the staff, to adjust the Logic Model in response to the findings of the evaluation team in order to maximize effectiveness of the project.

Once finalized and launched, the project model will be sent to the national foundation with a request for any information the foundation may have on other models for reducing lead hazard in the nation and for review as a replicable model for other communities.

Constituency Involvement in Evaluation: The Logic Model of evaluation includes constituents of the program in all aspects of evaluation.

Chapter 15

Developing a Budget and Budget Narrative

As you're developing the program, you'll also need to develop the budget needed to support the objectives. Perhaps there is an accountant within the organization who can work with you, but more often you will be responsible for writing the budget and budget narrative yourself. This chapter gives you the information you need to develop a grant budget.

How Much Can You Request?

Federal requests for proposals always list the total amount of money the department expects to have available for that project and a ceiling amount that they will grant to each successful project. Foundations, on the other hand, give a range of grant sizes and a typical grant. So they might write in the guidelines or catalog: "Range: $500 to $5,000. Typical grant size: $1,000."

When wealthy individuals who don't have a foundation give financial gifts, it's based on this formula, in this order:

1. Who asks
2. How they ask
3. What they ask for

While foundations do not operate based on "who asks," sometimes decisions that don't necessarily make sense to outsiders are made for reasons known only to those on the inside.

When to Ask for More

Follow your best intuition and best information about previous giving when you want to solicit a local foundation. Or simply ask the program officer directly if he can recommend a way to increase your request.

Remember our freelance grant writer, Maggie? She once called a program officer and asked if they'd consider 5 percent of a capital campaign. The program officer told her that if this was for an organization the foundation would generally support, they might consider 10 percent, and said Maggie could apply for 10 percent with the understanding that she might get less.

Never ask for cents in a grant proposal, such as $272,241.22. And never use cents in your budget presentation—stick with whole dollar amounts. Also, try to round up or down to the nearest $5 or $10 for your budget line items.

When Less Is Better

On federal or state grants, never exceed the highest amount on the range of grant funds. In fact, it's wiser to ask for less. It's also wise to ask for an unusual amount, such as $272,241 if the published cap is $300,000. An unrounded number infers that you are asking only for the funding absolutely necessary to implement the project. It also tells them that you have gone into great detail in your search for pricing on budget line items.

Match Requirements

Match requirements are those monies required to "leverage" or qualify for a grant. That means that the applicant must, through its operations budget or other donations—such as in-kind donations of time, space, products, and/or staffing—offer a certain amount of funds in order to qualify for the grant. Most often, match is required up front by federal and state granting agencies. It can also be stipulated in the grant agreement established by foundations after you have received notice of a successful application.

Match Tied to Sustainability Plans

Match is also linked to sustainability plans. For instance, the RFP may state that in year one, the applicant must provide a 25-percent match ($25 for every $100 requested); in year two, a 50-percent match; and in year three, a 75-percent match.

FACT

One good way to provide part of a cash match, particularly if you are asking for staff salaries in the grant, is to have a willing applicant donate the new staff person's benefits package as a cash match. (Benefits are usually calculated at 25 to 30 percent of the salary.)

These requirements are meant to encourage the applicant to begin planning immediately to incorporate the project into its annual budget by year four, when the grant expires. It also has the result of discouraging applications by organizations that are more interested in pursuing grant money than in implementing and sustaining a necessary service.

Read the fine print in the RFP regarding matching requirements. Is it a combination of allowable expenses, or must it be a cash match?

Federal Financial-Match Example

An RFP from the U.S. Department of Education says applicants receiving grant funds must maintain and document local resources at the following ratio:

- **Year one:** at least 10 percent of total project cost
- **Year two:** at least 20 percent of total project cost
- **Year three:** at least 30 percent of total project cost
- **Year four:** at least 40 percent of total project cost
- **Years five through eight:** at least 50 percent of total project cost
- **Years nine through twelve:** at least 65 percent of total project cost

The eligible applicant's share may be obtained from any source, including funds made available for programs under Title I, and may be provided in cash or as in-kind goods and services. All match items must be designated for the purposes of this project and must not be used to provide match to any other project.

To determine match, the requested amount is divided by the percentage that is the federal share of the project. Thus, a first-year project requesting $125,000 in federal funds will need to match with at least $13,888 ($125,000 divided by .90 = $138,888). To maintain that level of funding in the second year, the match would need to be increased to $31,250 ($125,000 divided by .80 = $156,250).

In-Kind Support

In-kind support refers to those things that the organization and its partners, if any, are offering in addition to or in lieu of money. In-kind support includes such contributions as the following:

- **Staff time:** This is necessary when staff participate in such things as collaborative planning with others and are not paid additional wages for that participation.
- **Space and utilities:** If an organization is providing office space for a staff person, rent, and utilities for the space usually qualifies as an in-kind donation. This amount is usually available from the organization's accountant, who has computed the cost of square footage and operational overhead (electricity, gas, etc.) to determine the value of a space donation. Telephone expenses may also be included in the cost per square foot.
- **Volunteer hours:** Volunteer hours can be computed based on the average amount you would pay for comparable services in your community times the number of hours you can guarantee will be allocated to this project.
- **Products:** Existing products (such as desks and computer equipment) that merely have to be moved to an office for a new staff person count as in-kind donations. New-product donations (for instance, software donated to a nonprofit organization) can be added as "cash match" if you document the value of the donation. Purchasing new equipment such as computers, furnishings, or telephones to support a staff position may be requested of grant funds or purchased by the applicant and offered as match.

Multiyear Requests

The RFP will define whether the program and the request must cover one or more years. Most foundations leave it open to the grant seeker whether to apply for one or more years of funding, but generally do not make grants longer than three years. Multiyear projects have their pluses and minuses. First, on the plus side, a project that is funded for three years is pretty much assured of continuation funding at the level it really needs to prove itself.

The only instance in which the grantor will take away second and third year funds is if the grantee does not comply with the grant agreement. Before that happens, however, the grantee is likely to receive a warning and a set of goals it must achieve prior to being given year-two funding.

The negative side of multiyear requests is that it's difficult to plan anything three years in advance, whether for programming or budget. Granting agencies understand this, however, and provide some latitude in the level of detail you must provide for second- and third-year budgets and details of the project.

In planning a three-year budget, you will have to accomplish two competing objectives. You must decrease grant funds over each of the years, and at the same time, increase costs (such as salaries) that are likely to go up each year. Here is a sample multiyear budget that Maggie prepared for one of her clients:

Expense	Year 1	Year 2	Year 3
Personnel	114,500	214,550	226,950
Operating	45,550	35,450	38,050
TOTAL	160,000	250,000	265,000
Grant funding	80,000	120,000	80,000
Match funding	80,000	130,000	185,000

In Maggie's multiyear-budget example, the organization planned to receive grants totaling $80,000 in year one to leverage (qualify for) a state money match of $80,000. In year two, it had to raise $120,000, and in year three, $80,000. Granting agencies are inclined to view grants that leverage other donations favorably.

Taking Care of Partners

If you are required to have partners in order to qualify for a grant program, then you must make sure that the partners are compensated for the services they provide under the project.

The federal Safe Schools–Healthy Students program grant, for instance, requires partnership among school districts, mental-health services, and police. It also requires the school district to be the primary applicant and fiduciary (the "accountant") on the grant.

The successful school-district applicant, therefore, must purchase the services of police and mental-health organizations in order to fulfill the requirements of the funded program. And while you are writing the grant proposal, costs for these services must be determined and calculated as part of the budget.

Other purchased services, such as evaluation, are also calculated before you submit the proposal, so it's best to ask for estimates when you meet with all the project partners to design the program.

Planning for Sustainability

Before seeking a grant, those involved must discuss the financial and programmatic needs that the project will have at the end of the grant period. Often, you can counsel them to request one-time purchases (such as computers, furnishings, supplies, or cars) from a grant and put less of the award toward ongoing costs such as staff salaries and benefits. They'll eventually have to pay staff salaries out of the organization's budget anyway, unless the project is abandoned. And, if the project is likely to be abandoned after the grant runs out, how valuable was it in addressing a need or problem? Should it have been proposed in the first place?

Sustaining programs after the grant period is the latest big issue with foundations and government funders. They have grown weary of helping to establish programs only to see them disappear for want of funds, energy, or commitment after their grant money is used. They are now requiring that every grant proposal include a discussion about sustaining the project after grant funds are expended. Here are some possible methods of sustaining programs:

- Charge a copay or small fee for services to offset costs.
- Charge as many one-time costs as possible to the grant (e.g., equipment, training, etc.) and begin to incorporate ongoing costs (e.g., space, staff, etc.) into the nonprofit's annual budget.
- Find an ongoing resource, such as a Community Mental Health Fund or Per-pupil allocation from the state that indicates a willingness or interest in funding the project after it has proved itself.
- Plan an annual fundraising event from which proceeds will support the project.

- Address the problem or need permanently within the time frame of the grant so there are no ongoing costs.

Writing the Budget Narrative

Whether you actually write the budget yourself or you receive one from your executive director or accountant, you do have to write the budget narrative. The narrative is your chance to explain how you developed this budget. Your narrative should include the following details:

- Calculations: If the project requires two full-time-equivalent (FTE) counselors, each working forty hours per week at $40,000 per year, you budget $80,000 per year. Over three years they will cost $240,000. (If you need two half-time staff per year, you should request one FTE.)
- Other sources of funding if any, and their use.
- Distribution of funding for the line item: "Part from matching funds, part from the grant request."
- Justification: "$40,000 annual is the average salary of a certified counselor in this area."
- Estimated or actual cost: "The cost of software packages is $222 each if purchased through the state plan for mass purchases. ABC, therefore, requests twenty packages at an actual cost of $4,440." Or you can say, "Software packages are estimated at $225 each times twenty for a request of $4,500."

ALERT!

Remember to include only the costs relating to the particular program and not ongoing administration costs that are not part of the grant proposal, unless you are applying for a general operating grant or attributing the cost to the "indirect" line item. You might even explain what will become of equipment after the project is over.

A budget includes both expenses and revenue; don't neglect to address the revenue side of the budget. Where will all the necessary funding come from?

Citing Other Sources of Funding

Whether you are or are not required to provide in-kind or matching funds, you must indicate where you will be receiving all the funding necessary to complete the project. Take a look at the example at the end of this chapter— it is a budget for launching a project that later received federal funding.

Another example is in the foundation grant proposal in Appendix D. The grant applicant stated the source of all matching donations in the budget narrative, including the $80,000 it received from a previously successful grant cited in the sample budget at the end of this chapter. If a budget narrative is not required, use footnotes in your budget spreadsheet to identify sources and values of other funding.

Sample Budget and Narrative

Note that in this sample budget for a mobile media-laboratory project, it has columns for total cost, money requested from the funder, the nonprofit's contribution, and a "community match."

Community match, in this case, is listed separately. It indicates that ABC nonprofit understands that, in order to completely implement the project, it must identify and apply for additional funding contributions above those requested of this funder and provided by the applicant.

Also note that although purchase of a van and equipment is the first logical step in the process of launching a mobile media laboratory, the funder has already indicated that it does not issue grants to support capital purchases. Therefore, the organization applied for funding based on the stated interests of the grantor and is determined to seek capital funding elsewhere.

A budget narrative is shown following the grid sample and describes the rationale for each line item.

Line Item	Total Cost (two years)	Requested of City Foundation	ABC Match	Community Match
CAPITAL PURCHASES				
Van and conversion equipment to include phone-switching equipment, storage, security, and generator	$30,000			$30,000
Laptop computers and DVD players, server, printer, and scanner	$20,000	$5,000	$5,000	$10,000
PROMOTION				
Van printing and signage, posters, press kits, rental promotion, television and radio spots, collaborative planning, and promotion with community partners	$20,000	$10,000		$10,000
STAFF				
Vista/Americorp and Community Volunteers (equivalent)	$40,000		$40,000	
One FTE supervisory/ teaching staff to develop curriculum, deploy and operate program, and train staff and volunteers	$60,000	$60,000		
MAINTENANCE				
Fuel, upgrades, Internet service fees, etc.	$10,000		$5,000	$5,000
OVERHEAD				
Staff and volunteer supervision, financial tracking and reporting, program oversight, and evaluation	$15,000	$5,000		$10,000
Totals	$195,000	$80,000	$50,000	$65,000

ABC Nonprofit provides $50,000 in-kind and cash match and requests a grant of $80,000 to launch the project described: $65,000 to fully implement the project and achieve the stated outcomes will be sought from ABC's community partners and foundations. Line-item detail follows:

Capital Purchases: ABC requires a van and equipment to launch the mobile media laboratory. A small portion ($5,000) of the total $50,000 capital expenditures is requested of the XYZ Foundation.

Promotion: The Mobile Media Laboratory is an opportunity for both ABC Nonprofit and the XYZ Foundation to build and enhance community relations. ABC, therefore, requests $10,000 from the XYZ Foundation for publicity, promotion, and community awareness. Furthermore, ABC will ensure that the project is called the "XYZ Foundation-sponsored Mobile Media Lab," a tagline that will be printed in all promotional materials and painted on the media van.

Staff: ABC has been granted the services of two Americorp volunteers whom it will assign to the project. The equivalent pay of an estimated $40,000 over two years is contributed by ABC to the project. ABC requests $60,000 from the funder to pay for two years' service from a project coordinator.

Maintenance: Ongoing maintenance and costs are charged to ABC and its community partners.

Overhead: ABC requests $5,000 of the $80,000 grant award to be allocated for fiscal oversight and program reporting.

Community Match: ABC Nonprofit and its technology planning partners described in this proposal are in the process of applying to area foundations and corporations for support of a comprehensive project to narrow the digital divide.

As a part of that overall plan, the mobile media-lab project will receive portions of support granted to the partners. Other funding sources will include rental revenues and reduced costs for staffing afforded by the use of community and recently granted Americorps/Vista volunteers.

Chapter 16

Other Grant-Proposal Sections

Every RFP or set of guidelines has, by one title or another, a section on the community or market need, a project description, an evaluation, and a budget. Beyond that, however, you may be asked to respond to numerous and varied questions. This chapter provides information on responding to these other frequently encountered topics.

What You May Encounter and Where

Although government grants, particularly federal ones, tend to want more detail in your narrative than foundations, you will find a wider variety of subjects to address among established foundations.

This is due, in part, to the establishment of a standardized common grant-proposal format by many Regional Associations of Grantmakers (RAG) and their member foundations. Since each foundation had input in the creation of the standard, the hybrid is far more comprehensive in its scope of questions than any one of the individual foundation's guidelines was before the standardization.

Many subject areas (educational programs, medical programs, technology transfer) have special questions asked in no other requests for proposals. For instance, educational-grant providers often require a section on professional development to ensure that teachers are prepared to deliver the program described.

Medical-grant RFPs may require a section responding to issues uncovered in an annual site visit and particular only to your clinic. You might be asked to address sanitation measures implemented or the availability of foreign-language interpreters during medical visits.

Technology transfers, medical grants, and experimentation grants always require sections on testing in human or animal subjects.

Specialized sections that may appear on some more technical RFPs require specialized, and often expert, knowledge of the subject matter. Seek assistance in writing these sections.

We've selected those sections that are most common and more applicable to a number of different types of projects. You are likely to encounter one or all of these at some point in your quest for grants.

Collaboration/Partnership

Both government and foundation grantors hold collaboration and partnership in high esteem; they believe there's a cost savings in collaboration. While technically that still has to be proved, it is a cost savings to them since they are not funding two agencies to do similar projects or to address similar needs among identical populations.

Whenever possible, use information about your community to make collaborative links between and among organizations. Local funders know when you don't attempt to partner because they know pretty much everything that is going on in the community. State and national funders will know you aren't talking to others when they receive two RFP responses from the same geographic area. Politically, the worst thing your organization or employer can do is know that another agency in town is developing a project similar to yours and not extend a request for partnership.

When You Partner

In a section on collaborations and partners, if requested, provide a narrative that:

- Lists the partners to the project
- Provides a brief description of each partner's role in the project
- Justifies the existence of the collaborative—why it was formed and "the beauty of it"
- Names a lead agency and/or a fiscal agent: The fiscal agent is the only organization that will receive funds. It will then purchase or pay for services from the other members of the collaborative.
- If appropriate, chronicles the history of collaboration between the organizations

ALERT!

Stating that the collaborative was formed to respond to an RFP requirement, even if it's true, is not a good idea. A collaborative should come together primarily to address a community issue, and only secondarily to seek grant funds to support its problem-solving efforts.

What If There's No Partner?

No partners or collaborators? Here's a short sample response from one such agency. Note that it addresses the need to coordinate services even though it does not directly partner with others:

ABC collaborates with hundreds of area agencies to develop and/or deploy the assistance necessary in order to improve the lives of individuals and families in the target areas. ABC's role is to work with neighbors and community-based organizations to identify priority concerns and necessary remedial services, and to secure those services from the existing system rather than to duplicate what already exists. ABC also provides community outreach and public awareness in the target areas for the services provided by other agencies.

Review of Literature

A review of the literature is exactly that—a review of the research on a topic, cited and stated to support your case and explain the reason you selected the model for service that you did.

Federal departments, such as the departments of education or health and human services, and some selected medical-project funders, are among those grantors that require a review of literature. Especially in highly specialized areas such as medicine or electronics, if you are not well versed in the field, it is best to work with a professional researcher and/or expert in the field. It is often critical in specialized areas that you cite all the literature available on a subject. For a layperson, that search can be as exhausting as it is exhaustive.

Following is an abbreviated sample provided by an expert resource to a grant writer.

Lead poisoning has become an increasingly significant public-health issue. According to the U.S. Centers for Disease Control and Prevention (CDC), nearly one million children in the United States have levels of lead in their blood high enough to cause irreversible health problems and to produce a variety of developmental challenges.

Research has shown that lead poisoning has a pervasive impact on the human body, impacting most of the physiological systems. Those most affected include the central nervous system, reproductive system, kidneys, and other (organs). At the higher levels, lead poisoning can cause coma, convulsions, and even death. But even at the lower levels, the presence of lead in the blood can severely limit a child's development. Some of the most significant consequences include diminished intelligence, limited neurobehavioral development, diminished physical growth and stature, and impaired hearing.

However, lead poisoning is completely preventable. Unlike many public-health challenges, the environmental hazards that contribute to lead exposure can be abated and the threat of lead poisoning reduced. The only requirements are a willingness to invest in at-risk neighborhoods and a commitment on the part of key stakeholders at a national, state, local, and community level.

During the past decade, a variety of efforts have been initiated in neighborhoods across the country to remediate lead hazards and track the impact of these remediation strategies on public-health indicators. In the City of Baltimore, for example, the city government has joined with nonprofit and development organizations to address lead hazards in the home.

The primary weakness of many of these efforts, though, is that they fail to make connections among key stakeholders. Most have very little direct involvement by residents of affected neighborhoods and/or lack the necessary investments on the part of national organizations. Also, many of the initiatives fail to involve stakeholders from the public-health or medical communities, or from research institutions, which prevents them from tracking the impact of their efforts or advancing knowledge of lead poisoning in the scholarly community.

A review of existing literature on lead hazards results in numerous publications on risk analysis, lead hazard control, primary prevention strategies, and global prevention strategies. Little literature exists on the development of broad-based collaborations to ameliorate exposure and risk or on the potential for effectiveness of such collaborative efforts.

Note that the introductory paragraph states the number of children affected from national data. The author draws on further medical research, detailing why lead poisoning is a cause for concern. And again, by drawing on national statistics and a review of literature on lead-abatement projects in other cities, the grant writer makes a case for how the proposed program will be different and why it is likely to be successful.

Reviews of literature for social or educational projects are much easier. Locate materials about the service model to use in your project description. Compare the selected service model with one or two others and tell why the one you selected is more appropriate to the needs of your population than the other. Cite your resources (if possible, four or five) and attach a bibliography to the narrative if requested.

Staff Qualifications

This is a relatively simple section to respond to. Use the resumes of those working on the project staff to summarize their relevant experience. If their resumes are outdated, interview them briefly about more recent accomplishments. If the staff position is not filled, write a job description; list the responsibilities the person in that position will have and the qualifications of a successful applicant for the position.

Try to be sure that the staff and the board of the nonprofit organization for a project reflect, in gender and ethnicity, the target population.

If you are requesting grant funds for a position, you must outline the job responsibilities and discuss at length the type of person the agency will be seeking. Be sure to include a brief plan for a personnel search and an equal-opportunity statement from the bylaws of your organization when requesting funding for staff positions.

Management Plans

The narrative describing management plans should center on the project rather than the entire organization. Do include, however, an overview of the organization and demonstrate where the proposed project fits into its mission and management structure. Illustrate reporting channels with graphs or organizational charts. Describe who is accountable for what aspect of the programming, and be sure to include a statement about fiscal accountability as a part of the management plan.

Let's look at a sample management plan. The following plan to improve and restructure a high school outlines the roles and duties of various personnel and administrators who will enable the district to meet its goals and objectives.

The high school principal will provide leadership in the high school community by building and maintaining a vision, direction, and focus for student learning. He will foster an atmosphere that encourages teachers to take risks to meet the needs of students. The superintendent and other administrators, with school-board members, will exercise leadership in supporting the planning, implementation, and long-range momentum of improvement at the school level. Teachers will provide the leadership essential to the success of reform, collaborating with others in the educational community to redefine the role of the teacher and to identify sources of support for that redefined role.

Planning and implementation for the high school restructuring improvement is under the leadership of sixteen committees composed of community representatives, out-district educators, teachers, parents, students, and administrators.

Each larger grouping of committees (such as "school environment" or "assessment/accountability") has selected one of its committees to participate with a leader to consider requirements for accreditation.

Ultimately, district administrators and the high school principal will be responsible for ensuring the success of the restructuring and its outcomes for student learning. However, the team approach ensures that staff, students, and community are responsible for the success of this effort.

Competing Programs/Agencies

Here's the Catch-22 on discussing your competition: If you list competing programs and/or agencies, you will have to say why they are not partners to the project. If you don't list them, the funder—particularly if it's a local foundation—will likely surmise that you are creating the project in a vacuum and deny your request.

Of course, the best-case scenario is when you have no competition. But most often that's only true if all of the competitors are part of a collaborative addressing the same issue. That leaves you with only one way to "win" this one.

Acknowledge what others in the community are doing, then describe the ways in which your organization or this particular project is different from what others are doing and/or ways in which the similar organizations remain specialized but are coordinating their efforts.

You can say: "LMNO, RST, and XYZ offer services for youth in the inner city; however, ABC is the only organization in the city to work in conjunction with the city police department and to provide police officers as mentors and coaches for youth in all of its programs.

"ABC's Camp was the first of its kind in the state to provide summer camping for low-income youth. Today, staff know of several camps providing experiences for at-risk and/or low-income children and adolescents, including GEF, LMN, and ZYX. Like the inner-city youth centers, however, ABC's camp has always been unique in that police officers participate with youth at camp as day counselors and coaches." With that, you've set your program apart from the others.

Constituency Involvement

You may be asked to describe constituency involvement in the design of the program, in its evaluation, in its execution, or even in all three. Also, you may see this same request with different phrasing. For example, schools are asked to describe "parent involvement" and hospitals to describe "patient input."

Foundations are no more eager than nonprofit organizations to "impose" services on a population. Involving those individuals most affected by the program in its design, delivery, and evaluation is a good way to both capture a funder's attention and ensure the success of the effort.

Consider this section this way: How would you feel if someone gave you a secondhand pair of shoes without ever asking you if you needed or wanted them? How would you feel if your local phone company came out with a statistic that said it had 100 percent customer satisfaction and you've had nothing but trouble with them? Wouldn't you say, "Well, they didn't ask me!"

Agencies should always talk up front with those who have a need to be sure that the statistics indicating need have a "face." That means that the program is designed in consultation with, rather than for, its beneficiaries. It's humiliating to be "provided for," and it is precisely this factor, many believe, that has spawned the so-called welfare mentality among the indigent and expectation of entitlement among the young.

Write about the involvement of program beneficiaries in your project description whether you've been asked to or not. This is a critical and politically charged issue for most funders, so even when they don't ask, tell them that you involve constituents or stakeholders in your program design and evaluation.

Make certain your client talks to the people who will benefit from the services and finds out if they need the services or even want them. Then write about their participation in the section on constituency involvement.

Sustainability Plans

Foundations and governments love to fund new and innovative projects, and in the past were reluctant to fund ongoing operations of a nonprofit organization. Today, however, some foundations are changing their approach and providing operating support to the nonprofit organizations deemed most critical to the continued vitality of their communities.

The biggest struggle among leaders in the nonprofit sector is finding operational funding to keep the doors open and the lights on, just so they can continue to do the good work they've already started. Often, they have created additional programs just to provide a portion of grant monies for overhead (or "indirect") costs. But that puts them in an awkward situation because the more programs they invent—assuming the programs work—the more they have to maintain.

You can understand that it can get a little tricky when you sit down to talk about how you're going to sustain a project over the long term, after it becomes institutionalized and, as such, the responsibility of an already stretched "operating" budget.

A Good Plan Is Vital

This section, nonetheless, is the make-or-break point of consideration among foundation trustees and grant readers. You must plan how you will put together the funding to sustain the program after the grant money is spent. You'll have to decide whether it will be through fees for service, partner funding, future grants or donations, operations, or, most likely, some combination of these income sources.

And often, you'll need a plan for sustaining the project for at least three years after the grant period ends.

The hard truth is that most projects really struggle when launch funding runs out. Often, they become a shadow of what they once were. The plus side of the equation is that the leadership of the organization can review its evaluation and eliminate what doesn't work. The negative side is that if a program works just the way it is, any adjustment will weaken it and the agency that operates it.

All that said, you are left with the responsibility of writing something as realistic as possible under rather unrealistic expectations.

Sample Sustainability Plan

As you'll see in the following sample budget for sustainability, the agency tries to balance declining grant funds with increased fees for services. It also plans to seek local foundation funding to replace declining government funding and contribute some support from its own annual budget.

Year One: $432,500 Budget (grant year includes one-time capital investment)		
45-percent local funding	ABC annual budget	$75,000
	Fees for service	$3,000
	Existing grant	$80,000
	Donations and discounts	$40,000
55-percent federal grant-funding requested		

Year Two: $175,000 Operating Budget		
100-percent local funding	ABC annual budget	$25,000
	Local grants	$100,000
	Fees for occasional services	$5,000
	Fees for regular service	$25,000
	Local underwriters	$20,000

Year Three: $175,000 Operating Budget		
100-percent local funding	ABC annual budget	$30,000
	Local grants	$75,000
	Fees for occasional services	$10,000
	Fees for regular service	$35,000
	Local underwriters	$25,000

Year Four: $175,000 Operating Budget		
100-percent local funding	ABC annual budget	$50,000
	Local grants	$30,000
	Fees for occasional services	$15,000
	Fees for regular service	$50,000
	Local underwriters	$30,000

This nonprofit was smart. The minute they were awarded a federal grant, they began meeting with local funders to talk about what they'd need in years two and three. Over the next year, they sent program officers media articles about the project and evaluation results, so they were well positioned to seek funding when the time came.

Status of Fundraising Efforts

This section is often requested in local grants. It is appropriate when you are raising a large total sum from several different sources. For instance, you'll be requesting $100,000 from the community foundation, $200,000 from area corporations and corporate foundations, and $50,000 each from a couple of key donors.

The grantor wants to know whether you have submitted proposals to those identified funders—remember, they know who they are and they talk among each other—and the status of those proposals (that is, proposals that are submitted, planned, pending, or funded).

A sample response for a capital project might read like this:

The state provided $37.1 million toward the center's development; private donors have provided $16 million. The capital campaign became public with $4 million needed. The XYZ Corporation Foundation has since committed $500,000.

Grant requests are pending with JJJ Family Foundation ($100,000 requested), NNN Foundation ($50,000 requested), and local philanthropist ($500,000 requested). Remaining corporate naming opportunities and a public "buy a brick" campaign are expected to raise the remainder of necessary funding.

Organizational History

Write this once, and you'll rarely have to write it again! No matter who the funder or what its priorities, the history of your organization is not going to change much and neither is the "slant" you put on the story. Be sure to put in highlights of the organization, as you'll note in the following example.

The City County Art Association was founded in 1910 by a City Federation of Women's Clubs, which recommended the establishment of an art collection as a basis for a future art museum. In 1911, an initial collection was assembled, and in 1924, the association occupied a Greek Revival residence, which was eventually renamed the City Art Museum (CAM). In 1981, the museum moved to its present site, a Beaux Arts-style Federal Building listed on the National Register of Historic Places and located in the city's downtown center.

CAM's core collection now consists of more than 6,000 works of art from all cultures and periods, with special strengths in European art from Renaissance to nineteenth century, nineteenth- and twentieth-century regional and American art, and works on paper including prints, drawings, watercolors, and photographs. The museum has always placed the highest importance on its public-education programs and continues to expand and diversify its classes, lectures, and events through collaborations and creative partnerships with other city institutions. The city's public sculpture program is supported by the museum's collection, which includes maquettes, drawings, and prints by major sculptors.

Use the history of the organization as a place to record changes in mission, growth of services, and other interesting and relevant facts. In some ways, the history can be used to justify the project, especially when you can cite continued growth or demand.

Funding Priorities

This section is the funder's way of asking, "If we can't fund you at the level you want us to, how would you like us to help you with a lesser amount?" There are several ways to handle this, as shown in the following examples.

When Less Won't Do

In this sample, the organization is steadfast in its request for funding at the level requested and offers only an alternative in the length of the grant period. Note that the writer emphasizes that a level of funding is necessary to meet the outcomes of the project and that any less would mean that those outcomes would not be accomplished as promised in the proposal:

> *The project proposed would require an XYZ Foundation grant of $600,000—$143,000 to complete the year-one outcome objectives; $253,000 to achieve the year-two outcome objectives; and $204,000 in the final year— to complete the project as described. An alternative would be to structure a five-year plan which would allow smaller per-year investments toward a slightly slower developmental process.*

When Any Amount Will Help

In the following sample response, the writer is saying, in effect, that whatever funding is available will be welcome and that the agency would appreciate the assistance of this funder in helping it get funding from other community sources.

> *Whether or not funding is available at the level requested, the coalition hopes that the foundation staff will consider assisting us in building a partnership of funders to share the three-year financial commitment necessary to achieve the stated objectives.*

Offering Choices

This final sample offers the grantor some choices.

If the XYZ Foundation is unable to grant the full three-year request, ABC Nonprofit offers two alternatives: the first two years' funding at $60,400 and $42,280 respectively for a total grant of $102,680, or the executive-director salary only, in decreasing amounts as follows: $45,000 in year one, $31,500 in year two, and $22,050 in year three for a total grant of $98,550.

Challenge Grants

This is more likely a question than a whole section in the grant proposal. The funder wants to know if you are applying for a challenge grant, meaning that you want them to put up funds that you can use to challenge or enthuse other potential donors.

For example, if you want to raise $50,000, you could ask for a $25,000 one-to-one matching challenge. A word of caution, however: Under challenge-grant agreements, if you don't raise $25,000 from other places, you don't get the $25,000 put up by the challenge funder.

ALERT!

A challenge grant provides money only in the event that you raise a like amount (or sometimes double amount) from others. Some foundations only offer challenge grants, some ask you if you would like one. In the latter case, don't ask for a challenge grant unless you are fairly certain you can raise the necessary match.

Say yes to a challenge-grant opportunity when you are:

- Launching a capital or fundraising campaign and want to use the challenge grant to attract attention among funders
- Entering the latter stages of a long fundraising campaign and want to challenge community donors to match one last gift
- Confident of your ability to raise the matching funds

If none of these is true, turn to a former First Lady for inspiration and, "Just say 'no.'"

Chapter 17

Capital-Grant Proposals

Most nonprofit organizations undertake a capital campaign at some time during their growth to fund the construction or renovation of a building or the acquisition of costly equipment. These efforts—which often require millions of dollars and several years to realize—especially need the assistance of a savvy grant writer to supplement the work of staff development directors, the capital campaign cabinet, and consultants hired to guide the effort.

What Is a Capital Project?

Capital projects are those in which the primary goal is to purchase, build, or renovate a building, or to acquire high-cost equipment. Often, capital-project revenue goals are in the millions of dollars. In these cases, the non-profit organization launches a "capital campaign" that requests money of constituents, businesses, foundations, and other community members.

FACT

The campaign cabinet may include some board members of the non-profit, but it should also include community members who are used to asking others for money and who are known to donate to various causes. In fundraising, unlike in grantseeking, "who asks" is always the most important factor in your success or failure.

A capital campaign begins with a feasibility study, usually performed by an outside campaign-consulting firm. The firm asks potential donors what they think of the nonprofit's chances of raising the goal amount of money and then makes recommendations to the nonprofit about how to manage the campaign. The consulting firm and the nonprofit often next convene a team of community members who form the campaign cabinet and make calls on potential donors. Meanwhile, a grant writer begins developing proposals to submit to local foundations. Often, grant awards form the earliest donations to a campaign, signaling to other donors in the community that the project has potential for success.

Some campaign-consulting firms offer grant-writing services as a part of their campaign consulting; others leave it to staff or grant-writing consultants but advise them throughout the process.

Who Gives to Capital Campaigns?

Unless the nonprofit organization is a national one, almost all the money raised for a capital project comes from local funders, including foundations, businesses, and individuals. Capital projects sometimes get funding from the state if the project is a large public-use facility such as an arena, hospital, or convention center. State and federal governments do not generally provide capital in response to a grant application; capital allocations are often made as agreements between representatives and civic leaders. A grant writer can assist a capital campaign in securing government dollars by adding equipment purchases into relevant programmatic proposals.

For instance, a school might seek computers for staff under the federal Safe Schools–Healthy Students grant program as a part of a goal to increase communication among teaching staff and implement standards-based outcome reporting. The purchase of those computers might then reduce the needed budget of a capital campaign to build and equip a new middle school.

The Kresge Foundation in Southeastern Michigan is currently the only foundation that provides capital-grant funds to organizations without regard for where they are located. For several years, the foundation has structured its grants around a "capital challenge" requiring its applicants to identify new sources of funding in their local communities to match the Kresge grant and close out the campaign.

The Grant Writer's Role

Though every community and every project varies in who gives what and in what amount, often, the grant writer will raise up to half of the campaign goal through formal proposals to local foundations. The grant writer may also be involved in writing a case statement for the campaign brochure and in crafting letters the organization will send to various individual donors.

Most grant writers, unless they are the directors of the nonprofit organization, don't get involved in organizing the campaign, performing the feasibility study, convening a campaign cabinet, or determining naming opportunities. Instead, these functions are left to the expert consulting firms to perform.

Naming Opportunities

Most capital campaigns include opportunities for donors to name the entire building, rooms within it, or other purchases made with donated funds. Some foundations like naming opportunities; others don't. Be sure to ask in your initial meeting with the foundation whether they wish their donation to be commemorated in a naming opportunity or in a more simple way such as a plaque in the building lobby.

Writing a Capital-Grant Proposal

Foundations do not give capital grants to purchase equipment or a building. They give grants *to enable* the nonprofit organization to do something important with the equipment or building. Remember that important distinction every time you write a capital-grant proposal. The most important thing to the audience is what the nonprofit will be able to do with what it purchases. Perhaps it will increase its capacity for providing service, enable staff to communicate and collaborate better with other organizations, or provide a new and necessary service. As with project grants, the outcomes from a capital-grant proposal must improve some currently undesirable condition.

Some foundations provide different guidelines for capital requests, and many ask for additional sections to be completed. For the most part, however, capital requests follow existing foundation guidelines, but the responses are somewhat different. Following are suggestions for how to approach the basic sections of a proposal when requesting funds for capital projects.

Problem or Need Section

You can copy the general case statement for a capital campaign into the need section of a grant proposal; they are that similar. Describe the need for the capital acquisition and use data to support your argument. A sample follows:

The Great River City Media Center (CMC), located on the west side of Great River, State, is the premiere public-access media organization in the United States.

Demand for CMC's services has increased as technology has changed. First, it added radio, then Internet and computer services, the I-VAN program for use in K–12 schools to teach digital filmmaking and editing, and a second television station, LiveWire 24, which broadcasts throughout the county with educational programming such as Classic Arts Showcase, NASA Direct, and Free Speech TV.

As programs and demand have increased, so has CMC's staff—from twelve in 1997 when it moved from the Reed Library basement into the second floor of the west-side library on Bridge, to thirty in the early 2000s, when it had staff dispersed to a rectory and church basement next door to the library and to Steepletown, a west-side nonprofit-organization complex. From 1998 to 2002, community members' use of CMC grew as follows:

- GRTV saw a 15-percent increase in locally produced programming. It grew from one broadcast channel to two and from one primary program to three with the addition of I-VAN educational services and Community Media Services video production and AV services.
- GRRadio grew from 65 to 80 volunteers; from 5 or 6 annual concerts to 25 to 30.
- GreatNet grew from 40 nonprofit "clients" to nearly 100.

CMC's programs and expansion would not be possible or necessary without the interest and commitment of community volunteers and public-access users. Before individuals or organizations get involved with public-access media, they attend an orientation about the CMC's radio, television, Internet, and media-literacy programs to determine their areas of interest. Though CMC has not promoted "orientations" in any formal way, demand for the introduction to the CMC's programs has grown in the past several years. Whereas, five years ago, an average of 19 people attended the monthly orientation, now attendance averages 30 per session. This brings in more than 300 individuals annually to the organization. The community looks to CMC to take on the latest technologies and is therefore increasingly drawing individuals interested in pod-casting, digital imaging, and Internet media.

Because the demand for I-VAN training in the schools has increased, CMC has done two things. First, it has established an I-VAN Club in the recently acquired storefront on Walter Street (formerly called the "annex") for the use of core-city young people. Second, it has developed teacher-training materials on DVD and CD that teachers can use to teach video production and editing in their classrooms. I-VAN staff are available by telephone and online to support teacher training and answer questions. In large part because of the success of I-VAN, CMC has identified a new niche that involves training K–12 teachers throughout the county to use media as a teaching and learning tool through the intermediate school district.

By 2002, CMC had outgrown its facility on Bridge Street. Staff were dispersed to three different sites, exchanging rent for CMC services. CMC began to explore possibilities for expanding in a way that would not disrupt services, but would, in fact, enhance them, and that would preserve the investment in technological infrastructure at the main office.

In 2004, the CMC was approached by key area funders and a neighborhood business alliance and asked to acquire and manage the historic Walter Theatre on the city's southeast side. The Theatre had been restored by a neighborhood organization approximately five years earlier. The restoration effort fulfilled the neighborhood organization's primary goal to serve as a catalyst for further revitalizing the Walter Street neighborhood. However, the Theatre had failed under several directors to sustain operations from programs, and its board of directors had looked for a resolution for more than six months before determining that it would surrender the property and a nearby facility they called the "annex" to an established nonprofit organization. The City Media Center appeared alone at the top of the list.

The acquisition of Walter Theatre and the annex was an opportunity to expand CMC's reach and visibility on both sides of the Great River and to fulfill several of the CMC's short- and long-range goals in that it offered:

- A venue for its many concerts, televised debates, and other programs
- Additional space that was desperately needed following program expansion that had placed staff in three different sites on the city's west side
- Storefront access to CMC's educational programs and a presence in one of the city's most economically depressed neighborhoods

Evaluation

Evaluate the programmatic functions of the capital project. If a new building will increase the number of people your nonprofit is able to serve, design a means for gathering data and demonstrating that you have increased capacity for service within a specified time.

There are some capital efforts that do not involve programs. They are often public-works projects such as new sidewalks or public art or some other urban-renewal effort. It's difficult to establish evaluation criteria or tests of such capital projects. If the project has been built, clearly that is success. If it hasn't, the grantee should return any grant funds previously pledged. Nonetheless, foundations want an evaluation section in their grant proposals. In these cases, keep it simple—say that the project will be judged successful if it is constructed on time and within budget.

Do not promise an evaluation just for the sake of evaluating. For instance, a downtown development authority promised to survey pedestrians about their opinions of a new artful sidewalk installation in the center of the city's shopping district. Why? What if all the pedestrians said they didn't like it? They certainly weren't going to raise more funds to tear out the sidewalk and redo it. If you promise an evaluation, even one that doesn't make sense, the funder may hold you to your promise.

Unique Proposal Sections

Depending on the donor's requirements, capital proposals may include questions that you will not find in a foundation's typical guidelines. Some common sections are relatively easy to complete or attach. They include:

- A list of cabinet members
- A list of donors and their amounts
- A list of targeted requests by name and requested amount
- Architectural drawings
- Purchase agreements
- Proof of regulatory compliance
- Narrative description of existing and planned facilities

When a nonprofit organization undertakes a capital campaign, all members of the board, the campaign cabinet, and staff are expected to make a donation. Foundation donors want to see that those closest to the nonprofit have faith in the campaign and are investing their own money, too.

Writing a Program Plan

The most important component to a capital-campaign grant proposal is the plan both for how you will raise the necessary funds and how you will use new equipment or facilities. Following is a sample plan:

The CMC's goal for growth, improvement, and acquisition of a venue was a perfect match with the request by the Walter Street Business District and other community agencies to explore and ultimately acquire the Walter Theatre properties. The capital campaign allows the acquisition and equipping of the Theatre, relocation of current staff who were dispersed in rented facilities, improvements and sorely needed updates to GRTV and GRRadio broadcast equipment, and high-tech network and broadcast connections between the two sites.

The Theatre acquisition formed Phase I of the capital campaign. In Phase II, CMC seeks to "electrify" the Educational Center and Theatre to allow for remote broadcast of television and radio, install a media-making environment, and equip the Theatre with cameras and a control room. The Theatre will continue to be used for film, live performances, video, lectures, fundraisers, and other community-use purposes, and performances can be broadcast in numerous ways.

CMC also plans to install a "hot studio" in a storefront in the Educational Center. It plans to link to the new city wireless-Internet canopy to allow local residents and Theatre users Internet connectivity for asset mapping, community communication and development, job-search assistance, economic development, distance learning, and creative-arts applications.

CMC has developed a drop-in computer center for local residents, based on an expressed need from neighbors. The Center houses desk-top computers and

CMC's twenty-station mobile computer lab that is part of I-VAN. In the Educational Center, students can stop in after school and casually explore computer uses such as media production, educational games, research, and homework applications. I-VAN staff operate the drop-in center and the I-VAN Club for neighborhood youth who use digital-editing equipment to create video projects about curriculum subjects and neighborhood people, events, and businesses.

GRTV has expanded its equipment lending, training, and post-production services at the Theatre.

The Great River Institute for Democracy (GRID) has held a series of educational films on topics including sustainable agriculture, water rights, democracy, and human rights, and hosted numerous community gatherings to discuss hunger, immigration, race relations, and other current-issue topics.

A large monitor in the window will promote coming attractions to the Theatre and feature the work of students in the I-VAN Club for passersby.

Also included as a part of CMC's two-percent for art is the Memorial Garden and Walkway, an artistic expression using bells as a theme based on an often-told story illustrating appropriate use of technology and asking people what they need.

Once the Theatre and Educational Center are fully equipped and operational, CMC plans capital-campaign Phase III to include improvements and sorely needed updates to GRTV, LiveWire24, and GRRadio broadcast equipment, including digital conversion and digital network and broadcast connections between the CMC's Bridge and Walter Street locations.

Phase IV of the campaign includes construction of a two-truck garage and a maintenance endowment to be held at Great River Community Foundation.

The phases are prioritized by organizational and community need. As individuals and foundations have donated, CMC has completed portions of the project in accordance with donor wishes.

Chapter 18

Write It Well

Good writing won't sell a bad program, but bad writing can sink a good one. In addition to knowing your audience and their wants and interests, you must write clearly, concisely, and simply—without oversimplifying—when writing grant proposals. In this chapter, you'll get some tips on how to get it right.

Use Everyday Language

Write plainly; you always have limited space, so you have to be brief and thorough. Often, the judges must read 20 to 100 proposals in just a few days. Yours will stand out and be memorable if your proposal is clear, concise, and jargon free.

Here are some tips for stating it simply:

- Don't add unnecessary adverbs. Use strong action verbs instead.
- Use short sentences.
- Avoid redundancy, particularly within a sentence. (You may note, however, that questions in various sections of an RFP are somewhat similar, and that forces you to be repetitive.)
- Eliminate strings of prepositional phrases.
- Cut the fat from your sentences. Rather than saying, "The project we began last year addressed the needs of at-risk three-year olds," write, "Last year, we addressed the needs of at-risk three-year olds."
- Use short and fewer nouns in a sentence.

Consider the difference between these examples taken from *Line by Line,* by Claire Kehrwald Cook (Modern Language Association, Houghton Mifflin Company, 1984).

"The inference that because high school graduates are more likely to be employed than dropouts, the differences may be attributed to the possession of a diploma is suspect since dropouts and graduates may differ in a variety of ways relevant to both graduation prospects and employment status."

Compare that paragraph with this:

"It is not necessarily the diploma that makes high school graduates more employable than dropouts; other differences may affect both their education and their job prospects."

Avoid Jargon

We've all been subjected to sociological changes in language. Two decades ago, the word "impact" was only used as an adjective for a sore tooth or as a noun describing a car crash. Now, it's not only accepted as a verb, but has also become overused to the point that it has lost its "impact."

ALERT!

To avoid using "impact" as a verb, learn the difference between "affect," and "effect," and use them appropriately. Usually, if you're tempted to write "impact," you want "affect," which means "to influence." When "effect" is a verb, it means "to bring about."

"Proactive" has been done to death, especially when used in the phrase "proactive rather than reactive." Just say your team will be "active" in addressing issues as they arise. It means the same thing. Or even better, "The team will actively address issues as they arise."

Some jargon is specific to an industry or focus and, because it is used among peers only, it tends to put off your reading audience. For instance, if you were to tell someone who hasn't read this book and is unfamiliar with the grant-writing process that you are reading the rubrics in an RFP, he or she could very well feel like you were trying to be secretive or trying to exclude them.

Other forms of jargon are idiosyncratic ways of expressing yourself. While these "tics" are perfectly appropriate in spoken language, they muddy writing. Avoid turns of phrase and redundant words and descriptions. Also avoid too many prepositions—"off of"—and lengthy, redundant phrases, such as "the reason is because" or "due to the fact that…."

Be Politically Correct

Using everyday language does not excuse street talk. Be politically correct, particularly when you are discussing individuals. Say "people with disabilities," not "disabled people." (Emphasize the person rather than the disability.) Don't sensationalize a disability with such phrases as "afflicted with," "unfortunate," "pitiful," or "victim of." And don't use the word "handicap" unless you're writing about golf. You want to emphasize the person's abilities. Say "She walks with crutches," or "He uses a wheelchair," rather than "He is confined to a wheelchair."

Use "able-bodied," rather than "nondisabled" when discussing people who don't have a physical condition that interferes with their ability to walk, see, hear, learn, or lift.

Use "people of color," "minority individuals," or terms such as "African-American," "Hispanic/Latino/Latina," "Native American," and "Asian" when you have to be specific about ethnicity.

Avoid Sexist Language

Use inclusive, nonsexist language by substituting "she/he" and "his/her." Better yet, you can avoid that awkward structure by changing a single-tense subject and verb to the plural. Then you can use "they are" instead of "he/she is." Avoid words that contain "man." Change "chairman" to "chair," "manpower" to "workforce," or "manmade" to "synthetic."

Another tired phrase is "at-risk youth." Substitute "teens," "adolescents," "young adults," "students," or "boys and girls" for youth when you're talking about programs for teens.

Explain Acronyms and Terms

You cannot assume that readers who will judge your proposal will know the same acronyms or buzzwords that are common to your organization or field of interest. While they may understand that "HUD" refers to the U.S. Department of Housing and Urban Development, what about CAC—Community Advisory Council—or R&D, which can refer to either Research and Design or Research and Development?

Make yourself clear. Give readers the full name or title on first reference, followed by the acronym in parentheses. After, and throughout the document, you can then use the full name or the acronym interchangeably.

Name Your Project

RFPs are often tagged with explanatory titles—"small-business innovation and research," "technology for the twenty-first century," "early childhood educational opportunities," or "leadership development for nontraditional leaders." That title appears on the cover sheet and again on assurances attached to the proposal.

Why not set your proposal apart from the others, particularly if it's something unique to your community? Instead of using a ho-hum title, try to find one that's catchy, memorable, or an acronym.

FACT

An acronym—always spelled out on the first reference—takes much less space when you're writing the narrative and filling out forms. It also makes a program more memorable for the judges. Try to come up with a memorable acronym for your project, derived from the first initials of the project's description.

A technology-planning group, for instance, might be called the Electronic Technology Infrastructure Planning Commission—and referred to as e-TIP. For an art project, formally referred to as "public art and community enhancement (PACE), you could use the tag, "Setting the PACE." And for an early childhood educational program, why not call it a school-time educational program (STEP)? Then you can dub the project "First STEPs."

Use Strong, Active Verbs

No one likes to read sentences constructed in the passive voice. That's when the subject of a sentence becomes the object or receiver of an action, and the writer uses a weak verb. Passive voice is particularly deadly in grant proposals. Yet, interestingly enough, it's incredibly common to see grants written in the passive voice.

People who work in the nonprofit sector often believe they must be modest and not toot their horns by telling others about their organization's accomplishments. Instead of writing, "We served 750 people," they'll say "750 people received services." When you have lots of that in a proposal, the reader gets the sense that services just occur magically.

Improve your sentences by changing passive sentences into active voice. It usually takes fewer words, and it gives your writing more vigor as well.

Present or Past Tense?

Your sentences should have strong present- or past-tense verbs. Don't say things like "XYZ would provide mental-health services for 300 individuals." That sentence implies that XYZ will provide services if, and only if, it gets the grant. Instead, be positive. Say, "XYZ will provide mental-health services." This says that the organization intends to address the problem whether or not it receives this particular grant. It also reinforces the idea that XYZ is an active community problem solver and that it is committed to delivering services people need. Finally, positive "will" statements can be taken directly from the proposal and placed into a grant agreement or contract as agreements.

Give your organization credit. Use its name as the subject/noun of nearly every sentence, or use the pronoun "we." For instance, "Last year, XYZ nonprofit provided food and shelter for more than 750 people," rather than "Last year, 750 people received food and shelter."

First or Third Person?

The voice of the entire proposal is a matter of style and, therefore, completely up to you, the writer. Some people think first-person voice is friendlier: "We are planning/We served/We will." Others stick with the third person throughout the document. "XYZ is planning to/XYZ served/The agency hopes to."

You might consider a compromise: Use the third-person voice for all government proposals, but write local foundation grants in the first person. The friendlier approach in foundation grants can be justified because members of your community will read your proposal. It is, therefore, very likely that a member of your nonprofit board knows at least one of the foundation's trustees.

When using a third-person narrative, do not refer to the organization as "they." An organization is an "it" and shouldn't be personified.

ALERT!

Whether you choose the formality of the third person or the friendlier first-person voice, make certain you use it consistently throughout the proposal. And, if you use the first-person voice, always be sure to make it plural: never "I"; always "we."

Speak with Authority

As in all other types of writing, writing what you know results in a stronger, more believable piece of work. You should also write with authority. Proposals are most often judged by peers, and you must be able to communicate with them as an equal.

In two sections of the RFP—the evaluation plan and reviews of literature—you must break all the rules about not using jargon and speaking plainly. That's because people who read evaluation sections and reviews of literature are looking for language that not only speaks with authority but also with expertise. In other words, evaluators have a language of their own, and their reviews of literature require the language of a Ph.D. You have to be conversant with it.

Some grants, in particular, require expert language. These are usually in very technical or medical fields, and they will be read by physicians and high-level Ph.D.s. Many of these RFPs are issued by the National Institutes of Health (NIH), and they require an entire section on using human beings as subjects of experiments. They also often require scientific explanations for the project you are proposing and a lengthy biography of at least one person, called the Principal Investigator (PI), who will lead all experiments or processes surrounding the project. In cases like this, the grants are typically awarded based on the PI's background, so it is important to make those credentials clear.

Chapter 19

Reviewing Your Work

The little details matter in a grant proposal. You've got the major items taken care of by now—the specifics of the program, the budget, the evaluation criteria—but you're not done yet. It is especially important to go over the proposal, focusing on the aspects that really give it that professional touch. This can make the difference between getting a grant and not getting a grant.

Spelling, Grammar, and Punctuation

No matter how good your spelling and grammar skills, you will need good reference books: a dictionary, thesaurus, and a stylebook or two (though no grant requires the use of one particular style over another). The Council on Foundations in Washington, D.C., has a stylebook particular to the philanthropy field, but it is geared more for those writing about philanthropy than to those writing to philanthropists.

ALERT!

Use, but don't rely on, spell check. Words can be spelled two ways, and while either will pass a spell check, only one is correct as it's used in your sentence. What could be more embarrassing than sending in a proposal from a "pubic" rather than a "public" school district?

If your readers are going to judge just the content of the grant, which is their most appropriate role, you must proofread for errors before submitting your first draft. Check tenses, check punctuation and run-on sentences, and check your spelling.

If you have enough time, walk away from your copy for a day or two. Then proofread it again—that's when mistakes will jump out at you. If you are rushed, ask someone you trust to proofread the document.

Page Counts Count

Instructions in the RFP or grant guidelines almost always provide page limits, a list of what must be included within the page limits, or what is exempt from the limits.

A typical set of instructions regarding page limits might say something like this: "The narrative section must be limited to twenty-five typed pages. The pages must be consecutively numbered in the lower right-hand corner, double spaced, printed on only one side of 8 ½" × 11" white paper with one-inch margins on all sides. The font size must be no smaller than twelve-point type. Page limits are for the narrative section only and do not include the title page, table of contents, abstract, assurances, budget form, or appendices."

Be sure to number your pages consecutively and to put the name of the organization and the city and state in all headers or footers. If a page gets misplaced, the proposal readers can either find it and put it in place or notify you or the granting agency that they cannot adequately score an incomplete grant application.

Using Headings

Once again, follow the directions. Use the same headings, and be sure to include the numbers, alpha characters, and/or Roman numerals used in the RFP. Do not, however, rewrite the instructions themselves or add the point value for each section.

Make the narrative as clear as you possibly can. Make your headings stand out by using bold, bold italics, underscoring, and other computer-enabled characters to separate sections, subheadings, and points. Do not use color.

Use bullet points for lists of items. However, here's a word of caution about bulleting. If the RFP instructions say to double space the proposal, everything—including the bulleted items—must be double spaced.

What Is a Rubric?

A rubric is created for the judges of grants, but is often made available to grant writers in the RFP. It's a way of presenting the evaluation criteria that assists the judges in scoring your grant.

Sections of the grant proposal—especially those done for government agencies—are usually assigned a number of points. For instance, a recently released federal grant provided 20 points for the need section; 15 points for results and benefits expected; 35 points for the approach/evaluation (project description); 10 points for budget; and 20 points for attaching the appropriate documentation and letters of agreement.

A more typical grant proposal might provide 25 points for need, 45 points for project description, 20 points for evaluation, and 10 points for the reasonableness of the budget. By the way, don't bother adding up the numbers; they are points, not percentages, and don't always come out to 100!

Evaluation Criteria

Judges use the evaluation criteria as guidelines when they award points to a project. These guidelines can be presented either as a list of criteria or as a rubric.

A rubric provides a scale for determining point awards to each section, according to how well it fits the description for that score. Following is a rubric for the abstract of an education proposal. The abstract in this case is worth up to 10 points.

Not Recommended	Recommended for Funding with Revisions (3–5 points)	Recommended for Funding (6–8 points)	Highly Recommended for Funding (9–10 points)
The project abstract is not included or is very incomplete.	The project abstract minimally describes the project; portions of the required elements are missing or are labeled "see attached."	The project abstract contains all elements required (content/structure of project; number of students potentially benefiting; student identification process; assessment and evaluation). If ISD applicant, application indicates which local districts will participate in project.	The project abstract contains all required elements and clearly and succinctly gives enough information so that the reader has an understanding of the scope, content, and structure of the proposed literacy achievement project and how it will be implemented and evaluated. If ISD applicant, application indicates which local districts will participate in project.

List of Criteria

Now let's look at a list of criteria. This list was established for a federal grant reviewer.

Criterion 1. Objectives and Need for Assistance (20 points)

1. The extent to which the applicant specifies the goals and objectives of the project and describes how implementation will fulfill the purposes of the Early Learning Opportunities Act (ELOA). The applicant must demonstrate a thorough understanding of the importance of early learning services and activities that help parents, caregivers, and child care providers incorporate early learning into the daily lives of young children, as well as programs that directly provide early learning to young children.

2. The extent to which the applicant demonstrates the need for assistance, including identification and discussion of its needs and resources assessment concerning early learning services. Relevant data from the assessment should be included. Participant and beneficiary information must also be included.

3. The extent to which the applicant describes its resources assessment and the relevancy of the results as the basis for determining its objectives and need for assistance.

4. The extent to which the applicant demonstrates how it will give preference to supporting activities/projects that maximize the use of resources through collaboration with other early learning programs, provide continuity of services for young children across the age spectrum, and help parents and other caregivers promote early learning with their young children. The applicant must provide information about how decisions will be made about who will provide each early learning service and/or activity funded through this grant.

5. The extent to which the applicant demonstrates that it has worked with local education agencies to identify cognitive, social, emotional, and motor-developmental abilities which are necessary to support children's readiness for school; that the programs, services, and activities assisted under this title will represent developmentally appropriate steps toward the acquisition of those abilities; and that the programs, services, and activities assisted provide benefits for children cared for in their own homes as well as children placed in the care of others.

Compare the Two

While a grant review is subjective, the evaluation criteria—however it is presented—is intended to make it less so. But the two different presentations of criteria somewhat encourage the reviewers to think differently.

FACT

Grant proposals written according to guidelines, rather than to RFP, are generally not "scored." They are judged by how well they fit the guidelines of the foundation and fill a need or resolve a problem in the foundation's target area.

For instance, in the rubric form of evaluation, the section begins with no points and earns more as it goes up the scale. Compare that to the criteria list, where the need section began with 20 points and then lost points if it did not meet the expectations of the reviewer.

In some cases, the RFP will contain only a list of criteria for selection and no outline for the narrative. Follow the list of criteria exactly, using it as your outline. When you are provided both, use the evaluation criteria as a way of reviewing your work and as a tool for your readers to use to help you strengthen any weaker sections of the proposal.

Enlist the Aid of Readers

A writer often becomes too close to his or her work and cannot be an objective editor. This is particularly true of grant writing since the audience is unfamiliar with the organization and because you have a limited space for explaining ideas and details.

You need two kinds of readers. First, you need readers with expertise in the field you are writing about. They are most like the final judges and will be ruthless about making sure that you meet the highest level of the rubric with your descriptions and explanations.

You also need readers who are completely unfamiliar with either the field or the organization for whom you are writing the proposal. If they don't "get it," you know you have more work to do. Use their questions or concerns to flesh-out ideas.

Using the Rubric or Evaluation Criteria

The evaluation criteria or rubric helps you and your readers judge your draft. Have others score the proposal just as they would if they were judges. Use their scores to help strengthen sections that need strengthening. Use the criteria to guide your writing, and if you can be objective, score your own proposal when the draft is complete.

ALERT!

In your schedule, be sure to build in enough time for review and revision of at least one draft of the proposal. Ideally, your team will read and judge two drafts before you submit the final. Give them at least three or four days with a draft—adequate time to review, digest, and provide feedback.

Once you receive all your scores, add them and divide by the number of readers to come up with an average. If you scored below 90 on a 100-point proposal, rework the sections in which you scored low. Ask your readers questions if you need more guidance during the revision process.

Competitive Priority Points

Many grant programs award competitive priority points for certain factors about the agency or its population. Usually, 5 points are available, over and above the score received on the proposal. They are awarded for such things as a high incidence of poverty among the population the organization serves, for being located in a designated economic-enterprise zone, or for some other criteria over which you have little or no control.

Even if you know you'll receive the priority points, do not add them to your evaluation scores. While the additional points can sometimes push you from "almost" to "funded," they don't strengthen your proposal or answer questions of grant judges.

Novice Applicants

Many federal grant programs are now awarding a competitive advantage to novice applicants. If your organization has never received a federal grant award, check the box on the cover sheet that indicates whether the organization is novice. While the proposal is not awarded additional points for being novice, it is given special consideration by the reviewers.

Chapter 20

Filling Out Forms

Writing the narrative may be the toughest part of completing the grant-proposal process, but the forms cannot be a last-minute task. In this chapter, you'll learn what to expect and how to plan to ensure that you're not running around on submission day trying to find an old-fashioned typewriter to complete nonelectronic forms.

20

What to Expect

The number and types of forms accompanying a grant package vary, but you will always have at least two: a cover sheet and a budget form. Neither can be entirely completed until the grant package is nearly finished. Budget development takes place concurrently with the program development and is not final until late in the process. The cover sheet usually contains a budget-summary section, so that portion will not be ready early. You can and should, however, read the cover sheet much earlier so you can determine what information you will need to gather in order to complete the form in its entirety. Other forms that may accompany grant-application packages include the following:

- Assurances
- Project-summary form
- Informational grids
- Checklists
- Certifications

Federal grant RFPs usually have a separate packet of forms. If you download the RFP from the Internet, be sure to also download the "application," which will be provided as a separate document.

Grants.gov permits electronic applications. When you submit electronically, you must have prepared your cover sheets and other documents so you can complete the electronic forms completely. If they are not complete, the Web site will reject your submission.

Cover Sheets

Cover sheets request all or part of the following information:

- Name of organization
- Name of contact person
- Brief summary of project
- Signature of board chair
- Federal tax ID and/or other special identity number
- Signatures of CEO/executive director
- Budget summary
- Address of organization
- Telephone, fax, and e-mail
- Type of organization
- Category of grant

Most of the information requested can be prepared in advance. You might want to fill out those portions of the form weeks before you have to submit the package. Following is a sample cover sheet for a foundation grant.

XYZ Foundation

Street

Anywhere, USA

Grant Application (please type or print)

Organizations requesting XYZ Foundation funds <u>must</u> submit a Treasury letter certifying 501(c)(3) tax-exempt status.

Date: _____

Organization: _____

Address: _____

Contact person's name: _____ Phone: _____

Contact person's title: _____

Purpose and objectives of your organization: _____

_____

_____

Normal funding/support sources: _____

Geographic area served: _____

Client group served: _____

Title of project for which funds are sought and brief description of project, its objectives, goals, and benefits to clientele and community.

_____

_____

_____

_____

Project dates: _____

Total project cost: _____

(continued on next page)

Amount and source of pledges/commitments to date: _____

_____

_____

Other funding sources (and amounts) applied to for this project: _____

_____

_____

Amount requested from XYZ Foundation: _____

Has the XYZ Foundation supported your organization in the past? _____

If yes, specify dates and amounts: _____

If funds requested are for a new or pilot project, how are sustaining operations to be funded?

_____

_____

_____

List XYZ corporate employees (or family) who are members of your board or volunteers in your organization:

_____

_____

_____

_____

List XYZ employees (or family) who are among your clientele: _____

Signed:_____

Date:_____

Identity Numbers

Cover sheets, particularly those supplied by federal and state grantors, request identity numbers. Foundations generally ask only for your 501(c)(3) letter and take the identifying number they need from that document. The identity numbers required by the government include, in some cases, the federal tax ID—as well as a special designation such as the number assigned a school district by the state—or the federal ID of a special-health clinic.

The federal government now requires a DUNS (Data Universal Numbering System) number on its cover sheets. This is a nine-digit number used to identify a business or nonprofit organization. The number provides access to financial information usually found in an organizational audit or other financial records and replaces the need to attach lengthy financial forms to your proposal. To look up your DUNS number go to *http://smallbusiness.dnb.com*.

Be sure to look up or apply for a DUNS number early in the grant-writing process. While the system does respond quickly to an application or query, on rare occasions it can take up to two weeks to be assigned a number.

If your organization does not have a DUNS number, you can get one for free by calling 1-800-333-0505 or registering online at *www.dnb .com*.

Assurances and Certifications

Assurances are included in most federal application packets. They outline the enabling legislation and its parameters and describe the things that the applicant must already do in order to qualify for a grant. As grant writer, all you have to do is make a copy of the assurance and have it signed by the appropriate person (usually the executive director, chief executive officer, or similar position).

Certifications are similar to assurances, but they also may request additional information. For instance, schools are asked to certify that they are drug and violence free. The form requests a list of recent expulsions or disciplinary actions for drugs or violence on school grounds as well as the signature of the superintendent assuring the government that the school is addressing the problem.

ALERT!

Sometimes you won't find instructions for writing a GEPA narrative within the RFP. If you are writing a grant proposal from a school district, be sure to familiarize yourself with GEPA requirements and prepare this narrative in advance as a part of your writing assignment.

Schools must also provide a narrative response to GEPA requirements. The General Education Program Act (GEPA) of 1994 requires all grant applicants to describe how they will provide "equitable access to, and participation in, its Federally-assisted program for students, teachers, and other program beneficiaries with special needs." The statute highlights six types of barriers that can impede equitable access or participation: gender, race, national origin, color, disability, or age.

ASSURANCES AND CERTIFICATIONS
STATE PROGRAMS

Assurance Concerning Materials Developed with Funds Awarded under This Grant

The grantee assures that the following statement will be included on any publication or project materials developed with funds awarded under this program, including reports, films, brochures, and flyers: "These materials were developed under a grant awarded by the State Department of Education."

Certification Regarding Nondiscrimination under Federally and State Assisted Programs

The applicant hereby agrees that it will comply with all federal and state laws and regulations prohibiting discrimination and, in accordance therewith, no person, on the basis of race, color, religion, national origin or ancestry, age, sex, marital status, or handicap, shall be discriminated against, excluded from participation in, denied the benefits of, or otherwise be subjected to discrimination in any program or activity for which it is responsible or for which it receives financial assistance from the U.S. Department of Education or the State Department of Education.

Certification Regarding Title II of the Americans with Disabilities Act (ADA), P.L. 101-336, State and Local Government Services (for Title II applicants only)

The Americans with Disabilities Act (ADA) provides comprehensive civil-rights protections for individuals with disabilities. Title II of the ADA covers programs, activities, and services of public entities. Title II requires that "No qualified individual with a disability shall, by reason of such disability, be excluded from participation in or be denied the benefits of the services, programs, or activities of a public entity, or be subjected to discrimination by such entity." In accordance with Title II ADA provisions, the applicant has conducted a review of its employment and program/service delivery processes and has developed solutions to correcting barriers identified in the review.

Certification Regarding Title III of the Americans with Disabilities Act (ADA), P.L. 101-336, Public Accommodations and Commercial Facilities (for Title III applicants only)

The Americans with Disabilities Act (ADA) provides comprehensive civil-rights protections for individuals with disabilities. Title III of the ADA covers public accommodations (private entities that affect commerce, such as museums, libraries, private schools, and daycare centers) and only addresses existing facilities and readily achievable barrier removal. In accordance with Title III provisions, the applicant has taken the necessary action to ensure that individuals with a disability are provided full and equal access to the goods, services, facilities, privileges, advantages, or accommodations offered by the applicant. In addition, a Title III entity, upon receiving a grant from the State Department of Education, is required to meet the higher standards (i.e., program accessibility standards) as set forth in Title II of the ADA for the program or service for which it receives a grant.

<u>IN ADDITION:</u>
This project/program will not supplant nor duplicate an existing early childhood development program.

Applicants not operating any component of the project directly must provide a letter of commitment and agreement, including the specifications of terms and conditions for delivery of services.

There is a written agreement between other eligible public nonprofit organizations or programs and the State that outlines provisions for the use of facilities for early childhood development program services (including such use during holidays and vacation periods; the restrictions, if any, on the use of such space; and the times when space will be available for the use of the applicant).

<u>(Competitive Grants Only) The following provisions are understood by the recipients of the grants should it be awarded:</u>

1. Grant award is approved and is not assignable to a third party without specific approval.
2. Funds shall be expended in conformity with the budget. Line-item changes and other deviations from the budget as attached to this grant agreement must have prior approval from a School Readiness Consultant of the State Department of Education.
3. The State Department of Education is not liable for any costs incurred by the grantee prior to the issuance of the grant award.
4. Grant recipients will comply with all subsequent legislation pending pertaining to this program.

Signature of Superintendent or authorized official: Date:

_____   _____

Budget Forms

The federal government issues two types of budget forms: one for construction projects and one for nonconstruction projects. All social-service projects use the nonconstruction budget form, as the federal government does not issue RFPs for construction projects for that sector. The Department of Justice and some other more specialized departments have different forms, but the information requested is mostly consistent from one federal agency to another. Budget forms for federal grants are available when you download an application package at *www.grants.gov*.

Foundations often provide a budget form and a statement saying that if your budget is in a different form, they will accept it.

Most budget forms ask for the following line items:

- Personnel
- Fringe benefits
- Travel
- Equipment
- Supplies
- Contractual services/staff
- Training/professional development
- Indirect costs

Indirect costs are a set percentage (usually 5–10 percent of the grant budget) allowed in the grant for the proposing organization's overhead and grant administration. Read the directions to make sure that indirect costs are allowed before completing the budget forms.

The following example is a budget form for an organization. Typically, foundations provide a similar (or even identical) form for the specific program or project being proposed.

INCOME	
SOURCE	**AMOUNT**
Support	
Government grants and contracts	$
Foundations	$
Corporations	$
United Way or other federated campaigns	$
Individual contributions	$
Fundraising events and products	$
Membership income	$
In-kind support	$
Revenue	
Earned Income	$
Other (specify)	$
List Top Five Donors	
	$
	$
	$
	$
	$
Total Income	$

EXPENSE		
ITEM	**Amount**	**%FT/PT**
Salaries and wages (for project budgets breakdown by individual position and indicate full- or part-time)	$	
	$	
	$	
	$	
	$	
Subtotal	$	
Insurance benefits and other related taxes	$ $	
Consultants and professional fees	$	
Travel	$	
Equipment	$	
Supplies	$	
Printing and copying	$	
Telephone and fax	$	
Postage and delivery	$	
Rent and utilities	$	
In-kind expenses	$	
Other (specify)	$	
Total Expense	$	
Difference (Income less expense)	$	

Fitting into the Spaces Provided

Increasingly, foundations and government departments are providing interactive electronic forms, which can be filled out and changed at any time. However, some cover sheets are still available only as hard copies. Though these hard-copy documents can be completed by hand, they look far more professional if completed on a typewriter. If you can find a typewriter. And if you have a lot of patience.

It isn't easy to line up all the little boxes and lines with the typewriter's keys and margin allotments. And, because you can vary type size and style only a bit on most typewriters, you'll find less space overall for keying in brief summaries, and even longer job titles, that must fit into the spaces provided.

You might want to make copies of the forms and complete them by hand first. Once you know what you want to write, type the responses on the originals. If you don't have a typewriter, check with your local library to see if they have a machine for public use.

With electronic forms that you get online, you have a bit more flexibility because you can change the size of the type or the font to fit into tight spaces. Forms sometimes allow a fixed amount of space for a brief narrative summary. And when you've entered about 200 or 250 words, you might discover the form simply won't let you write any further. Therefore, before you even get started, you'll want to develop a tightly worded, concise narrative summary.

Use the word or character-count function provided in most word-processing programs to make sure your text will fit into the space allotted on electronic forms or submissions.

Getting Signatures

As with support letters, you must begin planning for forms as soon as you receive the RFP. All of them request the signature of the chief person in charge of the organization, so you must coordinate schedules to get those signatures. Most forms also require the signatures of finance directors, program managers, and/or board presidents. Don't be surprised if you spend an entire day tracking down all of these individuals to get their signatures.

Here's a tip: Have officials sign their names in blue ink so you and the granting agency can tell quickly which is the original copy and which are the duplicates. Use this tip when asking officials to sign forms, support letters, audit reports, and other documents requiring original signatures.

You must always submit one original application and whatever number of copies are requested if you are submitting paper copies to the federal government. The original must contain original signatures from all the parties requested.

Chapter 21

Packaging and Submitting Your Proposal

Finally, you've completed the narrative and you're ready to complete the grant application package. Add the finishing touches, write the abstract, compile the last of the forms and attachments and ship or deliver it to the funder. Whew! You're almost done! This chapter outlines the last of the steps in the grant-writing process.

Writing an Abstract or Summary

Though an abstract or summary is one of the core components of all grant proposals, it's placed here because most grant writers find it easier to write the summary after the proposal is completed. Instructions for an abstract will be very succinct. The funder will want a brief description of the project, the need for the project, and the means of delivering the project (such as a collaboration or a qualifying statement about the applicant organization). In other words, they want a one- or two-sentence summary of each of the lengthy sections of your grant proposal.

The directions for the abstract will include a note regarding length either in number of words you are allowed or in terms of a page limit. You're rarely allowed more than one page, however, and often even less. Sometimes an abstract form is supplied by the granting agency. This will include a header with the name of the organization and its identifying number and sections for summarizing specific parts of your narrative.

Write the abstract last. You've already done the work, and you just have to go into the narrative of the proposal and find some succinct sentences or paragraphs and paste them into the abstract. Then write just a few sentences to "glue" it all together.

Following is a 250-word abstract introducing the applicant and need for the project, describing the project components, and summarizing the budget and request.

The school district is a public school system serving approximately 9,200 children and young adults in K–12, alternative education, preschool, and adult-education programs. The secondary (post-middle) schools in the east-state district include High School A (grades 10–12), which has a total enrollment of 2,450. The alternative education programs, BB for ages eighteen to twenty who have missed their graduation dates, and CC for ages fourteen to eighteen who have not yet missed their graduation date, enroll approximately 200 students.

Approximately 200 students enrolled in the high school program would qualify for alternative education, as indicated by failure rates, state Educational Assessment Program scores, language barriers, and other indicators of need, but current alternative programs are at capacity.

The district proposes a House School Program that would expand opportunities for failing students in the current grade 9–12 buildings (that is, increase enrollment slots from 200 to 250), focus on career pathways, nurture an effective learning environment, and provide additional specialized assistance required by at-risk adolescent students. The restructured program will include student assignments to "learning families" in the House School; focus on career development; a family-liaison worker; on-site security; enhanced opportunities (extended school day and block scheduling) for accumulating necessary credits; socialization opportunities such as anger management; improved teen-parenting curricula, the Teen Outreach Program (TOP) curricula; a focus on asset building with adult mentors, and a series of retreats, camping experiences, or other challenges designed to build friendships, individual confidence, teamwork, and leadership skills.

The district provides $__ in-kind and match, and requests a one-year grant of $____ to support the transition.

Writing Cover Letters

Federal grants and state grants really don't require cover letters, but it's a nice gesture, even if you suspect they may be tossed in the trash by the person who opens the package. Cover letters are very appropriate for local foundations as this is your opportunity to make a personal link between the board or staff of the foundation and the board or staff of the nonprofit organization.

Start every letter with a "Thank you." It's a much nicer greeting than "I have enclosed," because it focuses on the reader rather than the sender.

The cover letter should be signed by the person in the organization who has the closest link to the funder. For instance, if a board member is a close personal friend of a trustee of a family foundation, ask that person to sign the cover letter. If there is no one with a personal link to the foundation, have the letter signed by the CEO or executive director.

Take a look at the sample cover letter below. This organization had previously received a grant from the targeted funder for the same program. Based on evaluation, the organization zeroed in on strategies that worked so they could reduce the cost and present the program for refunding.

Date
Program Officer
ABC Foundation
Street
City, State, ZIP

Dear Program Officer:

Thank you for reviewing the enclosed three-year proposal for XYZ Nonprofit in city, county, state. The model for this program has been revised recently to build on past strengths of the program and to be responsive to community needs. It now calls for one of two services, which will be selected by the parents: telephone-call support from a trained volunteer, or home visits from a paraprofessional provided by one of the collaborating partners. We have also focused our services on first-time parents of infants and plan to provide consistent prevention services for up to three years of home visits or one year of telephone support.

These changes and others, as I've stated, are based first on what works, and second on cost efficiencies. The new model, like the previous one, will ensure that children develop optimally and that parents develop the skills and access the community resources they need to prevent child abuse and neglect. Services will be offered to approximately 1,800 new families each year.

We are respectfully requesting ABC Foundation support of $1 million over three years, which will be used to leverage other private and public funding to support the program's annual $1.2 million budget.

Please contact me with any questions or to set a time to meet for discussion of the project. Thank you for your attention and time.

Sincerely,
Organization Director

Using Color, Photos, and Other Graphics

Graphic elements are always nice, as long as they can be included in the document and be contained within the page limits. Charts and graphs can be used to illustrate a process, to define the management structure of your organization, or to describe the workings of new inventions. In general, however, avoid the use of color graphics or photos, and try to avoid the need to illustrate your concept in color—use shading or line art instead. There are two reasons for this: First, if you must make copies in color, it is more expensive. Second, even though you've attached the requested number of copies, the funder often makes more copies, and they will not make color copies. In general, consider color prohibited unless you are instructed otherwise in the RFP.

Using Dividers, Binders, or Bindery

Once again, let the directions dictate your course. Most often, however, the grantmaker will prohibit bindery or special covers. Instead, they will direct you to staple the pages together or enclose them in a rubber band.

Stapling can create a problem when you have a lot of pages to fasten together. You can use a heavy-duty stapler that can staple through at least 150 pages. Rather than investing in equipment that you may use only infrequently, go to your local shipper or copy shop and use one the business provides for customers.

Sometimes the instructions ask you to three-hole punch your original and copies and to secure them with clips or rubber bands. That means that the granting agency intends to create binders for the reviewers. If you want to avoid having to hole-punch dozens or even hundreds of pages, you can buy a ream of prepunched paper for printing your proposal.

When a funder is not specific about binding or dividing copies, you are free to package your proposal as you wish. There are a number of different ways to do this:

- A three-ring binder with dividers for each section. (This method is particularly effective when you have large grant proposals of more than 100 pages, such as those for medical or dental programs.)

- Wire or plastic bindery with a full-color cover or a simple cover with titles, logos, and other appropriate information
- A pocket folder with a cover letter in one pocket and the proposal and attachments in the other
- Binder clips

For the most part, keep your packaging simple. Often, even though you send the requisite number of copies, the granting organization must make additional ones. In these cases, they'll have to unbind or unstaple your grant packages.

Attachments and Appendices

Attachments and appendices are generally allowed (and sometimes required) and rarely count against your page limits. Sometimes the granting agency will limit the number of pages in your appendix and attachments. In this case, select the very best of your optional or limited attachments, such as support letters or media stories. Examples of attachments include:

- IRS determination letter—proof of 501(c)(3) status: required by foundations
- Board roster: required by most foundations
- Letters of support: required by most grantors, especially when you are proposing a collaborative structure
- News articles about the program: not required
- Annual report of organization: not required
- Organizational charts
- Maps
- Most-recent audit statement and report: often required by foundations; not required or wanted by federal government

Appendices might include such things as:

- Progress reports
- Formal needs-assessment reports

- Survey results
- Translated materials

Appendices are not required by most foundations. Only a few federal grant programs request appendices, and they will be clear about the content.

With the exception of the National Endowment for the Arts (NEA), few federal or state grant programs allow attachment of film or video. Most foundations don't appreciate video attachments unless they specifically request them. If you have an interesting, relevant video, place it on your Web site and reference its availability in your proposal.

Electronic Submissions

More and more, both the government and foundations are offering—and in some cases mandating—electronic proposal submission. Most still accept either a mailed document or the electronic submission, and some require both an electronic submission and mailed supplementary documents. Benefits of submitting your proposal electronically include:

- An extra day to complete the application
- No cost for mailing/shipping, unless for supplementary materials
- Most electronic-submission services will prompt you if parts of the application are missing
- E-mail confirmation of receipt of the document

Drawbacks may include the following:

- Unreliable connections to server
- Sometimes no means of saving the text, so must be completed in one sitting
- Registration can be complicated and time consuming

Electronic submission of documents requires that you create PDF files of your IRS designation letter, audit, and other required attachments. Usually, when you work in the electronic-submission format, you may go back and change the text as needed. Until you are finished, do not select the button that says "submit."

A couple more important points about using Grants.gov:

- Grants.gov requires a password consisting of upper- and lower-case letters, numerals, and symbols. Be sure to put your password in a safe place where you can look it up when needed.
- Grants.gov does not accept registration by individuals, so if you are an independent grant writer, the organization you are working for must register its own name, password, and contact information. You will not receive confirmation of submission, but your client will.

Making and Marking Copies

Government grants always tell you in the RFP how many copies to submit. They will also often tell you that the stated number is not required but "will facilitate review." This is really just a nice way of saying, "Send us the exact number of copies we requested." Foundations often do not say how many copies they'd like. Either call the program officer and ask, or submit one original packet.

Those agencies that require copies also require an original. Be sure that your original document is clearly marked as such. Use one or more of the following ways to indicate the original document:

- Add a sticky note with the word "original" to the original document.
- Print the original on stationery-quality paper and the copies on copy paper.
- Add colored sheets to the top of each proposal, with one color for the original and another for all copies.
- Attach a cover letter on organizational letterhead on the original document only. Do not attach a copy of the cover letter to any of the others unless it's requested.
- If binding, add a note to the cover of the package. Or make one color cover for the original and different color covers for the copies.

Shipping and Delivery Options

Other than electronic submission, there are three ways to deliver grants: personally, by mail, or by shipping service. The best choice among the three is the one that guarantees you'll meet the deadline.

For local grants and sometimes state grants (if you live in or near the capital city), the best option is hand delivery.

When the grant RFP states that a grant must be postmarked by a date, you must use the U.S. Postal Service. Dates entered into a shipping form do not count! When the RFP states that the grant must be received in the grantor's office by 5:00 p.m. on a certain date, you have to select the method that is most certain to get it there.

Since you will often be working on a grant, its forms, or its attachments on the very last day before it's due, you will probably usually use overnight shipping as a means of delivery to remote destinations. Use UPS or FedEx for these shipments. Unlike the postal service, these shippers provide a tracking number so you can know for certain when the grant has arrived. Please be aware, however, that if the shipper fails to meet the deadline, you can recoup the cost of shipping, but not the hours of labor and the potential for a large grant award. If at all possible, try to ship the grant two days before it's due.

When a grant is due on Monday and you are using a shipping service, try to ship on Friday. Cost for pickup and shipping on a Saturday can sometimes be double that of Fridays. Plus, if you ship on Friday, you can take the weekend off to rest before you tackle your next grant-writing project.

The most critical thing about wrapping up the grant is ensuring that it arrives on time. Know the time of the last mail pickup or how late your overnight shipping service is open. Check to make sure the hours aren't going to change, and keep track of Sundays and holidays that can delay shipping.

Chapter 22

Next Steps

You've met the deadline and shipped the proposal. Big "Whew!" and congratulations! Take a brief breather, then prepare to tackle the next steps. If the grant is awarded to you, congrats! There's lots to do. But even if you don't receive the grant this time, there are steps you can take to ensure you have a better chance the next time.

What's Next?

Sometimes the RFP will state the process and timeline from submission through declination or funding, but more often it won't, especially in the case of federal grants.

You can ask local funders about their grant-making cycles and will likely learn of the next trustee meeting and a deadline for notification of failure or success. Federal grantors don't like to be very specific because they want flexibility to respond to acts of Congress that may increase, deny, or reduce the funding allocation for the grant program.

Some grantmakers like to perform site visits, meeting with someone from the organization at some point after receiving your proposal. Be prepared to respond orally to questions related to the program you're proposing during a site visit.

But don't let the lack of response or the time it takes for the grantor to go through its decision-making cycle slow down your efforts. Above all, don't just sit and wait, especially if you have a large program. Since they often require that you find multiple funding sources, immediately begin to refine and reframe your grant proposal so you can submit it to other funders.

Once a major proposal is written, the work gets easier. That's because lots of sections (for instance, the need statement) can be reused again and again. That saves you a lot of time and effort when you are redeveloping a proposal and sending it to different funders.

Simultaneous Submissions

Unlike in the world of publishing, simultaneous submissions are perfectly all right in grant proposals. In fact, in some cases, it's mandated or at least expected.

In some areas, the major funders meet regularly to discuss what part each wants to play in capital campaigns or major community initiatives. In this case, if you haven't submitted proposals to all the major funders, you risk offending one, or worse, being cut out of funding from all of them for lack of planning and communication.

It's also perfectly appropriate to submit portions of a project to various funders all at once or to submit a federal grant proposal at the same time that you are seeking local support. In fact, this too is often expected. You will have to seek funds to sustain a project over its first several years, so why not try to raise as much as you can to see it through the start-up? Funders are almost always more interested in new projects than they are in ongoing ones, which they come to see as "continuing operations."

If the Proposal Is Denied . . .

No one likes to hear the bad news, but the truth is that hundreds, sometimes even thousands, of applications for funding are denied for every one that is granted. Often the funder will tell you in the declination—and for that matter, the congratulatory—letter how many responses they received to the RFP. You'll see statements such as, "Of 378 applications, we were only able to select the twenty-eight that scored 92 points and above." That should provide some measure of comfort to you.

FACT

It is possible to get rejected several times by different foundations as you search for funding for a particular program, but don't give up. If you have a good program, you will eventually be able to find the perfect fit between your project and a funder.

The good news is that you can try again—both with another type of proposal and, frequently, by resubmitting the failed proposal when the opportunity presents itself again.

Why Proposals Fail

There are several reasons that a proposal can be denied, including the most obvious and usual—that it did not score high enough to be in the top portion of projects submitted. Other reasons are not so obvious. For instance, proposals can be turned down because of any of the following:

- The client received a grant recently from the same funder, and the funder wishes to give others a better chance, even though it likes the project you are proposing.
- It's not your turn. Some grants, particularly those that are provided annually by states, appear to be distributed based on a rotating system of every three or four years.
- The organization did poorly on a past evaluation or failed to comply with the grant agreement on a past grant, even if the grant was from a different funder—don't forget, they often communicate with each other!
- The funder has a political agenda. Unfortunately, this often comes into play, particularly in state grants where one geographic area of the state is continuously favored over another. It may be only because that area has stronger representation or lobbyists.
- The project did not fit the guidelines closely enough.
- Your community does not have the highest incidence of need, compared to most others.
- The funder's priorities shifted or the program emphases changed between the time you submitted the proposal and the time it made grants.
- A similar project was just funded in your specific geographic area. It's unlikely a national funder will invest in two projects to serve the same general population.
- You failed to follow the directions. In this case, of course, you won't be able to help but blame yourself. But you will learn from it, and be more careful next time.

Requesting Reviewer Comments

Local foundations often will tell you what went wrong in the decision-making process during the trustee meeting. There is little you can do unless foundation staff give you some tips about reframing your proposal and invite you to resubmit the proposal.

In the case of state and federal grants especially, the first thing to do about a failed grant is to request reviewer comments if they were not shipped with the declination letter. Send a letter to the granting agency on your organization's letterhead. Include the number of the program, the date of the proposal deadline, and a polite request for reviewer comments and scoring.

Reviewer comments can range from a sheet of criteria with a square for a score and two lines per criteria for comments, to several full pages of narrative reviewer comments on each section of the proposal.

FACT

Reviewer comments are critical to helping you improve your grant-writing skills. Even if the organization isn't interested in reapplying, you'll benefit from reviewing the comments on the proposal. It will give you insight on how to improve your chances with other grant requests in the future.

You'll find that if there were three reviewers, scores and comments will differ, sometimes drastically, between them. Where one reviewer might give you full points for a section and make no suggestions for improvement, another may cut your points by half and find fault with nearly everything you've done. Then they seem to switch views in the next section of the proposal. Your final total proposal scores from each reviewer, however, should fall within a few points of each other.

You may not contest low scores—even in the rare instance that only one of your reviewers has scored the proposal poorly. However, these comments are invaluable as a roadmap for strengthening your next attempt.

Rewrite and Resubmit the Proposal

Following is a compilation of reviewer comments from one Small Business Innovation and Research (SBIR) grant review. Note how some appear contradictory.

Strengths

- Could be a clear advance in prosthetics
- If successful, this work would be significant

Weaknesses

- Idea is not new
- Wide body of literature not addressed
- Literature on specific control devices not referenced
- Market overestimated
- Price seems low
- Unrealistic workload
- Suggest first demonstrate technical feasibility of concept

You will have several months to absorb reviewer comments and contemplate how you will address their concerns in your next attempt. When you sit down to rewrite the proposal, ignore the strengths, or positive comments and address the weaknesses.

Some very technical grants, like the SBIR, require you, on a second application, to respond directly to reviewer comments and state how you've addressed the concerns they had with the project when it was first presented. However, most of the time, you will use the reviewer comments to improve your proposal in a much-less structured way. In the previous example, a resubmission will require the writer to research further the literature on prosthetics and prosthetic control devices. He or she will have to work closely with a financial expert or business consultant to develop more realistic market estimates and potential pricing. Then, the writer will have to work on the project plan, reducing it to something that can be accomplished in a shorter time. Or, as an alternative, the writer might encourage the inventor to do as much as he or she can prior to resubmitting the grant so the entire experiment is further along and he or she can limit the project plan to a technical feasibility study.

Focus specifically on reviewer comments and address each throughout the revision—even if only one reviewer cited the topic as a weakness and another complimented it. If the evaluation section was weak, take it to the local university and speak with a professional evaluator. If the need section was weak, locate more data to support your case. If the project description requires more detail, work with project staff to strengthen the approach.

As a general rule of thumb, one revision and resubmission is mandatory with the permission of your client or employer. A second, if your revision is denied, is all right. If the second revision is also turned down, however, you may need to look at developing an entirely new project. Clearly, the weaknesses lie with what you are proposing, not how you are proposing it.

You Got the Grant—Now What?

There's a saying among leaders of nonprofits: "Darn, we didn't get the grant. Darn, we got the grant." Of course, everyone is happy to hear that they submitted a successful proposal. On the other hand, now the real work begins—implementing the project and fulfilling the work plan.

The first thing you, as grant writer, are most likely to need to do when your organization gets the grant is review and possibly revise the project budget. Often, six months have passed between submission and the confirmation of funding, and things have changed. The organization may have purchased some requested equipment or implemented some phase of the project with other money. And often, too, the granting agent requests a new budget for final approval.

Sometimes you'll get the grant, but it's for less than the amount you requested. The funders do this for a number of reasons. They may have decided to fund more projects than they originally anticipated and want all of you to reduce your overall budgets by 10 percent—you choose where. Or maybe they've declined a line item in your budget because they didn't want to fund that particular thing.

Experienced grant seekers understand that they often don't get the full amount they requested and, therefore, they have a backup plan for filling in budget gaps.

You can apply for a local grant to supplement a federal one. You can make up the shortfall from the organization's operating budget. Or, with permission from the grantor, you can reduce the service you intended to provide or the number of people in your target population to compensate financially.

Writing a Media Announcement

Once you've gotten a grant, you'll want to do a bit of publicity in the local media. Local grants often require a media announcement as part of the grant-agreement contract. Just as with grant proposals, media announcements—also called press releases—are formulaic. Always begin with a headline such as "Media Release." Then provide contact information (the name, address, e-mail address, and phone number of the person in the organization who fields questions or can tell the media more about the project).

Also in the heading, you have to say whether the release is immediate or to be held until a certain date so the media know they may not release the information to the public prior to that stated time. Center a headline that announces the grant and the amount to be received. Then start the story with a dateline, just like those in the newspaper, that includes today's date and the city and state.

A two-page news release is more than sufficient. And it absolutely should always include at least one quote from project staff or leadership. If possible, use another quote from the granting agency. Describe the project in a way that makes it sound exciting. Signal the end with three number symbols centered after the last paragraph (# # #).

Following is a sample media release about the federal grant proposal included in Appendix C. Specific identifying information has been deleted or made generic for this example.

30 November 2003
MEDIA RELEASE
For Immediate Release
For More Information:
John Doe at (222) 555-1212
Address
E-mail

ABC Receives $250,000 from U.S. Department of
Education for Mobile Media Lab

November 30, year, City, State. The ABC Nonprofit (ABC) today announced receipt of a $250,000 grant from the U.S. Department of Education for its

Mobile Learning Lab for Information Education (MML). MML was planned and launched preliminarily with an $80,000 Ameritech/SBC grant provided earlier this year. The federal grant enables ABC to equip a van with computers, cameras, and wireless connectivity and to develop curriculum for kindergarten through twelfth-grade educational-enrichment programs and operation of digital editing software.

MML is a painted van equipped with twenty wireless laptop computers and sixteen video cameras that will travel to city and suburban neighborhoods and schools to provide computer training, Internet access, and video-production training. Audio, video, and computer data can be routed back to the ABC for possible transmission on FM radio, cable television, and streaming on the Internet.

"These funds will allow us to share high-tech resources in low-income neighborhoods, so MML is now one of the foremost projects we have to help us in our effort to close the digital divide," said John Doe, executive director of the ABC.

Under the direction of Americorp VISTA volunteers and staff, MML is piloting programs at a local school and will be ready for full launch in city and suburban schools by the start of second semester. The van and programs will also be provided to neighborhood associations, youth centers, and other programs for homeless or low-income families throughout the city.

ABC is a nonprofit entity with the mission to "Build Community Through Media." Affiliates of the ABC include TV, radio, Internet, and information democracy.

#

The Progress Report

Many grantmakers require that you submit periodic reports of your organization's progress with the program that has been funded. Unless you are also implementing the project, take your list of goals and objectives and interview your client about their progress toward each. Include the following topics in all progress reports:

- Progress toward stated goals and objectives
- Changes in the environment, funding, staffing levels, or other factors that limited progress and the ways in which they did

- Unanticipated successes and the reasons for them
- Anecdotal evidence of success (stories from participants)
- Long-term sustainability plans and steps taken in the interim to sustain the project
- Use of funds
- Any special terms or conditions of the grant agreement
- Lessons learned

The federal government has developed a standard reporting form for many of its grants. On them, you report progress toward the benchmarks, objectives, and/or outcomes you promised in your proposal. The reports require little narrative. Try to download a reporting form before you write a federal proposal so that you are sure you are framing your outcomes in a way that can be measured on the reporting form.

Chapter 23

Writing Grants as a Career

Are you thinking about becoming a full-time grant writer? Maybe you aren't sure what skills you need and what it takes to be successful. You can make a career out of writing grants, whether as a professional full-time staff member of a large organization or a freelance grant writer.

Basic Skills of Grant Writers

While some freelance writers develop proposal-writing skills to tap into the nonprofit market for their work, you don't need to be a professional writer to write grants. Nor do you need to have a particular style when you write. But you do need to appreciate brevity and simplicity, and you have to be willing to work at refining your writing style in that direction. Of course, you can't forget the basic areas of aptitude that any writer should have:

- Sentence structure
- Good grammar
- Correct punctuation
- Accurate spelling

In other words, you need all the skills you learned and have used ever since you completed eighth grade. And when in doubt, like any good writer, you'll know when to consult a dictionary, a thesaurus, or a grammar book.

Think Like an Entrepreneur

There are a number of other skills a grant writer brings to the profession that you either already have or will develop as you learn more about the field. These skills are almost more important than your ability to write. To be successful, you should be able to think entrepreneurially. That means having the ability to identify an organization's needs and to see how you can use your skills to help them meet their needs. You already demonstrated that you have an entrepreneurial spirit when you purchased and started reading this book. In other words, you saw a need to add grant-writing skills to your resume, and now you are learning how to do it to help fill that void for others as well as for yourself.

You must also learn to develop good client relations and become skilled at negotiating, just as you would in any other business. You'll want to become a good consultant or advisor to your clients. You've noticed through reading this book that successful grants most often come from making good matches between the funder and the services provided by a nonprofit. In other words, just as you had to decide what you could provide your clients—based on their needs—you have to be able to help them to think strategically and thoughtfully about which grants they should pursue for their service programs. And those choices have to be based on what the grant provider clearly wishes to accomplish with the money it distributes to charitable organizations. You want to help your clients find the best all-around matches for everyone.

Keep Track of Your Community and Research

A grant writer who is involved in the community, has helped develop programs for other organizations, or just keeps up to date on what's going on locally is an invaluable asset for his or her client. You will always be able to tap that background and knowledge when you have to put together collaborative proposals or assign project responsibilities. It also helps to know who the movers and shakers in your community are; they are experienced individuals who know how to get things done.

You'll also discover that if you are creative as well as practical when it comes to developing programs, you have another valuable asset your clients need. Sometimes they are just too close to their project or organization to see what seems instantly obvious to you as an outside consultant, if only by virtue of your experience. For example, if a school is designing a program to reduce delinquency, they might not be thinking about how girls fit into that picture and what's important to them in their various developmental stages. If you can remind them of the latest research that demonstrates that young women, especially those in middle school, need programs in which they do not have to compete with boys for the attention of their adult mentors, your client might decide to include girls-only clubs or activities in the project that they want funded.

Getting Started

Maggie was a freelance writer looking for a larger market for her work. She read books on grant writing, spoke with a professional grant writer, and even attended a workshop offered by the local United Way organization on writing grants. The problem was that she had only one nonprofit organization among her clientele; the others consisted predominantly of for-profit businesses and local publications. She telephoned her contact at the non-profit agency but received a cool reception. "It isn't you or your work," the contact said. "It's that these grants are critically important to us. We can't really afford to take a chance."

Maggie wondered how she'd break into a market that she knew would be lucrative when even her nonprofit client refused her assistance. She decided to reduce some of the risk for the nonprofits by offering to write a grant for free. Over the next week, she contacted another nonprofit she knew a bit about. "I'd like to volunteer to write a grant proposal for you," she said. "Do you have experience?" the executive director asked. "No, but I intend to get it by writing one for you," Maggie said. "Sorry," replied the executive director.

Finally, Maggie looked up a Request for Proposals and wrote a grant proposal based on the criteria in that proposal and her information about her client nonprofit agency. Then she tried again. She telephoned a third non-profit in the community and volunteered her services.

When the executive director asked if she had experience, Maggie said, "I've only done one, so I'll need your guidance." The executive director was thrilled. "We do have an RFP (Request for Proposals) right now. It's due in thirty days, and yes, we'd love some help! When can we meet?" Maggie was in.

The vignette above is true. It is not easy to break into grant writing for the same reason that the field is lucrative for freelance grant writers. Grant proposals have great value and are taken extremely seriously by nonprofit organizations.

ALERT!

Train your clients and staff of nonprofit organizations to send you "heads-up" letters announcing upcoming grant opportunities or upcoming RFP releases. Or sign up to receive notifications from Grants. gov and the foundation center, and notify your clients. Prior notice helps the grant writer advise the client, provide ample time to prepare a program and proposal, and identify and meet with potential community partners.

Maggie continued to market her grant-writing services over the following year, and she grew more and more successful at securing clients and work. Before the year was out, she didn't even need to market anymore. Nonprofit directors started passing around her name, and she got as much work as she could handle.

Other Ways to Open Doors

Like Maggie, you may have to donate your services the first time to open the door to your grant-writing career. As an alternative, you might subcontract with a professional grant writer in your community who can supervise your work and provide guidance for strengthening the final proposal. Or you may have an existing nonprofit client who is willing to work with you through the first proposal.

If possible, select some of the easier grant formats—usually local foundations or your local government—to get you started. This will limit the total number of hours you volunteer, and it will also provide you with a base of experience that you can use in marketing for more extensive work in the field.

Business and Science Clients

Businesses seek skills similar to those of grant writers. You might see a business in the classified section advertising for a proposal writer, and some individuals market their skills as "proposal," rather than "grant," writers. In general, businesses must often respond to requests for proposals—for services or products—in the same way that nonprofits respond to requests for proposals for new programs that address a particular issue. Occasionally, however, businesses must write grant proposals for specific types of requests made by government agencies or other businesses. Since very few businesses have a grant writer on staff, they will require the services of a professional freelance grant writer. Architectural firms are one exception. Many of the larger firms have proposal writers on staff to provide the narrative description and the other information required that they use to supplement presentation drawings and estimates.

Proposal writers and grant writers perform nearly identical services—one for the for-profit and the other for the nonprofit sectors. Use your grant-writing skills to market proposal-writing services in for-profit industries, or if you already write for businesses, use your writing skills to help nonprofit organizations improve your community.

A Word of Caution

Sometimes individuals apply for a very select grant, such as a Small Business Innovation and Research (SBIR) grant from the federal government. It provides Phase I grants of up to $100,000 and Phase II grants of up to $500,000 to entrepreneurs and inventors so that they can further develop their ideas for products that have some social application, as well as market promise.

For the most part, however, individuals are not the best market for your business. It is best for them to write the grant proposal themselves. The granting organization is funding the person behind the idea, and thus reviews the grant with an eye for that person's level of expertise, experience, and familiarity with the field. There are myriad other criteria that they use to judge the merit of the applicant and the proposal. The SBIR is judged by Ph.D. reviewers in science, medicine, technology, and/or engineering. The grant writer must be an expert in the field, along with the inventor, if he or she is to write with authority to this audience.

Another factor you should consider before taking on individuals as clients is that individuals often lack the money to pay the professional grant writer. If you want to donate your time and effort, you can easily find projects that are more fun and more interesting than those requested by a struggling inventor or entrepreneur.

Generalist or Specialist?

Some grant writers specialize. Medical grant writers, for instance, write for hospitals, medical researchers, clinics, and other health-related organizations. Some grant writers specialize in writing only educational grants for schools or colleges. Others focus on issues such as child abuse and neglect. There are grant writers who concentrate on business or scientific research grants and others who prefer to write only one type of grant, perhaps for federal funding. You won't find them interested in taking on foundation grants or vice versa.

FACT

Unless you're an expert, you may not have the skills needed to write proposals for professionals in science, medicine, technology, or engineering. Their proposals will be read by peers in these highly specialized professions and should include language and vocabulary they are accustomed to using with peer professionals.

Should you specialize? There are a couple of ways you can tell. Which of the two following checklists best describe you and your approach to work?

○ I like to learn new things.	○ I am a master of one or two subjects.
○ I learn quickly.	○ I have an extensive vocabulary in my field.
○ I enjoy meeting new people.	○ I want to work with people who share my interests.
○ I want a broad market for my work.	○ I want to contribute something of value to my field.
○ I am passionate about my work.	○ I am passionate about my subject.

If you fit best into the left column, you are a generalist. You will be embarking on a field in which you'll never want for work. If you agree with the statements in the right column, however, you are a specialist, and there's likely to be a great need for your help in your field of interest.

Range of Services

Grant writers don't have to limit themselves to grant writing. There's an array of services that you can offer clients that complement the actual writing of proposals. These can include such things as designing programs, planning and facilitating meetings, negotiating collaborations, searching for grant sources, writing media releases and packets, planning marketing strategies, and developing other written materials such as progress or evaluation reports. And don't forget, there's always a need for ongoing consulting and advising your client.

Another thing to consider: Grant writers who have established a solid reputation in their communities may find themselves called upon to review proposals written by new writers. That gives them an opportunity to be an editor and mentor to those entering the field. Local foundations may also call on an established grant writer to review proposals before the director presents them to their board of decision-makers.

Potential Earnings

As a grant writer, you can earn as much or more than other freelance writers, even though you're working for the nonprofit sector. All clients expect to pay for the things they value the most, and nonprofits truly value grant writers. The more successful grant proposals you write, the more valuable you become to your clients and potential clients.

You are working with organizations that have limited budgets, however, so be fair. Give them a not-to-exceed project fee for every grant proposal. For instance, if you plan to charge by the hour, review the Request for Proposal (RFP) or guidelines, estimate how many hours it will take to completely write, review, and develop the proposal, then add a few more hours to cover contingencies. Using your highest estimate, inform the organization that it will not cost any more than that figure to complete the project. Of course, there may be times you've underestimated a project and make less than you wanted. But as you gain experience with various types of proposals, and get to know your clients and their work, you'll find that as often as not, you'll complete the project in far less time than you had estimated.

Base your fees on your hourly rates, but give clients with limited budgets a guarantee that costs will not exceed a certain amount. Even if you find that you have exceeded the time you would have allotted the project, you should not exceed your estimate when you bill. Nonprofit organizations do not have a lot of flexibility in their budgets.

There is no way to estimate what a grant writer can earn. It depends on whether they are employed full time as a grant writer or they freelance, whether they are specialist or generalist writers, whether they take in several projects a year or just one or two, where they live in the United States, and myriad other considerations. A best guess for full-time employed grant writers within nonprofit organizations is the salary of a mid-level manager. Freelance grant writers can charge their hourly rate, whatever they and their local market dictate, and often earn more than full-time employed grant writers.

How Long Should It Take?

As a general rule of thumb, you can figure an experienced grant writer will estimate the hours for a project within the ranges listed on the chart below. These estimates include meetings with clients, filling-out forms, writing budgets, writing the grant proposal itself, and making revisions. Minor expenses such as shipping, mailing, or mileage are not included.

Item	Time required
Federal grants (one department)	40–60 hours
Federal grants (more than one department)	90–120 hours
Specialized grants (medical or research science)	100–180 hours
Foundation grants (assets of less than $20 million)	3–8 hours
Foundation grants (assets of more than $20 million)	10–20 hours
Corporate-giving program grants	Similar to foundations
State/local government grants	10–20 hours

Until you become accustomed to the process, it will probably take you longer to write your first few grants. It's also likely to take more time when you write a grant for a new client. But as you work with them on developing subsequent proposals, you'll find that you accumulate "canned" text that you can use over and over again. For instance, several paragraphs in your need statement must describe the organization and those it serves. Once a client approves what you've said and your first grant for them is successful, there's no need to "reinvent the wheel." It will save you a lot of research and writing time if you plug in those paragraphs when you tackle their next proposals. You can reuse them again and again with only minor updates and revisions.

ALERT!

Never accept a grant-writing assignment for a percentage of the final grant award. First, you will not be paid unless the funding is awarded, and second, a financial stipend for grant writers is rarely allowed under the terms of the grant award agreement.

Meet Funders Periodically

Try to meet annually or biannually with funders. Get to know the people at the local foundations. This can help as you get started with your career, so you'll know better what they're looking for in a proposal. Things change. You may meet with the program officer of a local community foundation who tells you that they based their decision about whether to present a proposal completely on the need section. If the writer didn't prove need right away and have evidence to support that position, they weren't interested. But over time this may change, and you may find that their focus shifts— for example, maybe these days they look for things that approach systems change. Now you'll know that you need to focus your proposals and your client's attention around a framework of systems change.

If you are freelancing, meet with funders as an independent writer rather than on behalf of a nonprofit client. Use the knowledge you gain in the meeting to help your clients frame their requests to local foundations.

Watch for Trends

You are in a perfect position to watch for trends in funding—locally and nationally. For many years, for instance, funders have emphasized, if not mandated, collaborative approaches to projects. They still are, but when that component was first introduced, it could have taken grant writers by surprise.

Recently, funders have emphasized project components such as professional development in educational projects, audience engagement for cultural projects, or systems change for problem-solving projects. Outcomes-based work plans and evaluations are another relatively new request from grantors. Today, funders are emphasizing sustainability plans, and some are even going so far as to change their approach to grantmaking away from funding start-ups and toward funding ongoing operations.

If you see two RFPs that ask for information about a new focus or that mandate a new criterion, chances are that other funders will soon be wanting the same thing. Think of those original two requests as being at the forefront of a new trend. Then, when the other funders hop on board—as they will—you and the organization you're working with will be ready to respond. You will be establishing yourself as essential to the clients you're working for, and your business will continue to grow!

Appendix A

Glossary

501(c)(3): IRS designation for nonprofit organizations, including religious, educational, charitable, organizations set up to provide social services. See "nonprofit organization."

509(a): IRS designation defining public charities.

abstract (also called project summary): Brief description of project, the need for it, and the means of delivering services.

annual report: Report published by a foundation that describes how grant funds were expended during the fiscal year.

application: Cover sheets and forms that must be completed as a part of the grant package.

assets: Holdings of a foundation in the form of cash, stock, bonds, real estate, etc.

assurances: Forms that must be signed and submitted to the federal government stating that the organization practices equal opportunity, has an environmental policy, or agrees to some other requirement of the granting department.

bequest: Money that is set aside and given to an individual or organization after a person's death.

budget forms: Line-item list of items to be funded, including personnel, wages and fringe benefits, projected travel expenses, training, etc. Form usually provided by grantor.

budget narrative: Details pertaining to the budget. Explanations and justifications of proposed expenditures, including calculations, other sources of funding, distribution of funding, estimated or actual costs.

building campaign: Fund drive to raise money for construction or repair of buildings.

bylaws: Rules that govern how an organization operates.

capital: Funding sought to support construction or renovation of a building or its infrastructure, or for large equipment purchases.

capital campaign: Drive to raise and collect money/funds that will finance an organization's building or renovation project.

case statement: Statement of need.

certifications: See "assurances."

challenge grant: Money that is donated to a nonprofit if other donors contribute a predetermined or matching amount.

charity: Nonprofit organization that operates for the purpose of helping/benefiting a certain segment of society.

checklist: Often funder provided, this lists the components that must be included in the proposal. Sometimes the checklist is submitted and sometimes it isn't. Check instructions.

cold calling: Going to a foundation and describing a need in the community and how your agency would like to address the issue.

collaboration/collaborative effort: Joining of several nonprofit organizations to address a shared goal or develop a joint project.

community foundation: Foundation established by one or two individuals who then enlist the aid of others in the community to contribute to the corpus—fund base—either through direct donations, legacies, or annual donations.

community match: Contributions provided by local donors to support items in a project not covered by primary grant.

competing agencies/programs: Others in the community that may have similar programs but are not partnering in the proposed project.

constituency: In the case of grants, most often the beneficiaries of a project or the target population.

corporate donor: A corporation that makes grants of cash or goods to nonprofit organizations.

corporate foundation: Company-sponsored, private foundation that contributes to the community by using a portion of its profits.

corporate-giving program: A company gift of merchandise or money

that came out of the annual budget for charitable giving, not from a separate endowment.

corporate grants: Money or merchandise that is given to nonprofit agencies by a profit-making business.

corpus: Money endowed to a foundation by a wealthy person, family, or corporation to provide funding for agencies that serve the community at large.

Council on Foundations (COF): National organization that supports philanthropy throughout the United States and provides services and publications to member foundations.

decline/declination: Foundation/government entity denies a request for funding a proposal.

direct costs: Actual cost to operate a proposed project.

discretionary funding: Money allocated to high-level staff or trustees of a foundation that they may grant on their own.

endowment: In the case of foundations, the corpus. Additionally, foundations may "endow" a nonprofit by providing money to be held in trust. The nonprofit then uses earned income from the trust to pay for ongoing maintenance or operations.

evaluation component/plan: Description of how you will assess the project and determine its success or failure.

excise tax: Annual tax that must be paid to the IRS by private foundations.

family foundation: Established by one or two donors/entrepreneurs to ensure that future generations continue to practice philanthropy.

Federal government departments: The following federal departments are most often those that make and administer grants for projects:

DHHS: Department of Health and Human Services

DOC: Department of Commerce

DOD: Department of Defense

DOJ: Department of Justice

ED: Department of Education

EPA: Environmental Protection Agency

NIH: National Institutes of Health

OSHA: Office of Safety and Health Administration

federal grant application kits: A set of forms that accompanies an RFP.

federal grants: Money that U.S. departments grant/give to nonprofits either through direct grants or through another agency, using pass-through funds.

federal register: Collection of all RFPs expected to be issued by the federal government in a given year. It is published or updated annually.

foundation grants: A source of funding from private or public charitable trusts.

funding cycle: The annual cycle by which foundations make grants (such as annually, tri-annually).

fundraising: Overall effort by an organization to raise funding, including but not limited to grant seeking, special events, year-end requests for support, bequests, and building relationships with major donors.

gap analysis: Used when there is not a lot of data to support need statement; looks at current situation, identifies desired outcome and what's missing, or the barriers to meeting goals.

goals: Broad, overall purposes of a project.

government grants: Tax dollars that the government (usually federal or state) redistributes to communities through programs.

grant: A financial or valued gift made to enable a project.

grant proposal: Documents written and used to apply for funding for a specific project or purpose.

grantee: Organization that receives a grant.

grantor: Organization that awards a grant.

grant-seeker workshop: Workshops targeted to specific RFPs and sponsored by a funding agency to provide additional information about the proposal process.

grant seeking: The process of reviewing possible funding sources and narrowing the field of likely prospects.

grant-writers workshop: Workshop held by a granting agency, usually state or federal government, to receive peer/expert assistance in developing your writing skills.

grant writing: The preparation of narrative, budget, and applications for funding.

guidelines: Usually provided by foundations, the outline of types of projects or categories of projects the funder will and will not be interested in funding. Guidelines provide directions for submitting an application for funding.

identity numbers: Tax identification or other identity number assigned to an organization by the federal or state government.

independent foundation: Usually founded as a family foundation; a large foundation led by a board of trustees nominated from within but generally not composed of remaining family members of the donor.

indirect costs: Costs that a nonprofit may take from project grants to pay a portion of overhead or operational expenses. Usually awarded as an allowable percentage of the project budget.

in-kind contribution: Support offered by agency and partners to project providing such things as staff time, office or other space, utilities, volunteer hours, and products.

IRS: Internal Revenue Service.

IRS designation: The letter indicating 501(c)(3) assignment status from the Internal Revenue Service. A copy of this document is most often required by foundations with the grant application.

LEA: Local Education Agency (such as school district, intermediate school district, etc.).

letter of inquiry: Describes a project and asks for permission to submit a grant proposal; the first step in the grant-proposal cycle.

letter of intent: Tells the granting agency that you plan to respond to an RFP.

letter of support: Written by a partner organization, community leaders, program collaborators, and recipient organizations in support of the proposed project for which you are seeking funding.

leverage: Money or items required to qualify for a grant.

management plans: Narrative supporting plans for managing a project.

matching-gifts program: The means by which the match requirement will be met. See "matching grant."

matching grant: A grant that's tied to the requirement that the applicant either use funds from its budget or raise donations of a certain amount in order to qualify for the grant.

multiyear requests: Grants that are applied for once but awarded for several consecutive years of funding.

need statement: Sets the stage for the proposal by describing your community, the target population, grant-seeking organization and what it does, and other relevant data that supports the need for the project.

NGO: Nongovernmental organization or a nonprofit organization that is in no way affiliated with government, except in that it might receive funds from government.

nonprofit organization: An organization designated by the Internal Revenue Service (IRS) as meeting the criteria (specifically, does not make a profit out of scale with its costs and performs a necessary function in society) for nonprofit status. Also referred to as a 501(c)(3), its IRS designation.

nonsupplanting funds: Funds that may not take the place of operating costs. For instance, if the organization is paying for a staff position, it may not, if it is prohib-

ited from supplanting, make the position a grant-funded one.

objectives: Measurable means of achieving the goals of a project.

operating support: Support for nonprofit operations (rent, utilities, staffing, etc.).

partnerships: See "collaboration."

pass-through funds: Funding that is available usually through a federal or state grant that is administered by a local government agency or local foundation.

payout requirement: Amount (usually 5 percent of corpus) that foundations are required to pay out in grants annually.

philanthropy/philanthropist: An organization/individual who donates money, goods, services, or time to humanitarian efforts.

post-grant evaluation: Project evaluation made at the end of the grant period.

preliminary proposal: Response to an RFP that calls for two papers: The first (preliminary) is used to judge which organizations may submit a full proposal for funding. Usually used for demonstration projects.

private foundation: Also known as a private charitable foundation; it engages in giving to community agencies money that comes from a wealthy person, family, or corporation.

private independent foundation: Often started by a family, but no longer controlled by donor or family members; administered by a board of trustees; the largest foundations in the United States; grants often made worldwide.

program officer: Person who reviews grant requests at a foundation and makes recommendations for funding or not to the board of trustees.

project budgets: Budgets for a specific project. Includes direct costs and indirect costs.

project manager: The lead manager for a project.

RAG (Regional Association of Grantmakers): Member organization serving foundations in a given region. Keeps catalogs and electronic databases of member foundations.

Request for Proposals (RFP): A document outlining the types of projects the funder might be interested in funding, the criteria a potential applicant must meet in order to qualify for the grant, and the directions for submitting your proposal.

review criteria/evaluation criteria: Guidelines or the rubric used by judges to judge the strength and value of a proposal and how that proposal will meet the grantor's objectives.

review of literature: Review of research on a topic/issue; cited, and stated to support the case for a grant application and the reason that the model of service was selected; required by federal departments and some medical funders.

RFP: See "Request for Proposals (RFP)."

rubric: A chart that presents the evaluation criteria and assists the judges in scoring your grant.

seed money: Initial funds that are used to start a project or fundraising campaign.

site visit: Often a visit by foundation staff to meet the staff and see the operations of a potential grantee.

staff qualifications: Summary of relevant service of staff who will administer proposed project.

state single point of contact: Person or office in your state that catalogs who has applied for what grants and assists grant writers by responding to questions during the application process.

support letters: Letters indicating contributions or support for grant applications.

sustainability plan: Applicant's plan for raising money that will continue program after the original grant expires.

tax-exempt organizations: See "501(c)(3)."

tipping: When a nonprofit organization receives most of its support from one donor, it may "tip out" of its nonprofit status.

trustee: A member of a foundation's board of decision-makers.

Appendix B
Resources

Grants.gov

Federal Register and links to federal agency Internet sites. Provides notices of federal funding availability, announces grant opportunities, and gives general information about grant programs. Requires enrollment to submit proposals online.

✍ *www.grants.gov*

Foundation Center

Provides notices of RFPs issued by foundations, a list of more than 65,000 foundations in the United States and search methods for locating foundations and their Web sites. Will provide free notice of grants available if you enroll. Also provides online message board for fundraisers and grant writers.

✍ *www.fdncenter.org*

Council on Foundations

Provides links to other sites such as Government Grant Sources and Private Sector Foundations. Links to Federal Register, Grants and Related Resources from Michigan State University, Resources for Grant Writers, State Grants, Schrock's Guide for Educators, Yahoo!'s Directory of Education Grants. Includes information about such things as Principles and Practices for Effective Grant-Making, Private Independent Foundations, Public Foundations, upcoming conferences and workshops, and Internet resources for nonprofits.

✍ *www.cof.org*

Fundsnet Online Services

Sources for grants, fundraising, grant writing, and philanthropy online since 1996. Categorized links to other sites.

✍ *www.fundsnetservices.com*

FundersOnline

Links to European Union institutions, philanthropy, news sites, searchable database of nonprofits, and research information.

✍ *www.fundersonline.org*

Michigan State University Libraries

Links to foundations, grant categories, and other useful information for grant writers and nonprofits.

✍ *www.lib.msu.edu*

Nonprofits.org

Internet nonprofit center. News and information for charities and donors.

✍ *www.nonprofits.org*

GuideStar.org
Provides IRS reports for both nonprofit organizations and foundations. Good source for analyzing foundation giving patterns.

✑ *www.guidestar.org*

Nonprofit Good Practice Guide
Online resource for nonprofit leaders and grant writers regarding all aspects of nonprofit business management.

✑ *www.npgoodpractice.org*

You'll also find many, many catalogs that list grants for particular kinds of agencies. Regional Associations of Grantmakers often release catalogs of foundations (and sometimes interactive CD's) that can facilitate research into geographically relevant grantmakers.

Appendix C
Sample Federal Grant Proposal

The following grant sample proposes a Community Technology Cen-
ter (CTC) grant project. This grant proposal was funded at approximately
$235,000 for one year as requested. The sample follows the outline of the RFP
for CTC projects and begins with a request to describe the ways in which the
proposed project meets the criteria in the federal statute for authorized Com-
munity Technology Centers. All identifying information has been deleted and
replaced with more generic information indicated by uppercase type.

a. Meeting the Purposes of the Authorizing Statute

The XYZ NONPROFIT in SOMEWHERE, USA seeks to equip a mobile
Community Technology Center that will respond to needs for technology
education from several areas of the community. In its weekly scheduled visits to inner-city and other schools, community centers, and neighborhood
associations, XYZ's new Mobile Media Laboratory will provide access to
computers and the Internet, to digital video cameras and nonlinear video-
editing programs, and to e-learning courses on the use of media tools, provided in both English and Spanish.

XYZ has selected a mobile Community Technology Center because it
enables the organization to reach into a broader area that could be served
by one building site. It also brings media to the people and overcomes transportation and social barriers shared by most targeted service recipients.

The Mobile Media Laboratory (MML) will also be used at meetings of
community groups, as a remote broadcast station for public-access television or radio, and as a vehicle for wireless Internet access, particularly in
those areas of the City that have either no or outdated technology infrastructure. It will travel to other cities in this or surrounding states, as requested,
to demonstrate effective remote routing and switching, and its educational
programs on media and technology.

Using an Ameritech grant for that purpose, XYZ has purchased a
sixteen-passenger van and has spent six months developing relationships
and partnerships with community organizations in need of MML services.
Some, most notably three area high schools and an area service center for

indigent/homeless adults and families, have requested assistance in improving job skills or facilitating job searches. The State's Small Business Development Center has expressed interest in discussing ways the MML might assist entrepreneurs, particularly those interested in developing and commercializing new life science, computer, or advanced manufacturing technologies. Primarily, however, the organizations that have been most eager to provide MML services to their constituents are local school districts and youth centers. All of these organizations are interested in during school or after-school programs for children, youth, and adults that provide homework help and incentives for learning, academic-enrichment programs, Internet access and exploration, e-learning tools and curricula, multimedia activities and tools that link student work with public-access broadcasting systems, and Web-page design and deployment. Several of the schools within the districts have requested either special software such as PowerPoint or have asked for English-Spanish curricula and training. On behalf of Spanish-speaking families, these schools have also requested access to e-mail systems so Hispanic families, who feel particularly isolated in the western part of the state, can communicate more regularly and without cost with their relatives in other states or countries.

The MML Project has four overarching goals:

1. To improve literacy skills among school children and low-income adults; build self-esteem among users; and introduce isolated populations to the larger network of available services at XYZ and other community sites.
2. To enhance existing school and after-school academic programs and attract additional and regular participation in these programs.
3. To remove barriers and embarrassment for adults who are "technology have-nots" so they can derive benefits from technology such as assisting children with school work, connecting with community resources, online shopping and research, accessing and using data for informed decision making, and others.
4. To integrate XYZ and MML services into a broader community plan to identify the digital divide locally, to map the existing and changing technology infrastructure on a Regional Geographic Information System (REGIS), and to develop a five-year technology plan and necessary partnerships to effectively narrow the digital divide in the City/County.

b. Need for the Project
i. Local Need

Somewhere, USA is the state's second-largest city with a population in excess of 200,000, and a County population of more than 500,000. According to the updated data from the U.S. Census, one out of every seven children and one out of every nine residents of the county live in poverty ($16,895 or less for a family of four). According to the state's League for Human Services, a family of four in the county would require an income of $34,000 in order to be economically self-sufficient.

Most of the minority population in the county is concentrated in the City of Somewhere, USA. More than 31 percent of the city's population is African-American, Hispanic-American, Asian-American, or Native-American. Less than 15 percent of the overall county population is minority. In the past ten years, the minority population of the city has increased while the majority population has decreased in the city and increased in the county.

Most of the poverty is also concentrated in the City of Somewhere, USA: 36.5 percent of households in the County earn less than $25,000 annually, whereas 46.5 percent of City households earn that amount. In addition, children in the Somewhere, USA Public Schools are more than twice as likely as those in other County school districts to receive federal free/reduced lunch benefits (66 percent of children in the 1998–99 school year and rising).

The map on the following page shows a large section of Somewhere, USA (shaded area) that local demographers and social scientists target as having the greatest need for technology infrastructure and access (census tracts 26, 28, 29, 30, 31, 32, 36, and 38). In this area are eight public elementary schools, one branch of the public library, and two neighborhood associations. Also in this area is the highest proportion of minority residents and the greatest rate of poverty: Church's community house serves the population of this area as does one of the Somewhere, USA Youth Group's centers.

In a 2000 survey of City residents, 59 percent of the population indicated that they had access to the Internet, while 41 percent either had no access or were unaware of any points of access.

A study from the previous year showed that only 70 percent of school children in the County used a computer at school. In a ranking of twenty school districts in the County for technology availability (hardware and software), teacher professional development, connectivity, and other attributes,

Somewhere, USA Public Schools ranked 18th, while another District seeking XYZ Nonprofit services ranked 13th.

Low States Educational Assessment Program (the state's standardized test—SEAP) scores correlate with children in poverty: In Somewhere, USA only 38 percent of children scored satisfactory on the SEAP of reading. Most other school districts averaged from 50 to 70 percent satisfactory scores, while the two districts that scored over 80 percent both have zero-poverty populations.

Somewhere, USA Public School children struggle on SEAP and other tests of educational achievement. The state's analysis of adequate yearly progress targeted 42 of 57 Somewhere, USA Public Schools for improvement in reading. An analysis of annual City's Achievement Test (CAT) reading results over the past several years, shows that the majority of Somewhere, USA Public School students consistently perform below the 50th percentile in reading. When the results are disaggregated, data reveal considerable gaps in achievement between majority and minority students and between low-income and moderate-/high-income students. The following table compares the percentage of elementary students performing at or above grade level (50th percentile) in reading in Spring, 2000.

The District's middle school population meets the criteria for at-risk: 71 percent come from low-income backgrounds; 68 percent are minority; 22 percent receive special-education services; 15 percent are bilingual. One thousand and fifty middle school students, or 36 percent, were on suspension for some time during the 1999–2000 school year. Sixty-three percent (63 percent) missed over twelve days of school, while 29 percent missed over thirty days of school. Fully two-thirds of the students are below average (50th percentile) in mathematics, science, and reading as measured by the city's achievement tests. Over 40 percent are below the 25th percentile. The statistics for later elementary students show similar demographics with again fully one-third of youngsters below average in reading, mathematics, and science on the city's achievement tests. The only significant difference is suspensions, which are below 5 percent at the elementary level. Clearly, Somewhere, USA Public Schools' students, particularly those from minority families and/or low-income families, require early intervention to prevent later academic failure and dropping out.

Early intervention must include after-school and summer-school supplemental instruction, particularly geared to increasing literacy skills. To ensure that children attend regularly and often, the program should be safe, entertaining, and enriching. More than 40 percent of families in the inner city do not have home computers. Their children's only access to computers is in their elementary schools, all of which struggle with outdated linkages to the Internet, a high ratio of children to available computers, and limited time and expertise for teaching computer skills or simply allowing children to explore on their own.

Their parents struggle to develop up-to-date work skills or to assist their children with homework. Worse, they are cut off from the flow of information that would enable them to make informed decisions about their and their children's lives, and about school, work, and democracy.

In the past year, several nonprofit, private sector, and governmental representatives have launched the technology-planning group around a mission to identify, map, and develop a five-year plan for narrowing the digital divide in the City and County. The XYZ Nonprofit Executive Director sits on the group and is a strong advocate for individuals residing in areas of the community where the technology infrastructure is either nonexistent or out of date. Because these areas are not always contiguous and because the need for literacy programs, media-literacy training, computer-skills training, and other media communications is so great, XYZ Nonprofit is proposing a mobile Community Technology Center that can be deployed to schools, community/youth centers, neighborhood associations, and other centrally located sites throughout the City and nearby suburbs. In this way, XYZ Nonprofit can serve the greatest number of individuals in need of technology assistance, can remove barriers of transportation or unease by bringing media to the people, and can help mobilize public opinion and action around the issue of closing the digital divide. XYZ Nonprofit views the Mobile Media Laboratory (MML) as a catalyst for deeper community involvement in the issues surrounding the information age.

ii. Response to Need

The XYZ Nonprofit's mission is "Building Community Through Media." XYZ Nonprofit and its affiliates serve most of the county with public-access television, radio, Internet, and Information Democracy services. XYZ

Nonprofit provides access to media for citizens and provides media services such as public service announcements, informational video-filming and programming, Web-page design and deployment, and/or Internet linkages for the nonprofit sector.

Staff and members of XYZ Nonprofit are concerned about equitable access to the Internet, computer training, and media communications and have long provided classes in media tools and media literacy from the XYZ Nonprofit site. However, since many individuals in the inner city are isolated from both information and such services as XYZ Nonprofit provides, staff now propose a mobile training van, which will be equipped with laptop computers, e-learning programs, television cameras, video-editing software, and Internet wireless links for communications. The van, Mobile Media Laboratory (MML), will be available anywhere in the county as scheduled, and XYZ Nonprofit is currently developing a rigorous weekly schedule of visits to the following organizations that serve children and/or indigent adults:

- Somewhere, USA Public Schools (currently scheduling for visits to eight elementary schools and one high school)
- Youth Group's two inner-city youth centers
- Church's Community House and its programs for inner-city children through seniors
- Neighborhood associations and nearby homeless shelters
- Suburban public schools (The suburb is contiguous to Somewhere, USA and has similar demographics to the urban core. Its school system serves nearly 9,000 children of varied ethnicity and socio-economic status.) (Currently scheduled to visit weekly one high school and two elementary schools.)

The MML will supplement available computers in after-school programs, allow high-speed Internet access with trained instructors and guides for children, provide cameras for filming activities in the schools and centers, and provide editing software so participants can edit videos and/or stream them directly to the station for airing on public-access television. XYZ Nonprofit plans to develop interactive curriculum on camera and editing equipment use and deploy it to the Web. This will ensure that children and adults wishing to use the video equipment also learn to navigate the Internet. The curricula will be deployed via the software, which allows continuous feedback loops for learners, self-paced learning, and multimedia display. Additionally, with assistance from curriculum specialists at Somewhere, USA and Suburban public schools, the XYZ Nonprofit will develop eight computer-based units of instruction (four early elementary; four later elementary) in the learning content areas, for enrichment and reading-improvement activities.

The television cameras and editing programs are near-universal motivators for learning. The Internet-deployed e-learning program can be geared to age, reading level, or learning style, and will be used to help children and adults improve their literacy skills while learning media skills.

In addition to improving literacy skills, the MML and its programs are integral to a larger community-collaborative technology-planning initiative that seeks to narrow and close the digital divide. The media lab will be used in that capacity to reach the disenfranchised members of the community, including children, and to provide them voices and vehicles for participating in the technology-planning process and numerous other community-improvement efforts currently underway.

c. Project Design
i. Goals, Objectives, and Outcomes

The goals, objectives, and outcomes of the proposed MML community learning project are as follows:

Goal 1: Improve literacy skills among school children and indigent adults; build self-esteem among users; and introduce isolated populations to the larger network of available services at XYZ Nonprofit and other community sites.

Objective a: Write curriculum for e-learning (subjects include video editing, radio hosting and transmission, and Web-page development) that is interactive and easy to understand.

Objective b: Define reading levels for each separate curriculum according to the skills the student will learn (i.e., higher reading levels for more difficult media skills).

Objective c: Train student assistants to assist low-level readers by demonstrating media-equipment operation and using e-learning curricula to supplement hands-on training.

Objective d: Provide e-learning curricula in Spanish for 15 percent of the local population that speak and read only that language.

Objective e: At end of 2001–2002 school year, hold a city-wide video-production competition and honor all participants at an awards dinner.

Objective f: With Somewhere, USA and Suburban public schools, develop eight thematic units of computer-based instruction incorporating the content areas of language arts, science, mathematics, and social studies, focused on reading for comprehension in all content areas.

Outcome: Those who participate regularly in the MML program will increase their reading levels by a half or one grade level (additional beyond that expected through school) by the end of the year.

Goal 2: Enhance existing school and after-school academic programs and attract additional and regular participation in these programs.

Objective a: Provide laptop computers and digital video cameras during school and after-school programs.

Objective b: Train participants to use video equipment and encourage them to explore online learning about video editing, radio hosting and transmission, Web-page design, and other computer and/or media skills.

Objective c: Provide attractive posters with announcements of MML schedule in individual schools.

Outcome: By the end of the year, all Somewhere, USA and Suburban public schools after-school programs served by MML will increase regular participation by at least 20 percent.

Goal 3: Remove barriers and embarrassment for adults who are "technology have-nots" so they can derive benefits from technology such as assisting children with schoolwork, connecting with community resources, online shopping, research, accessing and using data for informed decision making, and others.

Objective a: Develop and promote a regular schedule of MML stops at inner-city neighborhood organization offices and community centers.

Objective b: Introduce media equipment with "thought starters" on how individuals might use the computers, digital video cameras, and/or media training to enhance their lives and their interfamily interactions/activities.

Objective c: Provide wireless connection to the Internet for areas of the city that do not have technology infrastructure.

Outcome: Participating community residents will report on presurveys and postsurveys a greater sense of connection to community services (e.g., library, government, schools, etc.) and a new value for lifelong learning.

Goal 4: Identify, map, and develop a five-year technology plan to help narrow the digital divide in the city.

Objective a: Program Coordinator and XYZ Nonprofit Executive Director will participate in a government/private/nonprofit-sector-led technology-planning group.

Objective b: Commission will identify and map areas of the City according to their respective technology infrastructures. Technology infrastructure maps will be integrated into the Regional Geographic Information System (REGIS) for use by citizens, local government agencies, technology providers, and funders.

Outcome: Graphic depiction of digital divide will mobilize public opinion around the issue and encourage technology providers and local funders to address identified issues.

ii. Linkages

The Multimedia Training Lab is in the final stages of planning and already has attracted high interest among those agencies and institutions that provide services to children, youth, and low-income adults and families. The following organizations have requested direct services from the MML but have little or no ability to pay for services:

Neighborhood District: An area of the city that provides, in a two-block-area shelter, clothing, a health clinic, and a food kitchen for indigent/homeless individuals and families. Neighborhood was among the first areas to request that XYZ Nonprofit establish a mini media center to allow radio and television training, Internet linkage and computer equipment, and training to those in the neighborhood. The mini media center has a live television broadcast line and is prepared to expand its program with the addition of supplemental equipment and e-learning opportunities.

Somewhere, USA Public Schools (SUPS): Serves approximately 22,000 students in K–12. Both the administrators and individual school-building staff have requested XYZ Nonprofit services for media training and/or computer assistance. Some of the schools require supplemental computer equipment, some require software availability (e.g., PowerPoint), some wish job-training programs, and some schools have media-training programs but lack equipment or up-to-date equipment, particularly for nonlinear video editing.

The Suburban Public Schools (SPS): SPS serves approximately 9,000 students in K–12 and has the most diverse range of socioeconomic status among students: Some come from $500,000 homes while others live in rent-subsidized apartment complexes. The District offers media training at the high school building but lacks transmission capabilities and up-to-date editing equipment or facilities.

Somewhere, USA Youth Group, Inc.: Established more than sixty-five years ago by then–police chief Mr. Big, it is believed to be the first police-sponsored youth program in the nation. Late last year it completed remodeling and construction of two youth centers on the City's southeast and west sides. Both centers have state-of-the-art computer laboratories that were intended for use by youth members to assist with homework or to improve computer literacy and skills. Neither laboratory is being used fully or wisely. Staff of the centers lack technical training and/or curricular programs; thus, youth use of the computer-lab resource is limited. Youth Group has requested XYZ Nonprofit services to assist in developing computer literacy and curricular programming and to supplement activities in the centers with media training.

Church's Community House: This full-service center provides day care, job training, senior meals and activities, and after-school programs in one of the City's most economically depressed south-side neighborhoods. It has requested a television broadcast line with links to XYZ Nonprofit public-access broadcasting and seeks to train youth and adults to use media and computer equipment, to develop and air its own television programming around center special events, and to supplement computer-training equipment and curricula for its job-training program.

In addition, XYZ Nonprofit is linked with numerous organizations and programs throughout the community, including but not limited to the following, which have also expressed interest in at least occasional use of the MML:

Technology Planning Group (TPG): A commission composed of representatives from nonprofit organizations, governmental units, and private-sector businesses, with a mandate to identify the current technology infrastructure on REGIS maps and develop a five-year plan for closing the digital divide. The TPG will be funded through at least two local grants for the first two years of the program and will seek additional funding as needed to implement its technology plan. The MML will assist in this effort by helping identify areas of the community where the infrastructure does not support technology and by mobilizing public opinion around the digital-divide issue.

The Strategy Group: TSG was conceived as a way to apply the principles of Continuous Quality Improvement to the larger community. Now in its fifth year, TSG is focused on a holistic and data-supported approach to problem solving. It models this approach currently by coordinating and enhancing efforts in the community to improve families' economic self-sufficiency. TSG holds at least two annual meetings of hundreds of community residents and would use the MML for creating interactive meetings (each table at a work session would have its own computer to enter decisions and comments and link to the server in the van) and to simulcast the meeting for view on public-access television as a means of informing those not in attendance.

Neighborhood Associations: XYZ Nonprofit has established relationships with many of the area's neighborhood associations either individually or through its relationships with the Somewhere, USA Police Department and City of Somewhere, USA. XYZ Nonprofit hosts a monthly call-in television program with the mayor of the City and has developed video presentations and other media-outreach programming for the police department. XYZ Nonprofit intends to schedule regular visits of the MML to each neighborhood association as a way of reaching into inner-city areas and assisting residents in becoming media and computer literate. This effort will also benefit the neighborhood associations as neighbors will increasingly look to the associations as gathering places and service centers with relevant programs. The neighborhood associations will also use the MML to promote, film, edit, and air media programs about special events such as art fairs, neighborhood clean ups, "take back the night," and others.

A State University: ASU is a local university that is involved in numerous community initiatives with XYZ Nonprofit. It is also the site of the state headquarters for the Small Business Development Centers that are now seeking a technology designation from the federal government. ASU has a well-developed community databank and is a source of evaluation tools, training, and processes for many programs in the City. The XYZ Nonprofit will call on ASU to assist in the evaluation of the Mobile Media Lab program, and will provide the MML as requested to assist ASU in its various endeavors.

d. Project Personnel

Mr. Executive Director (ED) is executive director of the XYZ Nonprofit, which oversees the operations of all XYZ Nonprofit affiliates and programs. ED was a founder of XYZ Nonprofit and has been with the organization since 1981. He has been named by the Somewhere, USA Jaycees as one of the top-five leaders in the City and in the State, has been a guest on national morning-television programs, and has published hundreds of articles on community media, free speech, and/or democratic principles. ED has been keynote speaker at several national and international symposiums, and has traveled throughout the world advising Third World nations on issues surrounding democracy and the media. He has worked as a juror for the national art exhibit, and has participated in an arts and Internet project, the Arts Integration Team, for the botanical gardens, and the Arts Integration Team for City's Art Academy. ED is chair of the A Media's board and its "Community Media Review" publication and is recipient of the An Award for humanistic communication.

The XYZ Nonprofit employs ten full-time staff, three of whom are racial minorities; three staff members are women. Its Board of Directors is also composed of diverse individuals: ten are majority race; two members are minority; three members are women. The XYZ Nonprofit's personnel policy states: "XYZ Nonprofit provides equal opportunity to all applicants without regard to race, color, religion, age, sex, physical or mental disability, national origin, marital status, sexual orientation, or any other legally protected status. In addition to complying with the letter and spirit of this policy, XYZ Nonprofit practices policies of recruiting, hiring, training, management development, promotion, and compensation based only on an equal-opportunity basis."

The MML will be staffed by one full-time project coordinator and two assistants. Equipment repair and linkages will be maintained by Net Services, which has a staff of two. The project coordinator will be responsible for scheduling the training van's stops and visits, for developing curricula and deploying it to the Web, for marketing the services available from the MML with other local nonprofit organizations, particularly those serving at-risk populations, and for reporting progress toward goals to the Executive Director and the XYZ Nonprofit Board of Directors. This person is not yet hired. The XYZ Nonprofit will make every effort to recruit a minority and/or woman for the project coordinator position and will ensure that the person will work well with the population to be served by the MML. At least one of the MML assistants, both of whom will work most closely with program participants, will be of minority race.

e. Management Plan

i. Timeline of Responsibilities and Milestones

The following is a chart that provides a timeline.

Date	Activity	Responsibility
July–August, 2003	Purchase MML vehicle	XYZ Exec. Director
	Design exterior and have vehicle painted	XYZ Exec. Director
	Arrange for e-learning software installation	XYZ Exec. Director
August–September, 2003	Develop written job description and responsibilities for project coordinator position.	XYZ Exec. Director
	Place advertisements for position in local newspapers (including those serving minorities)	XYZ Exec. Director
September, 2003	Screen and interview applicants for project-coordinator position	XYZ Exec. Director
	Recruit additional applicants if needed with evaluators	XYZ Exec. Director
	Establish evaluation tools and processes for MML and programs	
October, 2003	Receive notification of CTC grant approval	XYZ Exec. Director
	Hire program coordinator	XYZ Exec. Director
October, 2003	Develop job descriptions and requirements for program assistants and post/advertise openings	Project Coordinator
	Interview and hire two program assistants, at least one of whom will be of a racial minority	Project Coordinator
October–November, 2003	Equip MML with digital video cameras, laptop computers, servers, appropriate software, and wireless connections to XYZ	Exec. Director and Project Coordinator
	Develop curriculum for online program teaching video-camera operation and editing software	Project Coordinator & TV Affiliate Director

Date	Activity	Responsibility
	Develop schedule of regular stops and programs for MML throughout city	Project Coordinator
November, 2003	Develop curriculum for online teaching of Web-page design and deployment	Project Coordinator
	Begin MML scheduled visits to schools, community centers, and other sites	Project Coordinator
December, 2003	Develop curriculum for online teaching of radio hosting, transmission	Project Coordinator and Radio Affiliate Director
January–February, 2004	Formally evaluate program and revise offerings, curricula, and/or schedules as recommended for improvement	Project Coordinator, Exec. Director, and evaluators
October, 2003–October, 2004	Continue regular visits to arranged sites and respond to requests for occasional visits to community, meetings, events, etc.	Project Coordinator
	Continue ongoing evaluation and program improvements	Project Coordinator
	Continue participation in planning commission to identify and map digital divide	Project Coordinator and Exec. Director
	As program demonstrates success toward objectives, encourage agencies receiving services to become more independent (i.e., to develop permanent on-site mini media centers)	Project Coordinator, Executive Director, & participating agencies
July–October, 2004	Identify year-two and beyond need for support and solicit support from local funders on behalf of agencies and/or XYZ and MML	Project Coordinator, Exec. Director, and participating agencies
September–October, 2004	Formally evaluate program and progress toward year-one goals and objectives for reporting to agency participants, federal government, other communities, and local funders as justification for continuation and/or expansion	Project Coordinator, Exec. Director
	Hold community celebration acknowledging student video productions	Project Coordinator

ii. Community Involvement In Program Operations

Monthly, XYZ Nonprofit will host discussion groups of representatives from all user agencies and schools where the MML is deployed regularly. Members will have open opportunities to suggest improvements or to request additional services or improvements to existing services. For instance, SUPS has already requested that the laptops be programmed with PowerPoint for one of its high school programs that requires a PowerPoint presentation before graduation. The school lacks both hardware and software to enable all students to fulfill this requirement, and even though some of the students have home computers, many of them do not have PowerPoint software. SPS has a high school class on television but lacks updated video-editing capabilities and software and has no means of airing students' work. If sites wish additional regular program visits by the MML, the project coordinator will arrange them to the extent possible.

In addition, the two educational organizations will advise on curriculum development in the content areas and for the media instruction and assist in determining appropriate reading levels of curriculum materials and e-learning tools. Curricula will be designed in the Software by the Project Coordinator with assistance from courseware developers at the Software Company prior to review and improvement by the school districts.

Twice during the year (midyear and end of year) all regular and some occasional agency users of the MML will be surveyed and/or interviewed by the outside evaluator from ASU to determine levels of satisfaction with the service, suggestions for improvement, need for continuation or expansion of services, and qualitative data on the Mobile Media Lab program's progress toward stated goals and objectives.

The community will be invited to a year-end event that is the culmination of an all-city student video-production competition. The event will include entertainment, video clips of all entries, full viewing of the winning entries, and food, and will be held at a centrally located site.

f. Resources
i. Facilities, Equipment, and Supplies

The Mobile Media Lab van will be equipped with twenty laptop computers, most likely Macintosh G4 PowerBooks, which have easy-to-learn and easy-to-use nonlinear video-editing software. The laptops will also contain desktop-publishing software for development of Web pages, announcements, or other activities; I-Movie and Moviemaker; Netscape, or another navigational tool; PowerPoint; and word-processing software. Each computer will be equipped with a wireless modem that interfaces with a wireless relay station on the van. Signals can be sent from any remote site to the

XYZ Nonprofit for deployment to the Web, television, or other medium. The Software will be used to develop curricula that can be deployed to the XYZ Nonprofit Web site for interactive e-learning about media tools; however, because it is being donated by the developer to XYZ Nonprofit and requires licensing, the course-development software will not be directly available on the laptops. Other curricula will be developed to reflect early and late elementary learning-content areas and will be downloaded to the laptops for use in enrichment programs.

The MML will carry fifteen digital video cameras. Completed video can be fed directly, via Firewall, into the computer for real-time viewing and editing or for transmission to XYZ Nonprofit.

The XYZ Nonprofit occupies the second story of the west-side Library. It houses Net Services, a computer service provider for nonprofit organizations; a computer laboratory that provides both scheduled classes and free use of computer equipment; the station television studio and video-editing offices; a public-access music radio station; and the Somewhere, USA Democracy Institute, a program that teaches media literacy around social issues (e.g., treatment of gender, race, cigarette-smoking promotion, etc.) and that logs local-media election coverage and reports findings to the community. XYZ Nonprofit currently owns and operates a mobile television-production vehicle that can be plugged into various television feed sites (b-lines) around the City. The MML will use the same and additional lines to deliver training and programs.

XYZ has received a grant to purchase the MML and to begin program development with an outside consultant. It has good relationships and a history of accountability with local funders and has already discussed potential for continuation funding with several local foundations. Pending evaluation of the year-one program and continued need, three of these foundations have encouraged the project startup and are willing to review subsequent requests for funding.

XYZ has a history of developing programs that are a progressive blend of social welfare and entrepreneurial response. This history has placed XYZ in good standing with local businesses, several of which have expressed interest in leasing the MML for events and training at their locations.

ii. Number of People Served and Cost Justification

Besides providing a vehicle and tools for transmitting community meetings and events to thousands of individuals in the community who are unable to attend such events, and besides its impact on the overall awareness of the community about issues and services surrounding information technology, XYZ anticipates providing regularly scheduled, direct multimedia training for a minimum of 800 individuals from the following sites:

- 320 students from SPS at one or more of the schools
- 80 students from SUPS High School
- 20 students from two OCPS elementary schools' after-school programs, including an elementary school where more than 80 percent of students are very low income
- 100 members of Youth Center
- 60 program participants from Church Community House (various ages)
- 20 Homeless District residents
- 200 community members from Neighborhood Association stops

Training for these individuals is expected to: increase reading levels; decrease isolation; cause fuller participation in the social network of the community or school; and/or develop or improve media and computer skills. Training will cost approximately $565 per participant (calculated by dividing the total program cost by 800 regular students).

iii. Project Continuation

Much of the cost of launching the MML and its programs is requested from the year-one grant. Ongoing costs include maintenance and fuel for the van, staffing, software/hardware upgrades, and an annual student video-production competition.

XYZ is prepared to incorporate the estimated annual cost of maintenance, repair, storage, and gasoline for the MML into its annual budget and has already done so for year-one programs. The cable franchise fee recently negotiated provides XYZ with both cable-access television support and some Internet support for the next fifteen years. Because part of the cable franchise fee will come from a portion of the cable company's "At Home"

Internet subscribers, the money may be used to sustain the cost of operating and maintaining the MML.

The remaining ongoing costs come to approximately $120,000 (staffing and awards dinner) and approximately $20,000–$30,000 annually for equipment/software purchase/upgrades, for a total of $150,000 needed each year to operate the MML and its programs. XYZ will encourage agencies and schools that use the MML regularly to include in year-two and beyond budgets a fee for service based on the number of hours requested and positive evaluation and need for continuation. It will also charge fees for service at large community meetings and events, as hosting organizations have the ability to pay, and will seek local funding of ongoing costs until the program is subsidized primarily by fees for service.

XYZ plans the following mix of funding sources for years one through five:

Year One:	$432,500 Budget
45% local funding:	XYZ annual budget: $75,000
	Fees for service: $3,000
	Existing grant: $80,000
	Donations and discounts: $40,000

Year Two:	$175,000 Budget
100% local funding:	XYZ annual budget: $25,000
	Local grants: $100,000
	Fees for occasional services: $5,000
	Fees for regular service: $25,000
	Local underwriters (competition/awards): $20,000

Year Three:	$175,000 Budget
100% local funding:	XYZ annual budget: $30,000
	Local grants: $75,000
	Fees for occasional services: $10,000

	Fees for regular service: $35,000
	Local underwriters: $25,000

Year Four:	**$175,000 Budget**
100% local funding:	XYZ annual budget: $50,000
	Local grants: $35,000
	Fees for occasional services: $10,000
	Fees for regular service: $50,000
	Local underwriters: $30,000

Year Five:	**$175,000 Budget**
100% local funding	XYZ annual budget: $50,000
	Local grants: $0
	Fees for occasional service: $20,000
	Fees for regular service: $50,000
	Local underwriters/donations: $55,000

g. Project Evaluation

i. Performance Measures

XYZ will contract with ASU's School of Public Administration for outside evaluation of the one-year pilot for the Mobile Media Lab program. The local evaluator will help XYZ strategically plan activities that will achieve the program goals and objectives; provide XYZ with data that can be used to make adjustments in service delivery and improve the overall program; and design and conduct an outcome evaluation to determine whether the program is achieving its intended goals.

Specifically, ASU evaluators will gather data (qualitative and quantitative) to measure the following:

- Number of individuals served at each site
- Rate of repeat use by individuals
- Baseline and year-end reading levels of users, correlated with repeat users

- Qualitative data regarding increased self-esteem among regular users
- Survey questionnaires for adult users to ascertain important uses for technology among the population and to gauge differences in feelings of isolation before and after using technology
- Qualitative data regarding increased community interest in the digital divide and other issues surrounding information technology
- Qualitative data on reasons and number of other agencies requesting regular services from the MML
- Qualitative data from teacher interviews on effect of computer-based enrichment classes in the learning content areas
- Student data from the Software indicating levels of proficiency and understanding of the information presented (e.g., Web-page design, using video cameras, nonlinear editing-software use, etc.)

Formal midyear and year-end evaluations will be posted on the XYZ Web site and distributed to all program participants and funders. Both evaluations will contain suggestions for improvement of the program based on interviews and data compiled by the local evaluator.

ii. Feedback and Ongoing Assessment

The evaluator will meet in January, 2003, with students, directors/administrators, users, and teachers to gather their input on the MML program and its progress toward shared goals. He or she will meet again with program participants at the end of the program to share evaluation findings and seek informal validation of the findings. In addition, XYZ will host monthly discussion groups of program participants to generate informal and regular feedback on the program and to report progress toward suggested improvements.

Appendix D

Sample Foundation Grant Proposal

The following grant sample proposes developing a countywide pediatric-asthma network that will help educate health-care providers, parents, and children about asthma management, using National Institutes of Health (NIH) materials. It also would provide intensive case management for low-income children who have moderate to severe asthma. The goal would be to reduce morbidity and mortality associated with pediatric asthma.

1. Executive Summary

The County Pediatric Asthma Network (CPAN) is a consortium of individuals from area health-care institutions and related agencies who, since 1993, have collaborated to improve pediatric asthma management among children. With pilot funding from 1996 to 1998, CPAN provided education for more than 5,800 physicians, nurses, school personnel, parents, and others who care for children with asthma, and intensively case-managed fifty children (ages five to nineteen) from low-income families.

The pilot project resulted in statistically significant changes: CPAN findings for 1997 indicate measurable improvements in knowledge about asthma, changes in behavior, and clinical outcomes for children. School personnel, children, and physicians increased their knowledge about asthma significantly as indicated on pre-education and posteducation tests. Children in the program significantly improved their use of metered-dose inhalers and other treatments. Perhaps the most dramatic improvement came in the clinical area, where the number of hospitalizations in one year fell from twenty to eight among the thirty-four youth who completed a full year of intervention; the number of days hospitalized dropped from fifty-seven to eighteen; and the number of school days missed went from 718 to 612.

These results were the motivation behind a recent CPAN long-range strategic plan developed with the assistance of the Direction Center. The plan calls for formalizing and strengthening the collaborative partnership, increasing public and health-care provider awareness and knowledge about asthma and asthma management, strengthening and expanding services to reach more and younger children from low-income families, and increasing research activities and dissemination of findings.

CPAN requests the assistance of the community foundation in formalizing and expanding the collaborative partnership to ensure that more low-income families that have infants or children with asthma will benefit from CPAN services.

2. Purpose
A. Needs/Problem Statement

Asthma is the most prevalent chronic pediatric disease, affecting approximately 4.9 million children and adolescents in the United States. The prevalence of asthma in the pediatric age group is increasing more than in any other age group as evidenced by a 56-percent rise from 1982 to 1991. Over this same period, the prevalence of asthma in those under eighteen years of age rose from 4 percent to 6.3 percent (National Center for Health Statistics, 1982–91).

Asthma is the most frequent reason for hospitalization due to chronic disease in children and teens, with an estimated annual cost of $712 million for treating asthma in those under eighteen years of age. That figure increases to $1.3 billion when parents' missed work days and outpatient visits and medications are added. In addition, asthma is the leading cause of school absenteeism, with ten million school days lost annually (American Lung Association of Michigan, 1994).

Asthma more commonly affects minorities, and with greater mortality, too. African-Americans have a prevalence of asthma that is 22-percent greater than whites, while age-adjusted asthma mortality data show that death rates in African-Americans are three times greater than in whites. Asthma also more commonly afflicts those in urban settings and those from poor households (Centers for Disease Control, 1986–90).

Eighty-three percent of the county's half-million population live in urban settings. In 1989, the county had 8,599 children and adolescents with asthma. Of these children, we can expect 7,149 to be from an urban area, 1,092 to be of minority background, and 791 to be from low-income families (United States Census Bureau, 1990). About 2,700 of the nearly 8,600 children have moderate-to-severe asthma. At least 2,400 live in households where they breathe second-hand smoke. These children are all at great risk. The estimated annual pediatric asthma costs in the county alone exceed $2.5 million.

ABC Children's Hospital, the regional tertiary and primary-care pediatric hospital and one of four hospitals that admit children in City, admitted 404 children with the diagnosis of asthma in 1996. Their illness generated a total of 1,141 hospital days and $1,276,895 in hospital charges, or an average of $3,161 per child. Of the 404 admitted children, 50.7 percent received Medicaid insurance and 2.3 percent were private pay (ABC Children's Hospital data, 1996). Finally, of those admitted children for whom ethnic data were available, 29.6 percent were of minority ethnicity.

During its pilot, CPAN provided asthma-management education for more than 4,000 parents, teachers and school personnel, health-care providers, and children with asthma, which proved valuable, statistically successful, and cost efficient. Staff also case-managed fifty children ranging in age from five years to nineteen years with very successful results, particularly in the areas of reduced hospitalization, improved overall health as evidenced by a reduction in school-days missed, and improved asthma-management behaviors, particularly among the children, though also among some parents.

CPAN plans to continue its educational outreach and seeks funding to add fifty children per year to its case-management roster (100 children in 2003, 150 in 2004, and 200 in 2005). All qualifying children will be from low-income families (using WIC standards for poverty). Qualifying age range will be expanded to include children younger than age five and their families. More than 50 percent of program participants have been of minority ethnic background, predominately African-American; it is anticipated that this involvement with the ethnic community will continue at the same or greater level.

B. Goals and Objectives

CPAN has two overarching goals: 1) to educate those caring for children with asthma—the physicians, nurses, school personnel, parents, and the children themselves—using National Institutes of Health (NIH) materials; and 2) to intensively case-manage low-income children with moderate to severe asthma. Achieving these goals will reduce morbidity and mortality associated with pediatric asthma.

Achieving the first goal consumes approximately 25 percent of CPAN's resources; accomplishing the latter requires the remaining 75 percent. CPAN believes it can best accomplish its two primary goals by implementing its long-range strategic plan. The plan outlines several goals and specific objectives; however, only those goals for which funding is sought from the community foundation are described below:

Goal 1: Formalize and expand partnerships and collaborations with other agencies that interact with the same population. Establish adequate staffing and communication channels to ensure formal, long-term partnerships that are in the best interest of the children served.

Objectives
- Maintain and strengthen linkages between and among CPAN, the County Health Department, City Public Schools, area hospitals and clinics, neighborhood organizations, home health-care agencies, pharmaceutical companies, the American Lung Association of State, State University, health-maintenance organizations, private practices, visiting-nurse services, area pharmacies, and family members of children with asthma.
- Expand beyond these partners to other agencies and school districts. The City and City Public Schools, among others, have expressed a strong interest in using CPAN's resources, both to in-service their personnel and for the case management of their students.
- Create and increase executive director staff to 0.5 full-time employees (FTE), 0.5 FTE, and 1 FTE for 2003, 2004, and 2005, respectively. The executive director will be expected to oversee the entire operation, including deployment of resources (including the CPAN

Speakers' Bureau), maintaining the service and educational missions, seeking future sources of revenue, and contracting with institutions and third-party payors.

- Create and increase medical social-worker staff to 1 FTE, 1.5 FTE, and 2 FTEs for 2003, 2004, and 2005, respectively. The use of a medical social-work intern for the past six months has proved invaluable. A social-assessment tool is being developed by CPAN to identify those families at highest risk.

- Create and increase clerical/data support staff to 0.5 FTE, 0.5 FTE, and 1 FTE for 2003, 2004, and 2005, respectively. As the case-management and data collection—for research purposes—increases, so does the importance of these positions.

Goal 2: Reduce pediatric-asthma morbidity and mortality within a targeted urban, low-income population with moderate-to-severe asthma through case-managed intervention.

Objectives
- Increase the case-managed population to 100 children per year, 150 children per year, and 200 children per year for 2003, 2004, and 2005, respectively.

- Establish protocols for identifying qualifying infants and toddlers for the program and share protocols with area practitioners, social-service agencies, and others who can refer preschool-age children to program. By the end of year one at least twenty-five infants/toddlers will be enrolled in the program; by the end of year two, at least one-third of participants will be under age five.

- Increase nursing staff to 2 FTEs, 3 FTEs, and 4 FTEs for 2003, 2004, and 2005, respectively. (The current CPAN budget allows for 1 FTE through June 30, 2004.) A priority in this objective is a nurse educator with a specialty in infant/toddler asthma management.

- Achieve measurable outcomes within this targeted population: reduce school absences by 20 percent, reduce hospital admissions by 50 percent, reduce days hospitalized by 50 percent, and reduce emergency-department visits by 20 percent.

C. Timeline

All objectives are established for the course of the next three years (2003–2005); most timeframes for completion are included in the objectives. CPAN is currently seeking funding from a number of sources to establish itself as a well-known, successful provider of asthma management for children from low-income families. Funding for the next three years is necessary until CPAN develops the linkages necessary to obtain government or insurance funding.

D. Partners

Since its inception as a pilot project, CPAN has enjoyed great interinstitutional and interdisciplinary collaboration. Indeed, CPAN consists of individuals from all four (now three) acute-care hospitals in City as well as staff from the American Lung Association of State, the County Health Department, State University, Health Organization, private practices, and visiting-nurse services. Physicians, nurses, respiratory therapists, social workers, pharmacologists, managed-care providers, educators, and family members of children with asthma are included in CPAN's membership.

Among its strongest and most consistent collaborators have been: 1) the Local Children's Hospital and Health Organization, which has supplied CPAN with health-care professional expertise, direction, and clerical support; 2) The American Lung Association of State, which has supplied CPAN with expertise, clerical support, and physical space; 3) Hospital Health Services, which has supplied CPAN with administrative and accounting expertise and a home; and 4) The City Public Schools, which has partnered with CPAN to educate City Public School personnel—principals, classroom, and physical-education teachers, school nurses, and school secretaries—to learn the optimal asthma care for their students.

As CPAN seeks to expand its services, new potential partners have been identified. Among those that have expressed an interest in participation are the County Intermediate School District, the City A Public Schools, City B Public Schools, City C Public Schools, and City D Public Schools.

E. Similar Programs/Agencies

There are no programs or agencies similar to CPAN in County and only a handful of such programs in the nation. In fact, at a recent convention for health-care professionals who specialize in asthma management, the City program was highlighted for several of its features: its broad partnerships, which cross the entire spectrum of health-care providers in the community; its focus on research, education, treatment, and evaluation; and its statistically significant results achieved in a relatively brief time.

It is the vision of CPAN's Board to become the "Region's model organization for asthma care, offering education, professional expertise, and advocacy resources to control this serious illness. Through stronger collaboration with institutions of higher education and health care, CPAN will improve the lives of infants, children, and adolescents with asthma," and to "become a nationwide model making its experience in research, education, and treatment available for replication by any and all interested professionals and organizations" (Long-Range Strategic Plan).

F. Constituent Involvement

Collaborating partners' specific contributions are described above. Individually, school personnel, health-care professionals, and parents of children with asthma frequently share specific problems related to the management of asthma for review and assistance from CPAN staff; however, most overall planning for services is done by the CPAN Board of Directors. The board at this time is composed primarily of health-care providers and representatives from other partner organizations, such as schools. Another goal of the long-range strategic plan is to diversify and broaden board membership to reflect community constituencies and represent program participants.

G. Staff Qualifications

Current staff are licensed medical practitioners. CPAN seeks to hire an executive director with a background in social services and/or health care to establish cross-partner communication linkages and quality-assurance procedures, and to establish and strengthen new linkages with other agencies that work with the same population group. Further, this person must be knowledgeable about managed care and insurance providers as he or she will be required to negotiate with these providers and with Medicaid to approve CPAN for reimbursement.

The nurse educator to be hired under the grant proposal will have a specialty in infant and toddler asthma management and treatment and will report directly to the Respiratory Department Manager at ABC's Health Services, as well as to the CPAN Medical Director and the CPAN board. He or she must be a registered nurse (RN) or registered respiratory therapist (RRT), with a bachelor's degree in nursing or related field necessary and a master's preferred. Past experience in community health, case management, and patient advocacy are important criteria.

CPAN will make every effort to recruit and hire qualified minority candidates for these positions.

H. Long-Term Funding Strategies

Once CPAN has an executive director, the organization can begin the lengthy process of identifying insurance and managed-care agencies and developing and presenting contracts for care. Sharing CPAN's clinical and behavioral outcomes with these organizations will be critical; naturally, it will enhance CPAN's position to have more than one year's data, significant as the year's data are. The executive director will also be charged with identifying a contact within Medicaid and exploring the feasibility of a proposal to the government for Medicaid reimbursement.

While these processes are put in place to ensure future funding, CPAN must continue to seek corporate and individual support. The executive director is important to this process as well and will be asked to identify potential donors, share our clinical-outcomes data, and solicit interim and permanent funding to expand services.

CPAN is also seeking funding from national and local foundations and from Local Hospital Health's Community Benefit Fund.

3. Evaluation
A. Defining and Measuring Success

Previous studies of asthma have cited improvements in educational, behavioral, or clinical outcomes when using educational interventions. CPAN is the first such study in the nation to demonstrate all three among its participating children. The children, their parents, school personnel, and primary-care physicians were taught about the effects, triggers, medications, equipment care and techniques, and management plans of asthma. These outcomes are provided below. Those that are statistically significant are indicated in italics.

Education Outcomes

Subject	Pretest Scores	Posttest Scores	P
Children	73 percent	93 percent	0.040
Parents	78 percent	84 percent	0.328
School personnel	80 percent	91 percent	0.001
Physicians	79 percent	94 percent	0.001

Behavior Outcomes

Behavior	Prestudy	Poststudy	P
Inhaled steroid use	19	28	0.004
Inhaled nonsteroidal anti-inflammatory use	16	9	0.016
Long-acting beta2 use	2	8	0.031
Short-acting beta2 use reduction		10	0.002
Tobacco exposure	23 no change; 3 increased	8 reduced	0.227
MDI/Spacer technique		30 improved	0.001

Clinical Outcomes			
Criteria	Prestudy	Study period	P
Hospitalizations	20	8	0.008
Days hospitalized	57	18	0.008
ER visits	58	50	0.470
School-days missed	718	612	0.260

The difference CPAN makes in the quality and duration of these children's lives is the measure of the program's success. CPAN, therefore, will continue to collect data with the use of group-specific pre-education and posteducation tests, prestudy and poststudy behavioral criteria, and measurement of clinical outcomes.

B. Dissemination

Results of the 1998 study have been compiled for presentation at the annual Academy of Allergy, Asthma, and Immunology and American Thoracic Society meetings. In addition, CPAN is preparing the data for sharing with area health-care professionals and the community.

C. Constituent Involvement

Constituents participate as members of pretest and posttest and study groups. CPAN staff have learned a great deal from their constituents. Clients of the program have been candid with CPAN about how to work in their neighborhoods and how to work with diverse populations. As a result, CPAN has twice modified its enrollment form to be easier to complete and more sensitive to constituent issues and has shaped its methods of approaching and assessing families based on the advice of early program participants.

The most common request of CPAN from constituents is to expand the program to encompass younger children; in fact, many program participants have younger siblings with asthma. Clients also require that staff reorder their asthma lessons to deal with more immediate problems. In many cases, staff work with clients to establish priorities before beginning educational plans.

4. Budget Form and Narrative

A. Grant Budget Form

A. Organizational fiscal year: July 1 through June 30

B. Time period this budget covers: Jan. 1, 2003–Dec. 31, 2005

C. Expenses: include a description and the total amount for each of the budget categories, in this order:

	Amount Requested from the Local Foundation	Total Project Expenses (2003, 2004, and 2005)
Salaries	$169,293	$626,642
Payroll Taxes		
Fringe Benefits	$42,323	$156,660
Consultants and Professional Fees		$21,750
Insurance		
Travel	$4,836	$10,881
Equipment (Office)		$4,500
Supplies (Office)		$2,300
Printing and Copying		$15,000
Telephone and Fax		$1,500
Postage and Delivery		$1,750
Rent		$18,000
Utilities		
Maintenance		
Evaluation		
Marketing		$1,000
Other (specify)		
Reference materials for library		$1,000
Peak low meters for each enrolled child		$3,600
Spacer systems for each enrolled child		$2,700
Professional development	$1,500	$3,000
TOTAL EXPENSES	$217,952	$870,283

D. Revenue: include a description and the total amount for each of the following budget categories, in this order; please indicate which sources of revenue are committed and which are pending.

	Committed 2003–2005	Pending 2003–2005
1. Grants/Contracts/Contributions		
Local Government		
State Government		
Federal Government		
Foundations		
QRS Fdn.		$50,000
ABC Fdn.		$150,000
The City Foundation		$217,952
LMN	$24,451*	$90,000
Family Foundation	$20,000*	
Health Department	$75,000*	$100,000
Corporations		
Individuals		
2. Earned Income		
Events		
Publications and Products		
3. Membership Income		
4. In-Kind Support	$120,505	
5. Other (specify)		
TOTAL REVENUE	$239,956	$607,952

*Committed only for 2003

B. Explanation

CPAN's request of the Community Foundation is for three years' funding for the following:

	2003	2004	2005
Salaries			
Executive director @ $50,000/year	$25,000	$20,000	$15,000
Nurse educator with early-pediatric emphasis	$35,360	$36,420	$37,513
Benefits/taxes (25 percent of wages)	$15,090	$14,105	$13,128
Travel			
Local mileage for nurse educator	$1,612	$1,612	$1,612
Professional Development			
Attendance at professional seminars and meetings for nurse educator and/or executive director as necessary	$500	$500	$500
TOTAL REQUEST	$77,562	$72,637	$67,753

Staffing

Adequate staffing is critical to achieving CPAN's objectives and goals for improving the health and outcomes of low-income children with asthma.

Cost for full staffing is calculated on market-rate salaries and includes payroll taxes. The Community Foundation is asked in this request for decreasing amounts over the next three years to support a 0.5-FTE executive director: $25,000 in 2003, $20,000 in 2004, and $15,000 in 2005. The person hired in this position will be responsible, with assistance from the board of directors, for establishing contracts with Medicaid and other insurance payors and for seeking alternate sources of funding until the position is self-sustaining. Base salary for this position is $50,000/year.

Also included in the grant request is three-years' salary for a nurse/asthma educator with a specialty in early pediatrics (infants and toddlers). CPAN plans to add this position first and to increase nursing staff by another FTE nurse/educator in 2004 and two nurse/educators in 2005 (total four new positions by the end of the grant period). Base salary for each FTE is $17 per hour or approximately $35,500 per year. Currently, CPAN's only nurse educator is supported by a grant from the Local Foundation, for which CPAN intends to apply annually.

Staffing positions not requested of the grant include a clerical/data-management coordinator @ $25,709/year (beginning half-time and increasing to full-time by 2005), and a medical social worker at $16 per hour or approximately $33,200 annually (beginning with one FTE and increasing to two FTE by 2005). A medical director's services are donated by Local Children's Hospital at a value of $75 per hour for 200 hours per year.

All positions assume a 3-percent cost-of-living increase annually. Fringe benefits include FICA, health insurance, disability, workers' compensation, etc., and are calculated at 25 percent of salaries.

Professional Fees

Professional fees are donated by the partners and include meeting expenses for the advisory council ($1,000 per year), administrative oversight provided by hospital's Health Services ($35 per hour for 100 hours in 2003, 150 hours in 2004, and 200 hours in 2005), and accounting services at $1,000 per year for three years.

Travel

Local travel is mandatory for the case managers/nurse educators. Mileage for the funded position of early-pediatric nurse educator is requested of the grant at $0.31/mile, 100 miles per week × 52 weeks. Mileage not included in the grant is calculated by the same formula and applicable to the current nurse educator and additional nurse educators as they are hired.

Office Supplies and Equipment

Office equipment includes computer hardware and software for the executive director and is not requested of the grant; supplies also are not requested.

Office Services

Copying and duplication is important to ensure seamless communications and to share information with parents and others charged with the care of children with asthma. This service is not charged to the grant request. Telephone and fax charges are expected to increase with the addition of another line at participants' request. This increase is not reflected in the grant request. Postage costs are estimated based on past experience.

Rent

Space for staff and program equipment is donated by the partners and is calculated at a rate of $12 per square foot for 400 square feet in 2003, 500 square feet in 2004, and 600 square feet in 2005. Utilities and maintenance are included in the cost per square foot.

Evaluation

Evaluation is ongoing and integral to the program. It is not calculated separately.

Marketing

CPAN plans a quarterly newsletter for participants and will seek the estimated $1,000-per-year cost for producing the newsletter from other grant sources.

Reference Library

CPAN hopes in year three to establish a small reference library for staff, other health-care professionals, and program participants at an estimated one-time cost of $1,000.

Health-Care Supplies

CPAN provides each child with a new peak flow meter (approximately $20 each with 20 percent allocated for loss) and a spacer system (approximately $15 each with 20 percent allocated for loss) upon enrollment. CPAN is seeking assistance with these costs or donated supplies from pharmaceutical companies and manufacturers.

Professional Development

It is important to remain abreast of changes in asthma treatment methods, educational information, and asthma management techniques, and to attend meetings of professional affiliations. Therefore, CPAN requests of the grant half of the $3,000 allocated for professional development over three years, to ensure that the executive director and early-pediatric nurse/ educator attend appropriate educational or networking conferences and seminars.

C. Other Requests

CPAN completed its long-range strategic plan in July, 2002, and immediately contracted with a local fundraising expert to assist it in establishing funding for formalizing the partnerships and expanding outreach and participation opportunities to children under five. Since then, CPAN has submitted requests on the invitation of John Doe to the ABC and XYZ foundations. Those requests are expected to be decided by the end of 2002. Plans also call for an application to the LMN Foundation and, pending responses from larger foundations, requests of several smaller foundations.

In addition, CPAN successfully applied for a hospital Health Community Benefits grant, which will provide $75,000 from October 15, 2002 to October 14, 2003 and may be renewable each year thereafter. It has also recently received a one-year $20,000 grant from the private Foundation at hospital's Health Services and a $48,903 grant from the LMN Foundation, which covers half of this year's and half of 2003's salary for the current nurse educator. CPAN intends to continue to apply to LMN for funding as needed when the current grant expires in July, 2002. An application for special-program assistance to purchase new bedding for children in the program was made to one of the trustees of the private Foundation.

D. Priority Items

If the entire amount cannot be granted, CPAN requests that the Community Foundation consider one of two alternatives: First, that it grant first-year funding and perhaps a portion of the second-year funding request to enable CPAN to begin formalizing its partnerships and expanding services.

Alternately, CPAN most urgently needs an executive director who can oversee daily management, communications, fundraising, marketing/public relations, and data-gathering activities and ensure quality control across the partnering organizations.

5. Organization Information

A. History

CPAN was founded in 1993 as a consortium of individuals from area health-care institutions and related agencies who sought to collaborate to improve pediatric asthma management. Pilot funding came from the Community Foundation, Hospital Foundation, Corporate Foundation, Private Foundation, ABC Hospital, and XYZ Memorial Medical Center.

In addition to providing successful public education about asthma management to more than 5,800 parents, children with asthma, school personnel, and health-care practitioners and providing asthma case management for as many as ninety-three children from low-income families in 2002, CPAN began community and professional awareness programs, data analysis and outcomes, a professional certification project, and patient educational resources.

Results from its 2002 program indicate significant success in most objectives and demonstrated the need to formalize the partnership so that CPAN can expand its services.

B. Mission and Goals

The mission of ABC County Pediatric Asthma Network is "to improve the lives of all infants, children, and adolescents with asthma by providing educational and professional expertise."

Goals in support of this mission were developed during long-range strategic planning and include:

- Stabilizing and strengthening the organization
- Increasing public awareness of CPAN and its programs
- Strengthening and expanding services
- Expanding and strengthening working relationships with agencies that serve urban, ethnic-minority children
- Stabilizing and broadening funding
- Increasing research activities and dissemination

C. Current Programs, Activities, and Accomplishments

Current programs, activities, and accomplishments are described in the proposal narrative. Selected additional planned activities include:

- Diversifying community representation on the CPAN Board of Directors and in its membership
- Establishing an advisory panel or ad-hoc focus groups composed of customers, providers, and community representatives
- Creating an organizational marketing plan
- Developing and providing certification standard for educators and health-care professionals
- Increasing access to insurance coverage and inclusion in managed care
- Developing and implementing a CPAN patient/practitioner-satisfaction evaluation program
- Disseminating the results of outcome-management programs through community and national professional media

D. Organizational Chart

The current partnership structure does not lend itself to the traditional organizational chart. Such a chart has not been developed and awaits adequate staffing.

Attachments:

Previous grants made to CPAN were handled by Hospital's Health Services, which acted as fiduciary agent. CPAN, therefore, cannot submit an audited financial report with this request. If the Community Foundation requests, it will supply an audited financial statement from the agent.

The following sample was submitted to the Kresge Foundation for its capital challenge program. Most foundations periodically examine and refine their program areas. The Kresge Foundation is in the process of altering the challenge grant program by the end of 2007. Be sure to check the Web site for current guidelines and priorities. Speak directly with a program officer prior to submitting your proposal.

3. NARRATIVE

Organizational Information

Appendix E
Sample Capital Grant Proposal

History

Great Rain Youth Centers, Inc., is a nonprofit organization incorporated in 1939 and founded by then police chief, Frank Sullivan. At the time of its incorporation, Youth Centers programs operated from a 40-acre Camp Sullivan and an inner-city youth center on Finney Street. It is believed to be the first or second program in the nation to combine personal-growth activities for at-risk inner-city youth with police-officer supervision, coaching, mentoring, and friendship. A 1942 issue of "The Saturday Evening Post" chronicled Youth Centers' early success in reducing the incidence of crime and delinquency among Great Rain's young people.

In 1953, Youth Centers expanded its services when it built the Westside Center. In 1958 it closed the Finney Street location and opened in its stead the Foster Center at 139 Crofton on the city's southeast side. Foster Center is still operating, but the Westside Center was demolished in 1989, and Youth Centers' programming in that area of the city moved to Southwest Elementary School.

Throughout the past 60 years, Youth Centers has provided a safe place for area youth to interact with, learn from, and become friends with police officers, and to find positive outlets for their energy and interests.

Since 1995 Youth Centers has had a new, enthusiastic and dedicated director who has breathed new life into the organization, its mission and its program. Under his leadership, Camp Sullivan now has a year-round camp director and camping program and greatly improved grounds and facilities. Both Foster Center and the Southwest School program have new programming, and, for the first time, an emphasis on programming for girls. The new Great Rain Police Chief strongly endorses the program and takes every opportunity to express his support, including giving a brief speech at half time of a professional basketball game at the City Arena last fall and participating as honorary co-chair (with former President of the United States), in the capital campaign to rebuild a Westside Center and renovate Foster Center.

Services

In 1997, Foster Center averaged between 600 and 1500 monthly contacts with children between the ages of seven and 17. During the same period, the Westside center at Southwest School logged nearly 1800 contacts per month. To be admitted to the facilities, youth must be members. A recent log of memberships indicated 600 current and active members. More than half of the members are teenagers, the other portion are pre-teens.

In addition to its daily recreational/educational programming at its centers, Youth Centers has, since 1991, provided police-officer and volunteer coaches for three Great Rain Rocket football teams, and in 1996 established three additional Youth Centers teams on the city's west side.

Camp Sullivan has an estimated 4,500 young people from low-income families each summer for the past nearly 60 years. Camp is a five-day residential program that operates from early June through August each summer and is now provided off-season leasing by community organizations and businesses. Some of the campaign cabinet members are former Camp Sullivan or Youth Center "alumni," who are eager to ensure that today's youth are afforded the same life-changing experiences they experienced as children.

Now in its 60th year, Youth Centers is poised on the edge of an exciting future, which includes recent improvements to Camp Sullivan and its programs, hiring of a year-round camp director and the creation of a year-round camping program, and some improvements to Foster Center and its programs. Programming for girls has grown by 500 percent in the past two years. Girls may now select from six activities (rather than the one offered previously) developed especially for them.

In addition, in the past year, Youth Centers has been approached by six other youth-service organizations requesting our collaboration on their projects. Currently, Youth Centers works with Native American Prevention Services in designing and offering a camping and youth leadership program for Native American teens, with Boy Scouts of America, and the Great Rain Recreation Department. The organization is considering offers to work as well with Latin American Services and United Methodist Community House.

As an organization, Youth Centers faces an issue common to other nonprofit organizations in that it must substantiate the prevention outcome of its programs. All staff and volunteers are being trained by outside professionals in outcome measurement, and staff are currently developing and implementing outcome measures for programs. The police officers on staff are eagerly learning education and prevention approaches as an alternative to what one officer calls, "the cuff and stuff" mentality many officers have. The community has also embraced the prevention approach as individuals have become more aware of the expense and loss associated with incarceration and treatment.

Another important issue facing Youth Centers is that of multiple service providers, particularly among those providing residential or day camp for special populations and/or low-income children. As a result, Youth Centers has established linkages and is sharing calendars and programs with several other camping programs and with the Great Rain Parks and Recreation Department.

As a member of the community, Youth Centers is an integral partner in combating a growing community crisis: currently one out of four juvenile arrests is female. These crimes are becoming more violent as well, but Youth Centers and its officer staff are developing programs intended to prevent delinquency among girls in the inner city.

The next stride toward a stronger future for at-risk youth in Great Rain, is improvement to the inner-city youth centers and expansion of programs for youth on the city's southeast and west sides.

Commitment to Diversity

The Board of Directors of Youth Centers is 22 percent minority; 22 percent female. The eight administrative and police officer staff are 38 percent minority; 38 percent female. Foster Center attracts neighboring youth most of whom are African American. The west side program at Southwest School draws participants from its neighborhood, which is 50 percent white, 30 percent Hispanic, 1 percent Native American, and 19 percent African American. In 1998, Camp Sullivan (which is an existing program of Youth Centers, though not the subject of this proposal), provided a 5-day camping experience for 329 youth as follows: 75 percent white; 25 percent minority.

Affiliations and Partnerships

Youth Centers operates as a partner with the Great Rain Police Department, and is the Department's most long-standing effort to develop relationships with youth and community members. Youth Centers will provide space for special programs of the schools, neighborhood organizations, and others near the new facilities, and will continue its strong relationships with area schools. The County Sheriff has recently offered to send two officers twice weekly to provide tutoring to youth involved in the Youth Centers' after-school academic program.

In addition to the collaborations and potential collaborations named above, Youth Centers has teamed with Great Rain State College (GRSC) to provide a youth soccer camp at which students and staff from GRSC provide coaching and Youth Centers program parameters and facility.

Maintenance Policy

Both current physical sites (Foster Center and Camp Sullivan) have maintenance budgets and depreciation schedules for buildings and equipment, which will be adjusted to accommodate the expansions when completed. A preventive maintenance plan is in place for the two vehicles owned by Youth Centers.

The maintenance and replacement budget has been tripled in the last three years, but still would not be considered "over and above" normal replacement expenses. It is Youth Centers' practice to use half of its depreciation and half of any surplus at year's end for capital purchase and replacement. Currently, Youth Centers depreciates $24,000 annually, although, other than the new bathhouse at Camp Sullivan, its buildings are nearly fully depreciated. A facility audit has not been performed.

Board of Directors

Member	Occupation	Company
A	Officer	ABC Bank
B	Director	Youth Centers
C, Treasurer	Retired	Accountant
Chief D	Police Chief	GRPD
E	Exec. V.P.	Manufacturing

Member	Occupation	Company
F, President	Probate Attorney	Law Firm
G	Reg. Director	Realty Trust

H	Owner	Vending
I	Owner	Steel Mill
J, Secretary	Owner	Sporting Goods
K	Crime Prevention Org.	Neighborhood Assoc.
L	Retired	
M	H.R. Manager	Plastics Co.
N	Retired officer	GRPD
O	Attorney	Law Firm
P	Radio host	WWWW
Q	Commissioner	City of Great Rain
R, Vice President	Owner	Wood Products
S	Director of Admissions	Business College
T	Management	Merchants Service Bur.
U	CPA	Self-employed

Project information

Project Description

Foster Center is 40 years old and in need of renovation and a 2800 square-foot expansion. The Center also needs to be equipped to provide new programs that meet the needs of today's youth—with technology access, an emphasis on educational goals and attainment, sports and recreation facilities and teams for at-risk girls, a fitness room, and opportunities for youth to develop leadership skills.

Renovation and expansion of Foster Center will enable the following new programs and offerings:

- A "learning center" where tutors—volunteers from the community and officers sent by the County Sheriff Department—can be matched to children in need of additional educational help. Boys and girls at the Foster Center need a quiet place to do their homework after school. The current facility has been overtaken by recreational needs and there are few "quiet areas" where students can concentrate on schoolwork. Youth Centers currently has a standing offer from the public school system that is willing to match trained tutors with at-risk children if Youth Centers can allocate space. Additionally the Great Rain Public School Special Education Program is interested in leasing this classroom during school hours when children are not using the center.

- Locker storage space and expanded bathroom and shower facilities for boys and girls. Currently there are no shower facilities for girls at the Foster Center, and neither boys nor girls have locker facilities for storing personal items. On any given night, one can walk into the Foster Center and find walls lined with the shoes and coats of dozens of youth that have no space to store these items.

- A computer lab where youth could become more familiar with emerging technologies (such as the Internet). Currently the inner city public schools in Youth Centers' areas of service are without much computer access and none of the schools have Internet access available to the children. The creation of a computer lab would take the first step in addressing this need.

- A youth meeting room where children could meet with police officers, counselors, parents and adult mentors to discuss school performance, family or personal and/or behavioral problems. The newly formed Youth Advisory Board would use the room for their meetings with a police officer to assist in planning activities for the center. The room would also serve neighborhood groups who need space for meetings and gatherings.

- Exercise/workout facilities to accommodate increasing demand. Cost for facilities such as these is prohibitive for inner city youth and located outside acceptable walking distance.

- A catering kitchen to serve staff and groups who use the center for banquets and other events that involve food.

Furniture, fixtures, computer, and sports equipment would be needed to accompany those changes. In order to operate throughout the summer months and to make both floors accessible by all children, the Foster Center would also need air conditioning installation and an elevator.

The original Westside Center was torn down in 1989 due to age and deterioration of the building. Westside programming, which is currently housed in the Southwest Elementary School, has outgrown the capacity of the school building. The Southwest School, while serving honorably as a temporary facility, has several problems. The Southwest location lends to the perception that Westside programming is restricted to elementary aged youth in Southwest School immediate area. Structurally, the school building is not designed for supervision of children engaged in a variety of educational and recreational activities. The gymnasium is extremely small and inadequate for older participants. As a result, youth between the ages of thirteen and seventeen rarely use the facility. This is the same demographic group that is likely to commit juvenile crime and is in need of safe alternative activities.

The planned Westside Center would offer many of the same amenities to the west-side community that the Foster Center offers to its neighboring community—high quality recreational and educational facilities in a safe, supervised environment. The new center is being built on property already owned by Youth Centers and will house the organization's administrative offices when completed. In addition to the same program offerings planned for Foster Center, the Westside Center will offer indoor and outdoor basketball courts. The indoor gymnasium will accommodate 150 seats for arts programs and large community meetings.

Youth Centers also seeks as a part of the capital campaign, two years' operational support for expanded programming. In both neighborhoods, Saturday and summer programs for at-risk youth are limited. Youth Centers would use most of the operational support to increase staffing and pay overhead expenses for these expanded hours at both centers.

The Youth Centers Board of Directors established a five-year strategic master plan in late 1997, which calls for the following outcomes, most of which are contingent on adequate facilities:

1. Increase overall program quality through ongoing training for staff, increasing staff numbers, and developing outcome-based measures for program quality.
2. Increase prevention component of programming.

3. Locate and focus programs and service locations to match juvenile criminal activity according to local law enforcement data.

4. Increase effectiveness in building character in youth and reducing juvenile criminal activity by providing consistent year-round programs and tracking individual youth through our programs. (Currently, Southwest School and Foster Center are closed in summer; Camp Sullivan will begin operating year-round for the first time this year).

5. Serve more youth (currently approximately 2000 contacts per month between both centers)

6. Serve a full range of ages from 7 to 17, focusing particularly on 13 to 17. (Currently, the Southwest School site serves very few adolescents and teens).

7. Increase services to girls to equal those available to boys. (Currently, we have one woman officer assigned to the facilities, but no locker/shower facilities for girls' programs).

8. Increase use of law-enforcement staff in full-time assigned positions and in part-time, volunteer and intern capacities. (The new Chief of Police has encouraged his police officers to become involved by offering on-duty time weekly for them to volunteer at Youth Centers).

9. Develop a youth-advisory board, youth newsletter, and "junior staff" program to provide more opportunities for youth voices in programming and operations.

10. Involve parents and families in the programming as volunteers and/or advisors. (The new study centers and computer labs will assist in this effort.)

11. Increase collaboration with other service providers, including schools to provide a wrap-around approach to the youth in our neighborhood locations. (New or expanded facilities should include other service and linkages to other resources).

Status of Architectural Plans

Plans for construction and renovation of both buildings are in the construction document phase. Foster Center plans are approximately 80 percent complete and are expected to be finalized by April 21, 1999. Plans for the Westside Center are approximately 20 percent complete and are expected to be finalized by the end of May, 1999.

Basis for Cost Estimates

Cost estimates are based on market conditions, R.S. Means Cost Data 1999, and verification by general contractors.

Regulatory Approvals

Local government requires only two approvals: site plan and zoning and approval by the inspections department. Both will be scheduled when construction documents are complete.

Effect of Completed Project on Overall Budget

Youth Centers' operational budget is broken into four cost centers. Two of the cost centers: administration and Camp Sullivan, (which comprise 82 percent of the annual budget) will be nominally affected by the campaign. Youth Centers' strategic plan calls for a part-time fund development officer to be hired after the campaign and the building plan calls for increased office space to accommodate additional staff.

The two youth centers constitute the other two cost centers. The current operational budget for Foster Center (the larger of the two programs) is $37,205. All operational expenses for the centers, including program and maintenance, are expected to increase approximately 185 percent. The cost projection of $68,500 per center is based on several factors, including:

- Staff is projected to increase to include four more part-time staff at 15 hours per week at a cost of $11,500 per year per center.
- Use of the centers six days a week, rather than five, year-round rather than just school-year months, increases center use by 150 percent.

Costs for two years' operations for both centers is included in the capital campaign budget.

Initial increases will be handled for approximately four years with the additional funds from the capital campaign and funds recently confirmed from a one-year Local Law Enforcement Block grant (LLEBG), which will pay for all four part-time staff and $10,000 for administrative and program costs. As community awareness raises over the next year through the capital campaign information, donor opportunities, and several planned 60th anniversary celebrations, we believe Youth Centers will benefit with a comparable increase in both the number and amount of annual donor giving. These increases will be used to sustain the operational budget for the centers within two to four years after completion of the buildings.

Drawings
See Attached
Fund Raising Information

Previous Fundraising
In 2005, Youth Centers received $225,299 in contributions; in 2006, it received $228,412. Contributions from semi-annual appeals comprise approximately $40,000 per year or 16 percent of the annual budget. Grants, an annual radiothon sponsored by the Variety Club, and other special events generated nearly 10 percent of the 2005 annual budget and 28 percent of the 2006 budget. Special events in the coming year are expected to generate approximately $80,000 as Youth Centers celebrates its 60th Anniversary.

Youth Centers has not attempted an endowment effort or capital campaign in the last four decades. However, it has completed two significant capital projects in the last three years: In 2006, $100,000 from the Variety Club radiothon and grants from local foundations allowed construction of a new bath house at Camp Sullivan; in 2007, it received $30,000 from Toys for Tots for construction of an adventure ropes course at Camp.

Youth Centers' annual appeal generates approximately $15,000 each year. Since the new director began his work at Youth Centers revenue has increased more than 160 percent: from $189,396 in 2005 to $283,052 in 2006, and to $306,428 in 2007.

Capital Campaign Goals

Youth Centers' campaign fundraising consultant developed the following budget for the capital campaign:

Private Contributions	$800,000
Corporate Contributions	753,000
Foundation Contributions	1,000,000
City/State	600,000
In Kind	210,000
TOTAL:	$3,363,000

Youth Centers has approximately 1,000 annual donors, and expects that the capital campaign will assist in expanding that base of reliable funders. To date, it has 19 gifts totaling $232,310 from donors who have not given previously or in the last ten years. Staff have been gratified to find that previous donors, after a tour and an explanation of what Youth Centers intends to implement in the coming year, appear genuinely interested in becoming involved with the organization again.

In the next several months, more than 40 volunteers are approaching 250 corporations and small businesses, more than half of which are new contacts, on behalf of the capital project and Youth Centers. We expect at least 50 percent of these businesses to respond favorably to a request for assistance and that these businesses, combined, will generate approximately $100,000 in gifts in the coming months.

Youth Centers has several strategies planned for reaching the public. Three 60th reunion or anniversary events are planned and 500 individuals are invited to attend one or more of the events. A video and historical exhibit of Youth Centers' first 60 years is on display at the City Museum Center and provides take-away materials regarding the organization and the capital campaign.

Rather than "selling a brick" as many organizations have done successfully, Youth Centers is generating "police badges" that, for a $25 donation, will bear the name of the donor and/or donor family and an I.D. number and will be mounted at the Westside or Foster Center as the donor chooses. Youth Centers projects that it will "sell" 1,000 badges, and that approximately 60 to 75 percent of those donating for a badge will be new donors to the organization. Because they will have a personal interest in the buildings and their programs, and their names will be added to the donor mailing list, many, staff believes, are likely to become regular donors.

Five Largest Gifts

To date, the five largest gifts include individual, foundation, corporate, and government donors, as follows:

State Senator and Mrs. Senator	$250,000
Corporate Foundation	$250,000
City of Great Rain	$200,000
Clothing Manufacturer	$150,000
Private Donor	$102,900

Expected Progress - Short Term

The capital campaign has generated $1.56 million in its first six months, to the date of this submission. The public kick off event was held in early March, 1999. A proposal for $105,000 is pending decision at the ABC Foundation and is likely to be determined—and hopefully awarded at least in part—in the next four to six months. Another proposal has been invited from the DEF Family Foundation. This organization was a donor for many years until approximately ten years ago, and younger family members appeared interested in renewing their involvement. The request for $150,000 is expected to result in a grant of at least $100,000 toward the capital campaign. Youth Centers has submitted a proposal to the State at the request of Board member and State Senator, requesting $500,000. The likelihood of the request being successful is difficult to determine at this time.

Forty volunteers have agreed to approach approximately 250 area businesses, approximately half of which have previously supported Youth Centers at some level. This effort is expected to generate approximately $100,000 in donations in the next few months. If all goes as expected, the remaining balance of the campaign by September, 1999 will be $1,053,000.

Youth Centers currently has an active grant with The Great Rain Foundation, which supplements the salary of a full-time, year-round camp director until revenues from rentals of the camp support his entire salary. When the grant closes (December, 2007), Youth Centers will be eligible—and has been encouraged—to apply to the Foundation for capital funds.

Constituencies Likely to Respond

A challenge grant from the Kresge Foundation would be extremely helpful in leveraging new donors from among the public and businesses that have not previously supported the organization. The Kresge Challenge would be used to leverage giving in the following areas:

Donor Constituency/Event	Anticipated Match
Parties hosted by cabinet members	$5,000
Program Alumni (requested at reunion events and through mailing)	$15,000
Second gifts from lead donors per their request	$175,000
Social Service Organizations (Kiwanis, Optimist, Black Social Workers Association, neighborhood organizations particularly in Youth Centers service areas)	$50,000
African American churches and congregations	$10,000
Smaller Foundations	$25,000
Businesses	$20,000
TOTAL:	$300,000

Campaign Committee

The 76-member campaign cabinet is 21.05 percent female; 18.42 percent minority, and is composed of friends of the organization and community leaders as follows: *(names withheld from sample)*

Effects of the Campaign

One of the goals of the capital campaign is to raise community awareness of Youth Centers and its programs, in the belief that this will increase the level of giving and provide a stable base of donors. The three most important effects of the fundraising effort are:

- To significantly raise constituency and financial involvement in the local youth centers. An intentional "push" in the final campaign targets neighborhoods near the centers and alumni of the centers or camp in the hope that Youth Centers will attain critical "grass roots" support for its programs.

- To build and strengthen relationships with current board members and alumni (or families of alumni) of the 60-year-old board, who represent a wealth of financial and personal support for Youth Centers.
- To establish Youth Centers as a vital and expanding youth-service entity in its community. Great Rain Youth Centers has not run a significant capital campaign in more than four decades. The success of this campaign and the accompanying publicity will demonstrate to the funding community and the larger community the credibility and value of Youth Centers. Our ability to initiate and sustain this major increase in programming and fundraising should yield comparable increases in future annual support.

Portion of Larger Campaign
The project is not a part of a larger campaign.

Naming Opportunities
N.A.
4.   ATTACHMENTS

Most Recent Audit
Attached

Long-Term Financing
Youth Centers will not require long-term financing.

Accreditation
Only Camp Sullivan, which is not a project for which capital funding is requested, has an opportunity for accreditation. As a part of its five-year strategic plan, Youth Centers will seek accreditation by 2001 from the American Camping Association. The Director has managed other camps so accredited and is familiar with the procedure and requirements to attain this accreditation.

IRS Ruling
Attached

Index

The EVERYTHING Series!

BUSINESS & PERSONAL FINANCE

Everything® Accounting Book
Everything® Budgeting Book, 2nd Ed.
Everything® Business Planning Book
Everything® Coaching and Mentoring Book, 2nd Ed.
Everything® Fundraising Book
Everything® Get Out of Debt Book
Everything® Grant Writing Book, 2nd Ed.
Everything® Guide to Buying Foreclosures
Everything® Guide to Fundraising, $15.95
Everything® Guide to Mortgages
Everything® Guide to Personal Finance for Single Mothers
Everything® Home-Based Business Book, 2nd Ed.
Everything® Homebuying Book, 3rd Ed., $15.95
Everything® Homeselling Book, 2nd Ed.
Everything® Human Resource Management Book
Everything® Improve Your Credit Book
Everything® Investing Book, 2nd Ed.
Everything® Landlording Book
Everything® Leadership Book, 2nd Ed.
Everything® Managing People Book, 2nd Ed.
Everything® Negotiating Book
Everything® Online Auctions Book
Everything® Online Business Book
Everything® Personal Finance Book
Everything® Personal Finance in Your 20s & 30s Book, 2nd Ed.
Everything® Personal Finance in Your 40s & 50s Book, $15.95
Everything® Project Management Book, 2nd Ed.
Everything® Real Estate Investing Book
Everything® Retirement Planning Book
Everything® Robert's Rules Book, $7.95
Everything® Selling Book
Everything® Start Your Own Business Book, 2nd Ed.
Everything® Wills & Estate Planning Book

COOKING

Everything® Barbecue Cookbook
Everything® Bartender's Book, 2nd Ed., $9.95
Everything® Calorie Counting Cookbook
Everything® Cheese Book
Everything® Chinese Cookbook
Everything® Classic Recipes Book
Everything® Cocktail Parties & Drinks Book
Everything® College Cookbook
Everything® Cooking for Baby and Toddler Book
Everything® Diabetes Cookbook
Everything® Easy Gourmet Cookbook
Everything® Fondue Cookbook
Everything® Food Allergy Cookbook, $15.95
Everything® Fondue Party Book
Everything® Gluten-Free Cookbook
Everything® Glycemic Index Cookbook
Everything® Grilling Cookbook
Everything® Healthy Cooking for Parties Book, $15.95
Everything® Holiday Cookbook
Everything® Indian Cookbook
Everything® Lactose-Free Cookbook
Everything® Low-Cholesterol Cookbook

Everything® Low-Fat High-Flavor Cookbook, 2nd Ed., $15.95
Everything® Low-Salt Cookbook
Everything® Meals for a Month Cookbook
Everything® Meals on a Budget Cookbook
Everything® Mediterranean Cookbook
Everything® Mexican Cookbook
Everything® No Trans Fat Cookbook
Everything® One-Pot Cookbook, 2nd Ed., $15.95
Everything® Organic Cooking for Baby & Toddler Book, $15.95
Everything® Pizza Cookbook
Everything® Quick Meals Cookbook, 2nd Ed., $15.95
Everything® Slow Cooker Cookbook
Everything® Slow Cooking for a Crowd Cookbook
Everything® Soup Cookbook
Everything® Stir-Fry Cookbook
Everything® Sugar-Free Cookbook
Everything® Tapas and Small Plates Cookbook
Everything® Tex-Mex Cookbook
Everything® Thai Cookbook
Everything® Vegetarian Cookbook
Everything® Whole-Grain, High-Fiber Cookbook
Everything® Wild Game Cookbook
Everything® Wine Book, 2nd Ed.

GAMES

Everything® 15-Minute Sudoku Book, $9.95
Everything® 30-Minute Sudoku Book, $9.95
Everything® Bible Crosswords Book, $9.95
Everything® Blackjack Strategy Book
Everything® Brain Strain Book, $9.95
Everything® Bridge Book
Everything® Card Games Book
Everything® Card Tricks Book, $9.95
Everything® Casino Gambling Book, 2nd Ed.
Everything® Chess Basics Book
Everything® Christmas Crosswords Book, $9.95
Everything® Craps Strategy Book
Everything® Crossword and Puzzle Book
Everything® Crosswords and Puzzles for Quote Lovers Book, $9.95
Everything® Crossword Challenge Book
Everything® Crosswords for the Beach Book, $9.95
Everything® Cryptic Crosswords Book, $9.95
Everything® Cryptograms Book, $9.95
Everything® Easy Crosswords Book
Everything® Easy Kakuro Book, $9.95
Everything® Easy Large-Print Crosswords Book
Everything® Games Book, 2nd Ed.
Everything® Giant Book of Crosswords
Everything® Giant Sudoku Book, $9.95
Everything® Giant Word Search Book
Everything® Kakuro Challenge Book, $9.95
Everything® Large-Print Crossword Challenge Book
Everything® Large-Print Crosswords Book
Everything® Large-Print Travel Crosswords Book
Everything® Lateral Thinking Puzzles Book, $9.95
Everything® Literary Crosswords Book, $9.95
Everything® Mazes Book
Everything® Memory Booster Puzzles Book, $9.95

Everything® Movie Crosswords Book, $9.95
Everything® Music Crosswords Book, $9.95
Everything® Online Poker Book
Everything® Pencil Puzzles Book, $9.95
Everything® Poker Strategy Book
Everything® Pool & Billiards Book
Everything® Puzzles for Commuters Book, $9.95
Everything® Puzzles for Dog Lovers Book, $9.95
Everything® Sports Crosswords Book, $9.95
Everything® Test Your IQ Book, $9.95
Everything® Texas Hold 'Em Book, $9.95
Everything® Travel Crosswords Book, $9.95
Everything® Travel Mazes Book, $9.95
Everything® Travel Word Search Book, $9.95
Everything® TV Crosswords Book, $9.95
Everything® Word Games Challenge Book
Everything® Word Scramble Book
Everything® Word Search Book

HEALTH

Everything® Alzheimer's Book
Everything® Diabetes Book
Everything® First Aid Book, $9.95
Everything® Green Living Book
Everything® Health Guide to Addiction and Recovery
Everything® Health Guide to Adult Bipolar Disorder
Everything® Health Guide to Arthritis
Everything® Health Guide to Controlling Anxiety
Everything® Health Guide to Depression
Everything® Health Guide to Diabetes, 2nd Ed.
Everything® Health Guide to Fibromyalgia
Everything® Health Guide to Menopause, 2nd Ed.
Everything® Health Guide to Migraines
Everything® Health Guide to Multiple Sclerosis
Everything® Health Guide to OCD
Everything® Health Guide to PMS
Everything® Health Guide to Postpartum Care
Everything® Health Guide to Thyroid Disease
Everything® Hypnosis Book
Everything® Low Cholesterol Book
Everything® Menopause Book
Everything® Nutrition Book
Everything® Reflexology Book
Everything® Stress Management Book
Everything® Superfoods Book, $15.95

HISTORY

Everything® American Government Book
Everything® American History Book, 2nd Ed.
Everything® American Revolution Book, $15.95
Everything® Civil War Book
Everything® Freemasons Book
Everything® Irish History & Heritage Book
Everything® World War II Book, 2nd Ed.

HOBBIES

Everything® Candlemaking Book
Everything® Cartooning Book
Everything® Coin Collecting Book
Everything® Digital Photography Book, 2nd Ed.

Everything® Drawing Book
Everything® Family Tree Book, 2nd Ed.
Everything® Guide to Online Genealogy, $15.95
Everything® Knitting Book
Everything® Knots Book
Everything® Photography Book
Everything® Quilting Book
Everything® Sewing Book
Everything® Soapmaking Book, 2nd Ed.
Everything® Woodworking Book

HOME IMPROVEMENT

Everything® Feng Shui Book
Everything® Feng Shui Decluttering Book, $9.95
Everything® Fix-It Book
Everything® Green Living Book
Everything® Home Decorating Book
Everything® Home Storage Solutions Book
Everything® Homebuilding Book
Everything® Organize Your Home Book, 2nd Ed.

KIDS' BOOKS

All titles are $7.95
Everything® Fairy Tales Book, $14.95
Everything® Kids' Animal Puzzle & Activity Book
Everything® Kids' Astronomy Book
Everything® Kids' Baseball Book, 5th Ed.
Everything® Kids' Bible Trivia Book
Everything® Kids' Bugs Book
Everything® Kids' Cars and Trucks Puzzle and Activity Book
Everything® Kids' Christmas Puzzle & Activity Book
Everything® Kids' Connect the Dots Puzzle and Activity Book
Everything® Kids' Cookbook, 2nd Ed.
Everything® Kids' Crazy Puzzles Book
Everything® Kids' Dinosaurs Book
Everything® Kids' Dragons Puzzle and Activity Book
Everything® Kids' Environment Book $7.95
Everything® Kids' Fairies Puzzle and Activity Book
Everything® Kids' First Spanish Puzzle and Activity Book
Everything® Kids' Football Book
Everything® Kids' Geography Book
Everything® Kids' Gross Cookbook
Everything® Kids' Gross Hidden Pictures Book
Everything® Kids' Gross Jokes Book
Everything® Kids' Gross Mazes Book
Everything® Kids' Gross Puzzle & Activity Book
Everything® Kids' Halloween Puzzle & Activity Book
Everything® Kids' Hanukkah Puzzle and Activity Book
Everything® Kids' Hidden Pictures Book
Everything® Kids' Horses Book
Everything® Kids' Joke Book
Everything® Kids' Knock Knock Book
Everything® Kids' Learning French Book
Everything® Kids' Learning Spanish Book
Everything® Kids' Magical Science Experiments Book
Everything® Kids' Math Puzzles Book
Everything® Kids' Mazes Book
Everything® Kids' Money Book, 2nd Ed.
Everything® Kids' Mummies, Pharaoh's, and Pyramids Puzzle and Activity Book
Everything® Kids' Nature Book
Everything® Kids' Pirates Puzzle and Activity Book
Everything® Kids' Presidents Book
Everything® Kids' Princess Puzzle and Activity Book
Everything® Kids' Puzzle Book

Everything® Kids' Racecars Puzzle and Activity Book
Everything® Kids' Riddles & Brain Teasers Book
Everything® Kids' Science Experiments Book
Everything® Kids' Sharks Book
Everything® Kids' Soccer Book
Everything® Kids' Spelling Book
Everything® Kids' Spies Puzzle and Activity Book
Everything® Kids' States Book
Everything® Kids' Travel Activity Book
Everything® Kids' Word Search Puzzle and Activity Book

LANGUAGE

Everything® Conversational Japanese Book with CD, $19.95
Everything® French Grammar Book
Everything® French Phrase Book, $9.95
Everything® French Verb Book, $9.95
Everything® German Phrase Book, $9.95
Everything® German Practice Book with CD, $19.95
Everything® Inglés Book
Everything® Intermediate Spanish Book with CD, $19.95
Everything® Italian Phrase Book, $9.95
Everything® Italian Practice Book with CD, $19.95
Everything® Learning Brazilian Portuguese Book with CD, $19.95
Everything® Learning French Book with CD, 2nd Ed., $19.95
Everything® Learning German Book
Everything® Learning Italian Book
Everything® Learning Latin Book
Everything® Learning Russian Book with CD, $19.95
Everything® Learning Spanish Book
Everything® Learning Spanish Book with CD, 2nd Ed., $19.95
Everything® Russian Practice Book with CD, $19.95
Everything® Sign Language Book, $15.95
Everything® Spanish Grammar Book
Everything® Spanish Phrase Book, $9.95
Everything® Spanish Practice Book with CD, $19.95
Everything® Spanish Verb Book, $9.95
Everything® Speaking Mandarin Chinese Book with CD, $19.95

MUSIC

Everything® Bass Guitar Book with CD, $19.95
Everything® Drums Book with CD, $19.95
Everything® Guitar Book with CD, 2nd Ed., $19.95
Everything® Guitar Chords Book with CD, $19.95
Everything® Guitar Scales Book with CD, $19.95
Everything® Harmonica Book with CD, $15.95
Everything® Home Recording Book
Everything® Music Theory Book with CD, $19.95
Everything® Reading Music Book with CD, $19.95
Everything® Rock & Blues Guitar Book with CD, $19.95
Everything® Rock & Blues Piano Book with CD, $19.95
Everything® Rock Drums Book with CD, $19.95
Everything® Singing Book with CD, $19.95
Everything® Songwriting Book

NEW AGE

Everything® Astrology Book, 2nd Ed.
Everything® Birthday Personology Book
Everything® Celtic Wisdom Book, $15.95
Everything® Dreams Book, 2nd Ed.
Everything® Law of Attraction Book, $15.95
Everything® Love Signs Book, $9.95
Everything® Love Spells Book, $9.95
Everything® Palmistry Book
Everything® Psychic Book
Everything® Reiki Book

Everything® Sex Signs Book, $9.95
Everything® Spells & Charms Book, 2nd Ed.
Everything® Tarot Book, 2nd Ed.
Everything® Toltec Wisdom Book
Everything® Wicca & Witchcraft Book, 2nd Ed.

PARENTING

Everything® Baby Names Book, 2nd Ed.
Everything® Baby Shower Book, 2nd Ed.
Everything® Baby Sign Language Book with DVD
Everything® Baby's First Year Book
Everything® Birthing Book
Everything® Breastfeeding Book
Everything® Father-to-Be Book
Everything® Father's First Year Book
Everything® Get Ready for Baby Book, 2nd Ed.
Everything® Get Your Baby to Sleep Book, $9.95
Everything® Getting Pregnant Book
Everything® Guide to Pregnancy Over 35
Everything® Guide to Raising a One-Year-Old
Everything® Guide to Raising a Two-Year-Old
Everything® Guide to Raising Adolescent Boys
Everything® Guide to Raising Adolescent Girls
Everything® Mother's First Year Book
Everything® Parent's Guide to Childhood Illnesses
Everything® Parent's Guide to Children and Divorce
Everything® Parent's Guide to Children with ADD/ADHD
Everything® Parent's Guide to Children with Asperger's Syndrome
Everything® Parent's Guide to Children with Anxiety
Everything® Parent's Guide to Children with Asthma
Everything® Parent's Guide to Children with Autism
Everything® Parent's Guide to Children with Bipolar Disorder
Everything® Parent's Guide to Children with Depression
Everything® Parent's Guide to Children with Dyslexia
Everything® Parent's Guide to Children with Juvenile Diabetes
Everything® Parent's Guide to Children with OCD
Everything® Parent's Guide to Positive Discipline
Everything® Parent's Guide to Raising Boys
Everything® Parent's Guide to Raising Girls
Everything® Parent's Guide to Raising Siblings
Everything® Parent's Guide to Raising Your Adopted Child
Everything® Parent's Guide to Sensory Integration Disorder
Everything® Parent's Guide to Tantrums
Everything® Parent's Guide to the Strong-Willed Child
Everything® Parenting a Teenager Book
Everything® Potty Training Book, $9.95
Everything® Pregnancy Book, 3rd Ed.
Everything® Pregnancy Fitness Book
Everything® Pregnancy Nutrition Book
Everything® Pregnancy Organizer, 2nd Ed., $16.95
Everything® Toddler Activities Book
Everything® Toddler Book
Everything® Tween Book
Everything® Twins, Triplets, and More Book

PETS

Everything® Aquarium Book
Everything® Boxer Book
Everything® Cat Book, 2nd Ed.
Everything® Chihuahua Book
Everything® Cooking for Dogs Book
Everything® Dachshund Book
Everything® Dog Book, 2nd Ed.
Everything® Dog Grooming Book

Everything® Dog Obedience Book
Everything® Dog Owner's Organizer, $16.95
Everything® Dog Training and Tricks Book
Everything® German Shepherd Book
Everything® Golden Retriever Book
Everything® Horse Book, 2nd Ed., $15.95
Everything® Horse Care Book
Everything® Horseback Riding Book
Everything® Labrador Retriever Book
Everything® Poodle Book
Everything® Pug Book
Everything® Puppy Book
Everything® Small Dogs Book
Everything® Tropical Fish Book
Everything® Yorkshire Terrier Book

REFERENCE

Everything® American Presidents Book
Everything® Blogging Book
Everything® Build Your Vocabulary Book, $9.95
Everything® Car Care Book
Everything® Classical Mythology Book
Everything® Da Vinci Book
Everything® Einstein Book
Everything® Enneagram Book
Everything® Etiquette Book, 2nd Ed.
Everything® Family Christmas Book, $15.95
Everything® Guide to C. S. Lewis & Narnia
Everything® Guide to Divorce, 2nd Ed., $15.95
Everything® Guide to Edgar Allan Poe
Everything® Guide to Understanding Philosophy
Everything® Inventions and Patents Book
Everything® Jacqueline Kennedy Onassis Book
Everything® John F. Kennedy Book
Everything® Mafia Book
Everything® Martin Luther King Jr. Book
Everything® Pirates Book
Everything® Private Investigation Book
Everything® Psychology Book
Everything® Public Speaking Book, $9.95
Everything® Shakespeare Book, 2nd Ed.

RELIGION

Everything® Angels Book
Everything® Bible Book
Everything® Bible Study Book with CD, $19.95
Everything® Buddhism Book
Everything® Catholicism Book
Everything® Christianity Book
Everything® Gnostic Gospels Book
Everything® Hinduism Book, $15.95
Everything® History of the Bible Book
Everything® Jesus Book
Everything® Jewish History & Heritage Book
Everything® Judaism Book
Everything® Kabbalah Book
Everything® Koran Book
Everything® Mary Book
Everything® Mary Magdalene Book
Everything® Prayer Book

Everything® Saints Book, 2nd Ed.
Everything® Torah Book
Everything® Understanding Islam Book
Everything® Women of the Bible Book
Everything® World's Religions Book

SCHOOL & CAREERS

Everything® Career Tests Book
Everything® College Major Test Book
Everything® College Survival Book, 2nd Ed.
Everything® Cover Letter Book, 2nd Ed.
Everything® Filmmaking Book
Everything® Get-a-Job Book, 2nd Ed.
Everything® Guide to Being a Paralegal
Everything® Guide to Being a Personal Trainer
Everything® Guide to Being a Real Estate Agent
Everything® Guide to Being a Sales Rep
Everything® Guide to Being an Event Planner
Everything® Guide to Careers in Health Care
Everything® Guide to Careers in Law Enforcement
Everything® Guide to Government Jobs
Everything® Guide to Starting and Running a Catering Business
Everything® Guide to Starting and Running a Restaurant
Everything® Guide to Starting and Running a Retail Store
Everything® Job Interview Book, 2nd Ed.
Everything® New Nurse Book
Everything® New Teacher Book
Everything® Paying for College Book
Everything® Practice Interview Book
Everything® Resume Book, 3rd Ed.
Everything® Study Book

SELF-HELP

Everything® Body Language Book
Everything® Dating Book, 2nd Ed.
Everything® Great Sex Book
Everything® Guide to Caring for Aging Parents, $15.95
Everything® Self-Esteem Book
Everything® Self-Hypnosis Book, $9.95
Everything® Tantric Sex Book

SPORTS & FITNESS

Everything® Easy Fitness Book
Everything® Fishing Book
Everything® Guide to Weight Training, $15.95
Everything® Krav Maga for Fitness Book
Everything® Running Book, 2nd Ed.
Everything® Triathlon Training Book, $15.95

TRAVEL

Everything® Family Guide to Coastal Florida
Everything® Family Guide to Cruise Vacations
Everything® Family Guide to Hawaii
Everything® Family Guide to Las Vegas, 2nd Ed.
Everything® Family Guide to Mexico
Everything® Family Guide to New England, 2nd Ed.

Everything® Family Guide to New York City, 3rd Ed.
Everything® Family Guide to Northern California and Lake Tahoe
Everything® Family Guide to RV Travel & Campgrounds
Everything® Family Guide to the Caribbean
Everything® Family Guide to the Disneyland® Resort, California Adventure®, Universal Studios®, and the Anaheim Area, 2nd Ed.
Everything® Family Guide to the Walt Disney World Resort®, Universal Studios®, and Greater Orlando, 5th Ed.
Everything® Family Guide to Timeshares
Everything® Family Guide to Washington D.C., 2nd Ed.

WEDDINGS

Everything® Bachelorette Party Book, $9.95
Everything® Bridesmaid Book, $9.95
Everything® Destination Wedding Book
Everything® Father of the Bride Book, $9.95
Everything® Green Wedding Book, $15.95
Everything® Groom Book, $9.95
Everything® Jewish Wedding Book, 2nd Ed., $15.95
Everything® Mother of the Bride Book, $9.95
Everything® Outdoor Wedding Book
Everything® Wedding Book, 3rd Ed.
Everything® Wedding Checklist, $9.95
Everything® Wedding Etiquette Book, $9.95
Everything® Wedding Organizer, 2nd Ed., $16.95
Everything® Wedding Shower Book, $9.95
Everything® Wedding Vows Book, 3rd Ed., $9.95
Everything® Wedding Workout Book
Everything® Weddings on a Budget Book, 2nd Ed., $9.95

WRITING

Everything® Creative Writing Book
Everything® Get Published Book, 2nd Ed.
Everything® Grammar and Style Book, 2nd Ed.
Everything® Guide to Magazine Writing
Everything® Guide to Writing a Book Proposal
Everything® Guide to Writing a Novel
Everything® Guide to Writing Children's Books
Everything® Guide to Writing Copy
Everything® Guide to Writing Graphic Novels
Everything® Guide to Writing Research Papers
Everything® Guide to Writing a Romance Novel, $15.95
Everything® Improve Your Writing Book, 2nd Ed.
Everything® Writing Poetry Book